The Bloody Vendetta

of Southern Illinois

Milo Erwin
& Jon Musgrave, Editor
IllinoisHistory.com
Marion, Illinois

Published by
IllinoisHistory.com
PO Box 1142
Marion IL 62959

Front Cover
Milo Erwin, Vendetta attorney, *Williamson County Historical Society.*

Cover Background
J. W. Landrum's Mill at Carterville in 1876, Warner & Beers' *Illustrated Historical Atlas of the State of Illinois.*

Library of Congress Control Number: 2005936827

International Standard Book Number (ISBN)
paperback: 978-0-9891781-0-5

Printed in the United States of America
2nd edition

In dedication to
Milo Erwin,
who had the guts to put this together
when he could have been shot,

and the

volunteers who keep history preserved at the
Williamson County Historical Society Museum
in Marion, Illinois.

About this edition

Welcome to the second edition of the enhanced version of Milo Erwin's *Bloody Vendetta*, or is it the sixth edition of the original book? It's not an easy answer. Milo Erwin first published his *History of Williamson County* in 1876 immediately following the major trials of the Vendetta. Of his volume, almost half of it dealt directly with that outbreak of violence. Compared to the last one, this 2013 version only adds a few more photographs and a postscript.

Erwin served as the defense attorney for a number of the defendants. He knew them well, not only as clients, but even friends. "I have been personally acquainted with most of the supposed members of the Vendetta from childhood," he wrote in the introduction of his coverage of the county's criminal history. For his history he had one goal: "I am not writing a record of passions and prejudices, but of facts, with the wrapping taken off, so that they can be seen as they are."

Unlike other local histories written by old men recollecting events gone by, Erwin was just 29 when he completed his manuscript. He saw history as a way to anchor the future.

> We have lived in the shadow of the gray hairs of our fathers. They have battled long and well to give us a country to live in, and we are the rich inheritors of all the glorious results of their self-denial and patriotic devotion. Let us prove ourselves worthy of the high destiny for which they offered themselves a sacrifice to common dangers and privations, by living honorable lives, and showing to the world that with affection we cherish their acts and hallow their memories.[1]

In writing the book Erwin proposed to himself, "as a maxim, that no man should be able from its pages to tell what political party I belong to; so impartially have I tried to write it." Though Republican in politics and friendly with the local Republican newspaper – he may have even been the

---

[1] Milo Erwin. Dec. 1, 1876. "Prefatory Address to the Young Men of Williamson County." *History of Williamson County, Illinois.* Marion, Ill.: Privately published. v.

anonymous writer of many of its Vendetta reports – he took his manuscript instead to the publisher of the *Egyptian Press*, James F. Connell, a staunch Democrat.[2]

The last of the Vendetta trials in 1876 ended in April, and it's likely that Erwin began preparation for his volume soon after that, though he references another trial from mid-August later that year. His research included talking with both older residents and the younger members of the Vendetta. "As I have not undertaken to invent facts, of course I had to draw from many sources," he explained. "I have tried to eliminate from the mass of facts such as would be most interesting to read and remember."

As far as historians can tell, Erwin apparently remained single all of his life and treated women with an extreme deference that will be easily noticeable as one reads this volume. He intended his prefatory address "to the young men of Williamson County." Of the women he made no mention, which is interesting as his elder sister had "assisted him" as he "drove over the county in a buggy" collecting the data for his history, and it was to her that he left his manuscript.[3]

Erwin wrapped up his writing in the late fall of 1876. He dated his prefatory address on December 1. Two months later on February 1, 1877, both county newspapers, the *Egyptian Press* and the *Marion Monitor* advertised the clothbound book for sale at $1 a piece – "A very interesting book for everyone to read is Erwin's History of Williamson."[4] By April paperback copies were also available for 65 cents.[5] In all, some 10,000 copies supposedly were printed for distribution among both the stores of the county as well as around the surrounding states where coverage of the Vendetta had

---

[2] Nannie Gray Parks. Research notes. Erwin File. Williamson County Historical Society.

[3] Feb. 7, 1946. "Manuscript of History Owned Here." *Marion Daily Republican.* Clipping found in the Erwin Family file at the Williamson County Historical Society. At the time of this article, Erwin's nephew W. F. Rummage, preserved the handwritten manuscript – "several hundred pages of note paper tied in rolls" – in a safety deposit book presumably in the Bank of Marion, the only financial institution in Marion at the time.

[4] Helen Sutt Lind. 1994. *Events in Egypt.* Privately published. 1:73.

[5] Lind 1:85; and Helen Sutt Lind. Summer 2002. "Milo Erwin alias Mark M. Stanley." *Footprints in Williamson County, Illinois.* Quarterly of the Williamson County Historical Society. 5:3. 21-25

been well-reported. Despite the large print run, few copies seemed to have survived. Fire destroyed most of the print run when a blaze swept through the offices of Judge George W. Young where they were stored.

By the turn of the 20th Century, few copies survived. In 1904, Hal Trovillion arrived in Herrin, Illinois, to operate the *Herrin Daily Journal* and the *Egyptian Republican*. He soon learned of Erwin's then almost-legendary book.

> For two years after our arrival in Herrin, we tried to get hold of a copy of this much discussed history. No one would admit possessing one, yet nearly everyone had read it. It seemed that as soon as the book appeared and became generally read, that both sides mentioned in it, set about to make away with every copy that could be found. For to have Erwin's history in the home was next to committing a crime, and besides it was a dangerous omen.

Luckily for Trovillion a man from a nearby mining settlement finally brought a copy to the newspaper office. The editor remembered the man "pulled from his pocket a small black volume, dog-eared and giving evidence of having been roughly or careless handled." For five dollars the man would sell it. For five dollars, Trovillion gladly paid.

> A month later this same man was found shot to death. His family had been implicated in the feud.

About eight years later Trovillion published Erwin's work for its first reprinting ever, changing little other than using a larger type and adding new headlines to some of the subjects. However, most importantly, he reversed the title from the straight-forward *History of Williamson County, Illinois* followed by a mention of the vendetta to *The Bloody Vendetta*, with a subheading of "Embracing the Early History of Williamson County, Illinois." In his "By Way of Explanation" in the reprint, Trovillion attempted to secure the support of those families involved.

> In behalf of the well known families connected with the terrible Vendetta which is here related it should be said that they are now among the best families in the community and some of the persons

named are counted at present, good citizens who have lived down all odium that once attached to their names.

Still, it wasn't enough as Trovillion recalled 29 years later.

> The edition sold like proverbial hot cakes at first. We were pleased and much encouraged, for it was our first venture in commercial book publishing.
> But soon something happened and sales slowed down. We began to get inklings that some of the old families on the prairies were much displeased that the book had been reprinted. Then we remembered the warning that had been given Erwin when he announced the writing of the story, and we recalled what some had cautioned us when we showed an interest to save the book from oblivion. These memories all came vividly back to us one rainy morning as we looked out of the office window and beheld Old Uncle William, as everyone referred to him, reading the ad for The Bloody Vendetta.

Regrettably, Trovillion didn't give William's last name, but he did describe him.

> He was the town's wealthiest man, a pioneer on the prairie, owned more property than any other man in the place, but dressed as if he were the community's poorest and neediest. He was the town's conventional and ever active protester of all propositions or movements that meant progress or cultural advancement for the town.

As Trovillion watched him through the window he recalled their last meeting where Uncle William adamantly stood foursquare against the establishment of a high school. "You only make a worse criminal when you educate a bad boy," he had ranted. "You know as well as I do that this here place is jist filled up with evil-minded lads..."

Eventually, Uncle William made his way inside to deliver his statement. "I don't like that," he told Trovillion firmly gripping the wrong end of the umbrella he carried and pointing it towards a poster in the window advertising the books. "It ain't fitten for this generation to read sich books. You had no right to print it again and reopen old sores that have been healing up." Finally, after tiring of his harangue Trovillion pointed out a simple truth to the old man that won the day.

> It's not worse on the on-coming generation, Uncle William, for us to reprint this book and distribute it than it is for you to own two copies of the original and loan them around to select friends to read, and pledging them to tell no one about it.

Uncle William stormed out of the shop and never spoke to Trovillion again. A few weeks later the recalcitrant old man died after falling from a load of hay and breaking his neck.[6]

Following the bloody events of the 1920s including the Herrin Massacre, the wars between the Ku Klux Klan and the Birger and Shelton Gangs, Trovillion once again capitalized on Bloody Williamson's infamy with a second re-printing in 1927. This one came with a new layout and style as well as additional copy-editing of Erwin's work. The sleek new red-covered hardcover book with gold-leaf lettering proved popular selling for just $2 a copy, a price Trovillion dropped to $1 by World War II when he tried to dispose of his remaining inventory.

In the aftermath of World War II, Trovillion pawned a number of remaining copies to the *Marion Daily Republican* for sale. "The demand for the book has indicated a wide interest in its content," reported the paper in 1946. At the time they noted that originally "its details of an unpleasant chapter in the county's history" made it a book of which local residents were not proud. However in recent years, likely because the county had celebrated its centennial in 1939, many had "come to recognize it for its historical value and the author's painstaking labors in recording the history of the early settlers."

The Williamson County Historical Society came out with the fourth edition in 1976 during the nation's Bicentennial and the book's 100th anniversary. Using the original as its template, the Society's version simply

---

[6] Hal Trovillion. March 1943 (or March 19, 1943). "At the Sign of the Silver Horse." *Egyptian Press* (Herrin, Illinois). 8. This particular clipping was found glued to an inside cover of Trovillion's second reprinting of *The Bloody Vendetta* in possession of Special Collections/Morris Library at Southern Illinois University-Carbondale.

enlarged the entire book from its original pocket-size dimensions to the more standard 5.5 by 8.5-inch size.

When I initially decided to do this project my first thought was to simply reprint the Vendetta portion of Erwin's book, maybe with some explanatory footnotes, and use Trovillion's title of *The Bloody Vendetta*. Instead the footnotes grew into page-long footnotes, and from there into chapters. As I sought to tie up loose ends and chase down interesting side stories the book continued to grow. When the page count doubled it was then and only then I decided I had stopped simply being the editor and had become a co-author.

A quick explanation is needed for you the reader at this point. Thirteen of the first 15 chapters are Erwin's work from 1876. Although I added new paragraph and even chapter breaks, I've left the writing style and 19th Century spelling alone. Thus be prepared for "drouth" for "drought" and "staid" for "stayed" as well as a half-dozen other words good spellers will swear are misspelled. What I have added to these sections are footnotes with additional information.

At two different points in Erwin's narrative I've add nearly two whole chapters dealing with the Ku Klux Klan. The Klan didn't just operate in Williamson County but Erwin limited his writing to only his home county leaving out important events in neighboring counties. As I thought this story would make more sense if included in chronological order I have inserted these chapters appropriately. The rest of the book is designed to fill in the blanks, tie up loose ends and to see what happened to the next generation of outlaws suckled on the vengeance of the Vendetta.

With two authors writing in two different centuries (and with another century in between) it can be tricky to keep up with statements in the present tense. When Erwin wrote of someone "now in Joliet" he meant in 1876, the time of his original writing and publication. "Now" or other present tense statements found in the footnotes throughout the book as well as the chapters I wrote or edited, refer to the early 21st Century at the time of publication in 2006.

Jon Musgrave
IllinoisHistory.com
July 8, 2006
Updated: September 12, 2013

Table of Contents

List of Illustrations

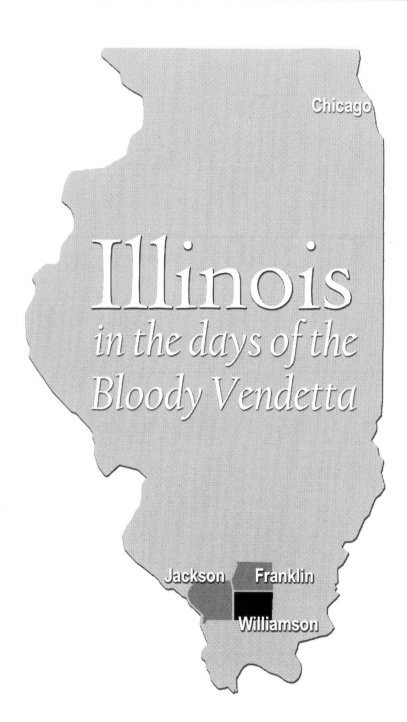

Chicago

Illinois
in the days of the
Bloody Vendetta

Jackson   Franklin

Williamson

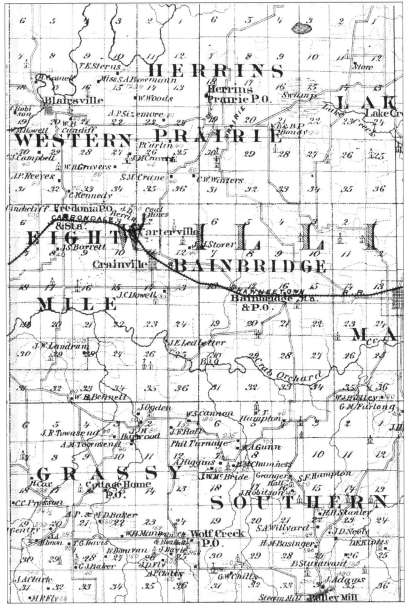

Illustrated Historical Atlas of the State of Illinois

Western Half of Williamson County in 1876.

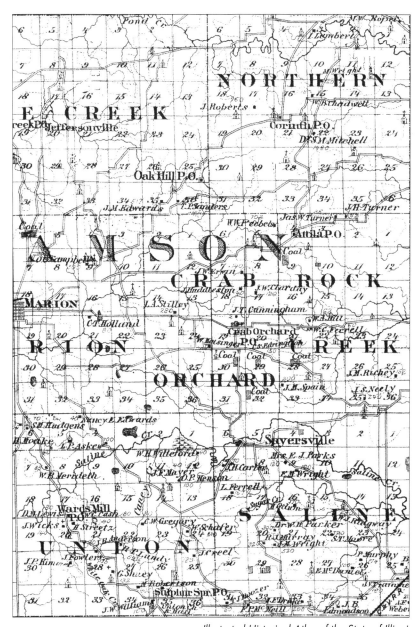

Illustrated Historical Atlas of the State of Illinois

Eastern Half of Williamson County in 1876.

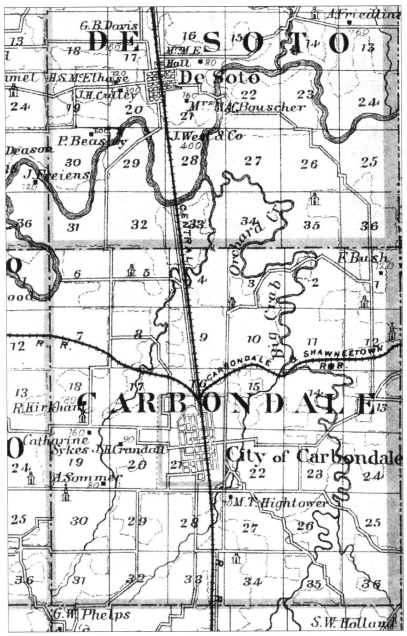

Illustrated Historical Atlas of the State of Illinois

Carbondale/DeSoto area of Jackson County in 1876.

Chapter 1. **Of Criminals**

I HAVE NOW COME TO THAT DIVISION of my subject, which must be more interesting to our neighbors than any other. And it is but fitting that I make a few egotistical preliminaries. I do not present this volume with the venal soul of a servile author, looking for competence or public favor. I was born a farmer, and am therefore independent. But so long as I claim the name of a citizen with my illustrious countrymen, a lasting obligation rests on me to assist in diffusing knowledge, elevating the standard of moral culture, rendering crime odious, and fastening the feelings of friendship on our people.

I have intended this feeble effort to lead in that direction. I have known this people from childhood. I believe, sublimated by education, they are capable of attaining nobler heights than have usually been ascribed to the people of "Egypt." I not only glory in my birth-place, but pass encomiums on the county, and say to the world that from my knowledge of the public spirit of our people, I can expect protection, honest dealing and liberty in Williamson County.

Linked to her by historic associations and proudly treasuring the memories of my fathers, the clearest duty of a modest youth like myself, whose unruly and turbulent boyhood has been subdued in the presence of this heroic people, is to assist in tearing down the curtains of darkness which hang like a mighty incubus around the crushed form of my native county, and bury them in the deep pit of contempt, where our citizens can stand by their grave forever and mutter thanksgivings to God, and invite an unsophisticated world to look with joy and pride upon a county redeemed from crime, and sparkling with brilliant gems of innocence and virtue.

If I could roll back the scroll of time, and wipe from its damning record the terrible scenes of blood which have bespangled it, and restore the lives of our murdered dead, I would consider it my bounden duty, though I sailed with bloody sails on seas of grief. But that scroll has been sealed for eternity, not to be unrolled until the echo of impartial justice shall resound in the sunlit chambers of Paradise.

I make this effort, prompted by motives, to assist in redeeming, if possible, our county from under the judgment against her, and prove to the world that our community is not composed of outlaws and cut-throats, but of a highly intellectual, honorable and moral people. I could wish to write a history by which the reader would be carried along the happy gales of pleasure, and never be drifted back into dark and bitter troubles, but I can not. Crime has darkened our county, like the shadows darken the earth, and our happiness has come to us only in fragments and detached parts. We have just passed through the deepest and crowning calamity of our history. Never was there such a shock to the feelings and sentiments of our people as the Vendetta caused. None believed that there was a heart so steeped in guilt as to conceive such crimes, nor a hand that dare commit the atrocious deeds. And yet I have to catalogue the deeds of a Vendetta, concocted by leaders and executed by fiendish emissaries, that has not a parallel in the record of crime. Here were men at whose blood-thirstiness even savages would blush, which brands them forever as the basest and bloodiest of incarnate demons.

Tacitus said: "Shame, reproach, infamy, hatred and the execrations of the public, which are the inseparable attendants on criminal and brutal actions, are no less proper to excite a horror for vice, than the glory which perpetually attends good actions is to inspire us with a love of virtue." And these, according to Tacitus, says Rollin, "are the two ends which every historian ought to propose to himself, by making a judicious choice of what is most extraordinary, both in good and evil, in order to occasion that public homage to be paid to virtue which is justly due to it, and to create the greater abhorrence for vice on account of that eternal infamy that attends it."

Plutarch says: "But as to actions of injustice, violence and brutality, they ought not to be concealed nor disguised." Rollin himself has written, "If the virtues of those who are celebrated in history may serve us for models in the conduct of our lives, their vices and failings on the other hand are no less proper to caution and instruct us, and the strict regard which an historian is obliged to pay to truth, will not allow him to dissemble the latter through fear of eclipsing the former."

Addison has said, "The gods in bounty work up storms about us, that give mankind occasion to exert their hidden strength and throw out into practice virtues which shun the day." If these virtues are worthy of record, the conditions which generated them are certainly proper for study. This necessitates a history of the storms which the gods work up around us. By reading which, "others who are about to get sootiness and filth from the smoke and flames of incipient storms, may take alarm and go and wash in the river of peace and come out white as pearls."

Who that reads this record of crime will not appeal to the ruler of human fates below, and record their protests in heaven above against such slaughter! I ask my countrymen if crimes that have sunk a county to the incandescent crater of perdition, ought not to be remembered. If you could cable the lightning from heaven, until its fiery forks kissed the flaming waves of hell, you would see nothing in its angry flames, as they zigzag athwart the pit of woe, throwing up a lurid glare, but the spectral mirage of murder ever standing up as a blazing memento that "sin is death."

I am justified by the great writers I have mentioned in giving the meanest as well as the noblest action of my countrymen. If I write of the guilty with merciless hands, from a heart as responsive comes spontaneously praise for the innocent. If not as eloquent and as touching, yet as warm, as full, as sincere, as such a tribute deserves. If you are sad at the deeds of bloody men, you will be buoyant at the faithfulness and heroism of virtuous men. I expect, out of a succession of events which possess all the traits of tenderness, splendor, honor, crime and debauchery, to write a romance without its exaggerations. It is a small difficulty to select an event, and swell it into a great tale, by fabulous appendages and spectral productions; for he who forsakes the truth may easily find the marvelous: but who is improved by it?

Samuel Johnson says, "Where truth is sufficient to fill the mind, fiction is worse than useless." Again, "The counterfeit debases the genuine." I am not writing a record of passions and prejudices, but of facts, with the wrapping taken off, so that they can be seen as they are. Though some of them are crimes that would make the bailiffs of Hades blush and turn pale, others are heroic acts that would sweep the zones of misery away.

I have abused no innocent man, nor palliated the guilt of none; but have intended that my whole course should savor of fairness and candor, more than anything else. Some have used strong arguments against our county, but I have not evaded the force of their reasoning where I was unable to refute it, either by a sweeping contempt for those who use it, or by charging them with misrepresentation, or by endeavoring to swing off the mind of the reader on some incidental point to the real condition of our county. To enter the arena of controversy with the great champions of crime, or even the little champions, is entirely beyond my ambition. Had that been my object it might long since have been affected. I do not care what this or that party may think of my feeble efforts. I feel very little anxiety or solicitude on that subject. I have written the truth as near as I know it, and will leave the result to the arbitrament of public opinion.

I have often been asked if I was not afraid that I would be killed if I wrote a history of the Vendetta. I answer, no! I have been personally acquainted with most of the supposed members of the Vendetta from childhood, and am a friend to all of them. I went to each one of them and asked him to tell me all he knew about the Vendetta, and each of them told me fully, fairly, honestly, and I believe truthfully, all I wanted to know. These people are all friendly now, and as gentlemanly as I ever met. Many of them I love and esteem, and to incur their ill-will is by no means desirable; but to court their favor at the expense of truth or right principle would render me guilty in the sight of God, and contemptible in the estimation of all good men. Since they were so kind as to give me information enough to write the whole truth, I deem it unkind and unjust to step aside from historic facts to hurl the shafts of envy, hatred and malice at any of them. Surely they have borne enough already, and I am satisfied that if no man gets inflamed at this volume higher than these young men, I will still be safe living in Williamson County.

Twenty-two of these parties are young men like myself, and I know of no country where finer-looking, honester, friendlier or more social young men can be found. I associate with them with pleasure. Many of them are my lasting friends, and I will not denounce them because they have been charged with crimes of which they were not guilty. For the guilty I have nothing but charity; yet some of them committed the high crime of murder without excuse. I shall commence with the first homicide that occurred in the county, and give a brief sketch of each one as it occurred, up to the present time.

Of the smaller offenses I have taken no notice, though they have been quite numerous and interesting. Some of them have been riots in which two or three men have been badly wounded. I estimate the number of assaults to murder that have occurred in this county at 285. Assaults with a deadly weapon, at 495; larceny, 190; rape, 15; burglary, 22; perjury, 20.

The first homicide occurred in 1813. Thomas Griffee was trying to shoot a bear out of a tree where the old court-house burned down in Marion, and he saw an Indian aiming his gun at the same bear.[7] Griffee leveled his rifle at the Indian and shot him dead.

The next murder occurred in 1814. Thomas Griffee had a man working in a saltpeter cave for him, by the name of Eliott, who was a little colored. He came into Griffee's one Saturday night, and a surveyor by the name of John Hicks raised a fuss with him, and stabbed and killed him. Hicks then ran away, and at that moment a band of Indians came up to Griffee's from the camp at Bainbridge, and wanted to go in pursuit of Hicks, but Griffee would not let them go. Next morning Griffee and John Phelps started in pursuit of Hicks; they came on to him at the Odum Ford, and Hicks snapped his gun at Griffee's breast, but was taken. [8] They took him to Kaskaskia, where the nearest Justice of the Peace lived, and he was "whipped, cropped and branded," and let go.[9]

In 1818 a friend of Isaac Herrin came to this county and found a man dead at the Stotlar place, unwept and unknown. This man was doubtless murdered by the Indians, and if so, was the only one ever killed by them in this county.

The next murder occurred in 1821 in Rock Creek Precinct, and was committed by Henry Parsons.[10] It was late one evening, when the trees were robed in the regalia of Spring, and the great molten orb was quenching itself in the wild winds as they come sweeping askant the rolling reach of upland, and the gentle mist was seemingly set to eddying by the rough elements, that this ruffian went walking down a little brook; his keen restless eye keeping a constant look-out, he saw a man through the deep green foliage, sitting on a

---

[7] The old courthouse Erwin mentions was built on the east half of the lot on the south side of the square where the currently-shuttered Tower Place restaurant is located, formerly Distinctive Interiors and before that Cox Furniture.

[8] Odum Ford was located across the Big Muddy River near the mouth of Pond Creek in the northeastern corner of Blairsville Township. It's not clear if the river crossing had a name at the time of Hicks' arrest as the Odum brothers didn't arrive in the area until the following year in 1815. The ford took its name from Dempsey Odum who lived on the Big Muddy in 1818. In the early 1830s he moved closer to Marion and helped stake out the first plat of the city in 1839.

[9] At the time of this murder the portion of what's now Williamson County north and west of the Big Muddy River belonged to Randolph County seated at Kaskaskia.

[10] Rock Creek Precinct represented the eastern two-thirds of Crab Orchard Township stretching from Poor-do (Attila) on the north south down to Dykersburg.

log across the brook. He fired on him, and the unknown hunter slipped off the log into the water, never to rise again. Parson buried him and his gun. He used to give as an excuse for this murder, that the Indians had murdered his father, and he intended to kill every one of them he could find, and he thought this man was an Indian.

There never came a more infamous devil out of the legions of horrid blackness than this man Parson. I give a sketch of him from the mere love of relief. He lived unmatched in the history of villainy; he did not seek wealth, but lived in the woods. He was a cold, calculating miscreant. His passions had no touch of humanity, and his brutal ferocity was backed by a kind of brutal courage. Like an animal, he never pardoned an affront or rivalry, and to be marked in his tablets on either account, was a sentence of death. But still he was really a coward, and pulled the trigger of death with a hand that shook. His crimes were all cool-blooded, and not chargeable to passion. Free from rules and reckless of life, feeling no kindness for aught that was human, hated and dreaded by men, detested and shunned by women, he would lay around Davis' Prairie and kill Indians.[11] With him the chambers of mercy had no relenting toward these blighted men of earth, but as a wasp is ever ready to inflict her sting, so was he ready to commit the crime of murder.[12]

On one occasion A. Keaster met him on the prairie, and he threw up his gun and told Keaster to stop, which he did. Soon after he heard the keen crack of his rifle, and then met him again. Parson told him he had just killed a bear back there and he could have it. But Keaster knew too well that down in the dark, thick bushes lay an innocent red man weltering in his own blood.

The little birds of different species flew across the open space and back again, turning and whirling in manifold gyrations over the scene, where the ineffable glories of sunset had been insulted by bloody murder. What a scene was this! An innocent, untaught man lying wounded in the bushes, dreading the return of his slayer! What a thrill of joy would have electrified his soul to

---

[11] Davis Prairie was one of the smaller prairies in early Williamson County, covering most of Section 23 in East Marion Township that's now south of Route 13 and east of Route 146. Davis Prairie Cemetery along Route 13 sits on the north side of the old prairie grounds.

[12] The 1820 census finds Parson heading a household between Stephen Stilley's and Thomas Trammell's. Parson's household includes one male 10 to 16, himself between 26 and 45; three girls under 10, one girl 16 to 25; and what's presumably his wife, who's shown between the ages of 26 and 45.

have seen a helping hand! Alone with his God and the winds and trees and flowers and birds, he died. The traces of his blood are hidden by the bushes and tall grass, but so long as Nature knows her own lament, will the cries of this murdered man be borne on the wild winds of heaven. I can not contemplate the character of a man but with astonishment that can look with fiendish complacency on the bleeding form of a brother man slain.

In 1823, Parson killed Parson Crouch. They lived on the Crab Orchard, near the Cal. Norman bridge, and Parson bought Crouch's improvements, and was to have possession as soon as convenient; but Parson got in a hurry, and told Crouch he must get out by Saturday night, or he would get stung with the "yeller jacket," a name for his gun. Crouch went to Equality that week for salt, and when he got within a quarter of a mile of home, as he was driving along in a bit of dark and lonely forest, this sloth hound shot him dead, from behind a tree. He was found with his pockets full of toys for his little children. Parson went to D. Odum's, threw down his gun and demanded a horse. Odum was afraid to refuse him, and he left the country. The whole country was raised and went in pursuit, but never overtook him. He went to Tennessee, and one of his sons came to this county years afterwards and said that a black dog had always followed his father, so that he could see no peace. He died a violent death. Thus "doth Providence with secret care often vindicate herself," and justice is continually done on the trial stage of life.[13]

In 1833, James Youngblood was at a rock quarry, on the Saline, and was making his dog kill a snake, when Gideon Alexander appeared on the bluff above and shot him through the breast. Youngblood rose and attempted to shoot Alexander, but fainted. Alexander ran down to him, helped him home, and protested that he saw nothing but a white spot down through the foliage, and thought it was a deer's tail. He waited on Youngblood constantly, and paid all bills. Youngblood lived five or six years, but finally took to bleeding at the bullet hole, and died on the cold, damp, dirt floor of his cabin. This was a curious case. Nothing was ever done with Alexander for this foul murder.

---

[13] Parsons appears to have moved to Carroll County in Tennessee which is about halfway between Nashville and Memphis as a man by his name and the same rough age appear in the 1830 and 1840 censuses there. That Henry Parsons' will was probated during the January 1844 term of the local court. Based on the three census records he was likely born between 1775 and 1780 putting him in his 40s at the time of the murder.

In 1841, Jeremiah Simmons got into a fight with J. G. Sparks, in Marion. William Benson, constable, interfered and stopped it. Simmons then commenced on Benson. The latter started home, Simmons ran after him with his knife; Andrew Benson came up at the time, ran up to Simmons and asked him to stop. Simmons looked over his shoulder and saw who it was, and stabbed backward, striking him in the abdomen, from which he died. Simmons made his escape. Benson offered five hundred dollars reward and the Governor two hundred dollars, for his arrest.[14] In about six months he wrote to his wife and was detected, and brought back from Iowa by Benson. He was tried and acquitted. His counsel were General Shields and General McClernand.[15]

---

[14] The *Illinois Republican* of Shawneetown printed the following reward notice:

"$200.00 REWARD — Will be given for the apprehension of Jeremiah Simmons, who committed an atrocious murder on the person of Andrew J. Benson, in the town of Marion, Williamson County, Ill., on Sat. evening the 4th inst. The said Simmons is about 30 years of age, stout, heavy made, big shoulders, weighs about 160-170 pounds, 5 feet 8 or 9 inches high; of a sandy complexion, coarse hair, thin lips, light sandy beard, round face and freckled, with tolerable dark or brown skin, heavy eye brows, light hazel eyes and a sulky sour countenance, grim looks and down cast, a man of but few words, seldom laughs or speaks, and when in company stands or sits by himself. Had when he left a white hat, napped with coon fur, dressed in homespun brown jeans, had a large rifle gun, sugar tree stock, a large butcher knife, made of a file. The above reward will be given to any person for the apprehension and delivery of the said Simmons or if confined in any jail in the United States, so that he can be brought to justice by me the father of the deceased. Williamson Benson, December 17, 1841." *Source*: Dec. 25, 1841. *Illinois Republican*; as quoted from Shirley Cummins Shewmake, comp. 1994. *Gallatin County, Illinois, Newspapers: Vol. 1 (1841-1843)*. Privately published. 28.

[15] His defense attorneys were future Mexican War General James Shields and future Civil War General John A. McClernand. In 1905, G. W. Chesley McCoy, provided another account of this incident which he said took place in the fall of 1841:

"Simpson got into a quarrel with Andrew Benson's father, and as the old man, who didn't want to quarrel, was going away, Jerry ran after him with a knife in his hand, swearing he would kill him. He and Andy were chums, and Andy ran up to Jerry and putting his hand on his shoulder said, 'O Jerry, you wouldn't kill father, would you?' At that Jerry struck backwards with his knife in his hand, probably not thinking or intending to hurt Andy, but only to shake him off, and the blade entered the bowels of Andy and killed him. Willis Allen, the father of Josh Allen, was one of the prosecution and James Shields defended him. Jerry was a man about 40. He broke jail and ran away, but was caught a year later and tried but acquitted by a packed jury." *Source*: J. F. Wilcox.

In 1854, John Mosley killed James Burnett, by striking him on the head with a club. The difficulty arose over a dog-fight. Mosley ran away, and was captured in Missouri by hounds following his trail. He was tried and sentenced for six years, but after one year's confinement was pardoned.

George Ramsey shot and killed Jack Ward in 1859. They had run a horse race, and Ward had won it, which made Ramsey mad. He threw a rock at Ward, then when Ward started towards him, shot him dead and ran away, and has never come back.

In 1859, John Ferguson, then a boy, went out into the country and found Ellen Reed lying in bed sick, when he shot her dead. He said his father had too much business with her. He ran away, and years afterwards came home and soon died.

In the same year, an unknown man was found hanging dead on the Crab Orchard, south of Marion. The facts about it were never known, but suspicion rested heavily on a man who lived near by in the bottom, at that time.

In the spring of 1861, an Irishman passed the house of R. T. McHaney, four miles east of Marion; McHaney came up about that time and found that the man had insulted his wife. He got his gun and shot the unknown Irishman dead. He was tried and acquitted on the ground of defending his family.

In 1862, Reuben Stocks, a soldier in the Seventy-Eighth Illinois Volunteers, had been transferred to a gun-boat and furloughed home; he brought several of the boys with him and conducted himself rather offensively to some people.[16] One day he was in Blairsville, and fell in with the "Aiken gang," some of whom he treated roughly. That night some men went to his house, on the Eight Mile, and called him up, telling him that they wanted him to go back to the gun-boat.[17] When he went to the door, they shot

---

1905 *Historical Souvenir of Williamson County, Illinois.* Effingham, Ill.: LeCrone Press. 175.

[16] Reuben may have been the younger brother to Henry Stocks, a man murdered a few years after the Vendetta. The two men were three years apart and living side-by-side in the 1860 Census of Williamson Co. Ten years earlier, Reuben isn't found in Illinois, but Henry, then 18, appears in the household of what may have been another brother, Benjamin Stocks, 23. All three men were farmers born in England.

[17] The reference to Eight Mile here refers to Eight Mile Prairie which straddled the Jackson-Williamson county line. The prairie gave its name to Twp. 9 S., Range 1 E., which is now Carterville Township.

him full of buck shot, from which he soon died. The perpetrators of this murder have never been discovered.

In 1862, when the One-Hundred and Twenty-Eighth Regiment left this county, and got to the Crab Orchard bridge, in Jackson county, Terry Crain got into a difficulty with John Burbridge, and struck him on the head with a stone, from which he died. Crain was not indicted until October 1875. He was arrested and admitted to bail on *habeas corpus,* in the sum of $15,000. In August 1876, he was tried, convicted and sentenced to fifteen years' confinement.[18]

In this same year, William Stacey stabbed and killed Henderson Tippy. They were boys, bathing in the Crab Orchard, near Marion, and got to fighting. Stacey was acquitted.[19]

In December 1862, James Baker was assassinated in Bainbridge Precinct.[20] He walked out one night and was shot dead with a shot gun. It was thought that this was done because he was telling where deserters were.

In 1863, James Emerson, an ardent Republican, was assassinated while hunting his horses in the woods, near Blairsville. No cause for his murder is known, unless it was his politics. The assassin is not known.

After George Aikin was frustrated in his efforts to sell out the One-Hundred and Twenty-Eighth, at Cairo, he went to Missouri, and got Allen Glide and Charley Glide, and came back here. These, and his son John Aikin, are the ones supposed to compose the "Aiken Gang." This gang flourished here in the spring of 1863, in the north part of the county, during which time several murders were committed, and no less than fifty of our citizens robbed. Dr. Bandy was taken out and whipped unmercifully, and George

---

[18] There's more on Crain's trial and his role in the Bloody Vendetta immediately following Erwin's account in the chapter, "Cleaning Up."

[19] From census records it appears that both boys would have been around 13 at the time. The 1860 Census doesn't show a Henderson Tippy, but does show an 11-year-old John H. Tippy living in what's now West Marion Township. He's the presumed son of Abraham Tippy based on that census record. The 1860 census of the county didn't list any boys with a surname of Stacey. However, the 1870 Census of Williamson Co., Illinois, found a 21-year-old William Stacey in Herrin.

[20] Bainbridge Precinct is now the western two-thirds of West Marion Township. The community of Bainbridge predates Marion and served as the first county seat. The intersection of the modern-day Old Bainbridge Trail and the Crab Orchard and Egyptian Railroad line marks the approximate location of the community.

Cox was attacked in his house and fired on several times. This band soon got so large that it became unwieldy, and they got to stealing horses. Several of them were arrested, tried and bailed, and left the country. Among the men arrested was James Cheneworth.[21]

In 1863, six men in disguise of soldiers went to Daniel Robertson's, in Lake Creek Precinct, and told him he must go with them to hunt a deserter. He said he would if they would go by for his brother, Joseph. They did so. About one-and-a-half miles from Joseph's, one man fired on Daniel, the ball striking him in the forehead, and he fell dead. Then, all six fired on Joseph, shooting four holes in his clothing, but he jumped from his horse and made his escape. They turned back, went to Peter Wascher's, and fired at him, and he at them, and he escaped. It was supposed to be some of this gang.

In 1863, James Stilly was killed by Ben. Batts. The latter was at work in his field, and Stilly came to him and they got into a fight, when Batts killed him with a hoe, and ran away.

In the same year, William Moulton was killed by some unknown assassin. Joshua McGinnis, Dock. Dickson, Thomas Murray and Henry Norris were arrested for this offense, but there being no evidence, they were acquitted. McGinnis may have been guilty, but the others were not.

One morning in 1864, Samuel Moore was found dead at the door of a saloon in Jeffersonville.[22] Parties had been drinking late the night before, and some one had killed him with a club. A man by the name of Washum was indicted, tried and acquitted; and his blood is unexpatiated to this day.

During this year, Vincent Hinchliff shot and killed James Prickett, a young lawyer of Grassy Precinct, at Blairsville.[23] Prickett was appearing in a case against the administrator of William Hinchliff's estate, and he and Vince

---

[21] See Chapter 17 for details on the Aiken Gang's activities that Erwin left out.

[22] Jeffersonville was the main village in Lake Creek Township (Township 8 South, Range 3 East) until the development of Johnston City on the new north-south railroad that now parallels Illinois Route 37. Though platted as Jeffersonville it's best remembered as "Shake Rag." The village was located within the area bounded by Corinth Road on the north, Shake Rag Road on the east and south and Old Frankfort Road on the west, all now on the eastern edge of Johnston City.

[23] Then as now, Grassy Precinct is the township in the south-western corner of Williamson County, home of Little Grassy and Devil's Kitchen Lakes. Cottage Home was the primary post office in the area located near the intersection of modern-day Grassy Road and Spillway Road.

got into a fight, with the result I have mentioned. Vince was tried and acquitted on the ground of self defense.

The last homicide of this year occurred on the 24th day of March. Several of the Parkers and Jordans got into a general fight in Marion, over an old feud, and William C. Parker shot and killed Richard Jordan. Two or three others were wounded. Parker ran away and has never been caught.

In 1865, Isham Canady was shot and killed, in Marion, under circumstances of such a justifiable nature, as to render the homicide almost an improper incident for a catalogue like this, because the killing was not the result of malice, but of a combination of circumstances which made it absolutely necessary at the very moment. The defendant was tried and acquitted on the ground of self-defense.

The next homicide of the year was that of Christopher Howard, who was assassinated near Herrin's Prairie, on Sunday, by some unknown villain, supposed to be on account of politics. He was a Republican.

In 1866, William L. Burton and Samuel McMahan were both shot and killed in a general fight in Sulphur Springs.[24] The fight grew out of politics. They were both Republicans. Dixon B. Ward was indicted for the killing, but there was no evidence of his guilt and he was acquitted.

In 1867, Horace Sims and John Latta got into a rough-and-tumble fight, at Sim's Mill, on the Saline, and Sims stabbed Latta in the thigh, from which he bled to death. Sims was tried and acquitted on the ground of self-defense, he being on the bottom at the time.

During this year, John Cheneworth was assassinated in the woods, near his house, in Herrin's Prairie. He was not found until several days after. Mr. Cheneworth was a still, quiet gentle man. William Chitty and one of his sons were arrested for this crime, but there was not a shadow of evidence against them.

At the November election, 1868, a shooting scrape occurred between the Stanleys and Cashes, in Southern Precinct, in which several shots were fired, and Wm. Stanley was killed.[25] Isaiah Cash was accused of this crime, but the

---

[24] The community of Sulphur Springs no longer exists but was located a couple of miles southwest of Creal Springs. Sulphur Springs Road now runs through the site.

[25] Southern Precinct is modern-day Southern Township, or Township 10 South, Range 2 East, now home to the U.S. Penitentiary at Marion. Pulley's Mill is the chief populated place in the township.

evidence tended to show that another man was guilty. This was an old family feud, warmed up by politics, the Stanleys being Republicans. In 1870 Isaiah Cash was driving along on his wagon, when he was assassinated, fourteen buckshot piercing his body. His slayer has never been known, but enough is known to say that suspicion has rested on the wrong man.[26]

One summer night in 1868, Charles McHaney and a boy by the name of Rogers got into a fight, five miles east of Marion, when Rogers stabbed and killed McHaney. He was tried and acquitted on the ground of self-defense.

In 1869 George Mandrel, a lunatic in Northern Precinct, met his father in the road, and slew him with an ax.[27] The scene was a bloody one, and Mandrel's lunacy is the only thing that saved his neck.

On the 1st day of January, 1869, Samuel Cover shot and killed Phillip Thompson Corder, in Marion. The difficulty arose about a difficulty between Cover and a brother of Corder's. Corder was striking at Cover with brass knuckles, when he was shot. Cover was then put in jail to keep him from being mobbed. He was afterwards tried and acquitted on the ground of self-defense.[28]

---

[26] See Charla Schroeder Murphy's "The Cash and Stanley Family Feud" in the Spring 2002 issue of *Footprints in Williamson County, Illinois*. (p. 14), for details about this relatively unexplored outbreak of violence that pre-shadowed the Bloody Vendetta.

"It seems that two men named Stanley and Cash had a difficulty previous to that time," reported the *Jonesboro Gazette*, "They met at the polls, and after fighting until they were out of the house, drew pistols and fired upon each other."

Despite the newspaper account, according to Cash family descendents Samuel Cash, a cousin of Isaiah, actually did the killing of William Stanley on Election Day, November 3, 1868. Stanley was 48 at the time of his death. Samuel fled to Texas at that point. Two years later unknown parties killed Isaiah. Then 24 years later in April 1894, Ed Cash, a son of either Samuel or Isaiah, lost his life to a mob as well:

"Ed Cash, son-in-law of Lon Perry, in Southern Precinct, this county, was called out of his residence in Texas Monday night the 9th inst. by a mob and hanged. After hanging, the body was fired into by the mob with their pistols and guns. Ed was in this county and worked on A. M. Townsend's farm last summer. He is the son of the Cash who, at an election several years ago, shot and killed Mr. Stanley in this county. The cause of the trouble is unknown here but it is supposed he (Cash) walked contrary to the Texas code."

[27] Northern Precinct is now Corinth Township in the northeastern corner of Williamson County.

[28] Seven years later the *Egyptian Press* reported that a Sam Cover of Grand Tower in Jackson Co., Illinois, had killed a man there on Dec. 8, 1876. Following the incident

On the 1st day of December, 1868, William Barham shot and killed Andrew J. Lowe, in Marion. Barham was a young man, afflicted with lunacy, and while in this condition stepped into Mr. Lowe's saloon, and shot him in the forehead. Barham was then arrested by B. F. Lowe, and lodged in jail. On the 7th day of September, 1869, he broke jail and escaped. Five years afterwards he was betrayed by a young lady in Tennessee, and arrested by Thomas Ballou, and brought to Marion. He was tried, found guilty of manslaughter, and sentenced for one year.

In 1870 Thomas Pinkney White, a prominent citizen of Herrin Prairie, was seen crossing his field in his shirt sleeves.[29] He was never seen again. At the back of the field where he went out, were signs of violence – a little blood and the tracks of two horses from there to Muddy River. It is evident that he was assassinated, but there are some who do not share this opinion. No cause for his running away was known to exist by anybody. He was an outspoken Republican, and his conduct in this line made him some enemies.

In 1871, Mastin G. Walker, an old and respectable citizen of this county, living seven miles northeast of Marion, was met on his farm by a ruffian, beaten over the head with the barrel of a gun, and slain. John Owen, an old man (one of his neighbors, with whom he had some trouble about land), was arrested, tried, convicted and sentenced for twenty-five years to prison; and is now at Joliet.

In 1871, Valentine Springhardt got into a difficulty at a mill in Marion, and was struck on the head with a large wrench and killed. The defendant gave himself up and was afterwards tried and acquitted on the ground of self-defense.

On the 15th day of April 1872, Isaac Vancil, the first white man born in this county, a man seventy-three years old, living on Big Muddy, was notified to leave the country or suffer death. He did not obey the order, and on the night of the 22d, ten men in disguise of Ku-Klux, rode up to his house, took him out about a mile down the river bottom, and put a skinned pole in the

---

he "fled the country." It's not clear if this is the same Sam though. The victim in the 1869 killing, Corder is believed to be Phillip Thompson Corder, Jr., son of P. T. Corder, Sr.

[29] The mines hadn't opened and the city of Herrin didn't exist yet, only a small post office and store sitting in the midst of a small prairie. White is also known to have taught at the first log cabin Bandyville School that opened in 1868 east of Herrin about a quarter mile from the current old school house that still stands at the intersection of Stotlar and Bandyville Roads.

forks of two saplings and hung him, and left him hanging. Next morning, when he was found, all around was still, blank and lifeless. The murderers are not known. I suppose that it must be a source of but little satisfaction to that infamous herd of desperate men to look upon that horrible scene, and feel and know that they are the guilty authors. They are hid from the face of men, but a just, certain, inexorable retribution awaits them. In the last day, God will make requisition for the blood of Vancil, which has stained Heaven with its vulgar blot. Until then we must submit to the arbitrament of time, and calmy wait with patience and resignation the unbiased inquest of the future. [30]

I know nothing of Ku-Klux, but conclude that they are bound by abhorrent oaths, for a squadron of devils could not drive them from their allegiance. It is a hard thing for a man to swear blind allegiance and implicit servitude to a master over both soul and conscience and never again feel the pure, untainted, dashing blood of freedom course his natural veins. Who can succumb to such a disgraceful yoke? Leon in his holy indignation could make no greater demand than this. A den of these infernal demons holding their hellish, midnight revelry, with their blood-shot eyes glaring with untold crimes, and their haggard visages bloated with an impress that tells of woe and mean distress, must be a nice gathering! It may be that some old bridge, on some lone creek, could tell a tale of a soul in mortal strait, and the constellation of the weeping Hyades dropped tears on a scene like this, where the trees have plead for mercy for some other man in the clutches of these mean, sneaking, low-down, white-livered scoundrels.

Vancil was an honest, hard-working man, but had some serious faults. Still, God gave all equal right to live and to none the right to deal death and ruin in a land of peace. Soon after his death eighteen men were arrested in Franklin county, charged with the murder; but were acquitted. Pleasant G. Veach, Francis M. Gray and Samuel Gossett were then arrested in this county, and admitted to bail in Benton. In a few days, Jesse Cavens, Wm. Sansom,

---

[30] Erwin identified Vancil as the first white child born in Williamson County, but immediately after the murder the April 27, 1872, issue of the Carbondale *New Era* identified him as the first white child born in Union County. However, Isaac's father and uncle didn't move their families to Union County until 1805, six or seven years after Vancil's birth in 1798 or 1799, depending on the account: *Source*: William Henry Perrin. 1883. *History of Alexander, Union and Pulaski Counties, Illinois*. Chicago: O. L. Baskin & Co., Historical Publishers.

Samuel Sweet, Jonas G. Ellett and John Rich, of this county, were arrested and lodged in jail at Marion. In eighteen days, Ellett and Gossett were bailed, and the others sent to Perry county jail, where they remained until December, when they were all tried in Franklin county, on change of venue, and acquitted. Some of these parties were indicted in the United States Court at Springfield, under the Ku-Klux Act, but all came clear. Colonel Ambrose Spencer prosecuted them, and he was, on the 6th day of January 1873, arrested for having them falsely imprisoned, and put in jail himself for a short time, and Jonas G. Ellett got $4,000 damages against him in this county.[31]

In 1872, James Myers was hauling, near his house on the Eight Mile, when he was shot from behind a tree with a shot-gun. He was taken to his house, and Samuel Tyner, one of his step-sons, with whom he had had a few words, was there and asked him what he could do for him. Myers told him to go for a doctor. He went to Dr. Hinchliff, and told him where Myers was shot, when he had not had time to find out. He had the day before borrowed a gun from Dr. Hinchliff, and it was found the next day where he had hid it. Young Tyner was arrested and admitted to bail. Myers not being dead, he ran away and has never been found. Myers died soon after.

In August 1872, Richard Allison shot and killed Samuel Absher, in a fight which arose about some chicken-coops, in Rock Creek Precinct. Allison ran away, and has never been caught. He stands indicted for manslaughter.

---

[31] Spencer was the son of John Canfield Spencer, a former Secretary of War as well as Treasury in the Tyler Administration of the early 1840s, during which time he lost his son Philip who had been hung for mutiny aboard the brig "Somers" off the coast of Africa in 1842. Following the incident with the Klan in Williamson Co., Ambrose Spencer moved to St. Louis and then to rural Missouri where he died on April 17, 1876, in the courtroom at Lynn. Without warning a man named Jeffries appeared in the room and shot Spencer three times, "once or twice through the head, the balls entering at the right temple and passing out through the top of the skull. The assassin made no attempt to escape, but gave himself up for trial." Just before firing Jeffries asked, "Colonel, what have you done with your wife and children?" Apparently, the two had fallen for the same woman, except that Spencer had won the lady's hand in marriage. *Source:* Helen Sutt Lind. 1995. *Events in Egypt: Newspaper Excerpts, Williamson County, Illinois, 1856-1878, Vol. 1.* Privately published. 50; quoting the April 13, 1876, issue of the *Marion Monitor* [Marion, Ill.], which in turn had reprinted an article from the St. Louis *Globe-Democrat.* At the time the Marion newspaper had justified the story predicting that it would, "be read with interest by many of our readers as the victim was once a citizen of this place, and while here made himself very conspicuous."

In April 1873, Francis M. Wise and William Newton, of Saline, were riding along the highway together.[32] They had bartered mules, and Wise wanted to rue, but Newton would not. Wise then shot him dead from his horse and made his escape. He is indicted for the crime of murder.

In 1874, Horace Carter shot and killed William Willeford, in Union Precinct, while attempting to arrest Richard Hilliard.[33] Carter was a constable, with a writ, and was shooting at Hilliard, and accidentally killed Willeford. He is now indicted for manslaughter, and under bond.

In 1874, James Gibbs and Dock Burnett, two young men, got into a fight at a party, seven miles south of Marion. They agreed to fight fair, and walked out with seconds. Burnett had a knife handed to him, with which he stabbed and killed Gibbs. Young Gibbs stood up and fought desperately with his fist, while Burnett was cutting him to pieces. He fell, and a cry went up to Heaven from the more tender-hearted in the crowd, at the cruel, murderous exhibition. Burnett fled the county, and a reward of $500 was offered for his arrest.

September 17, 1874, Stewart Culp, a respectable citizen of this county, was on his way from DeSoto, when he was shot and killed. He lay in his wagon with his head and one arm hanging out. His neck seemed to be broken. His horses went home with him in that condition. Nothing is known of his murderers.[34]

---

[32] Saline Precinct is now Stonefort Township in the southeastern Williamson County.

[33] Union Precinct was all but the northern tier of sections in modern-day Creal Springs Townships. Creal Springs itself not existing yet. Ward's Mill and Sulphur Springs post offices were the two in existence.

[34] Culp was Milton Stewart Colp (1820-1874). According to Barbara Burr Hubbs in her 1939 *Pioneer Folks and Places* he had once owned Laban Carter's farm that's now Carterville. The 1870 Census found Colp living in southwestern Franklin County. He was 51 then would have been around 54 or 55 at the time of his murder. His son John (1849-1920) later opened a number of coal mines in the county and gave his name to the village of Colp north of Carterville. A descendent of Vancil's stepson recalls that family stories suggest the Klan visited a Mr. Colp before Vancil's murder. Stewart may have been killed because he had testified for the prosecution in the Vancil murder trials.

Two days after Colp was murdered, someone shot Simon Bishop near Osage a few miles north of Blairsville in southeastern Franklin County. According to the newspaper account published on July 26, 1874 in the *Jonesboro Gazette-Democrat* he had served as a witness in the Vancil murder case, most likely in the state prosecutions

During this same year, William Meece was assassinated by Samuel Keeling, who shot him in the back at church, in Northern Precinct. They were both young men, and had had a fight a few days before. Keeling escaped, and one year afterwards he was arrested in Kansas by John Fletcher, and brought back to Marion. He changed the venue in his case to Saline county, and was tried and sentenced for life to prison.[35]

The next homicide that occurred in this county was that of Capt. James B. Murray, who was walking along a street in Marion, when he came to where Leander Ferrell was sitting. He made a halt, and was fired on by Ferrell. Several shots were exchanged between them, and Murray fell, mortally wounded, and died next morning. Ferrell was arrested and bailed on *habeas corpus,* and was tried in 1876, and acquitted of manslaughter. Murray was a large, powerful man, cool and deliberate, but a man of the greatest courage. Ferrell has been a quiet, peaceable citizen. They had several difficulties before, in which Murray came near killing Ferrell.

In the summer of 1876, John Kelly and Samuel Lipsy got into a fight in Cartersville, and Kelly stabbed Lipsy in the back.[36] Lipsy afterwards died, and it is now claimed from the effects of the wound. Kelly is in jail awaiting a trial.

---

since he is not mentioned as attending the federal trial. *Source*: Summer 2004. "The Murder of Isaac Vancil." *Footprints in Williamson County, Illinois.* Marion, Ill.: Williamson County Historical Society. 7:2. 14.

[35] The Feb. 11, 1875, issue of the *Marion Monitor* provided a few more details to the killing, though some are contradictory noting that Keeling had killed Meece at the "residence of Mr. Fitzgerald in Northern Precinct last winter during religious service. Keeling escaped, went to Nebraska where he has been known as Mitchell until his arrest by John Fletcher of Northern Precinct."

Later after the trial at Harrisburg the May 18, 1876 issue of the *Egyptian Press* of Marion provided more details: "Sam Keeland, who killed William Meece in March 1874 was sentenced to life. The act took place in the night time in a private residence where a congregation of people were holding religious worship at the request of old Mr. Fitzgerrell who was confined to his bed of sickness ... while the people were signing and extending the hand of fellowship to Mr. Fitzgerrell, Keeland stood with the door partially open (he was inside the house). When young Meece gave his hand to Mr. Fitzgerrell, Keeland fired the fatal shot. He fled to Kansas and was captured."

[36] Cartersville is an early form of Carterville, back when the village was still, in the minds of many, that of Laban Carter's.

Chapter 2.   **The Two Sides**

I HAVE NOW COME TO THOSE troubles which were known as

"THE BLOODY VENDETTA,"

And first, I will give an account of the families that. have been suspected of belonging to the Vendetta. And first of the Russells: Phillip T. Russell, who settled on the Eight Mile Prairie in 1817, brought with him three sons, James, Samuel and Jefferson. Jefferson Russell's family consisted of himself and wife, and eight children: Harriet, Winfield Scott, Nancy, Adelade, Mary, John R. , Thomas J. , and Hope. Four of these girls are married, but none of this family have been implicated in the Vendetta but Thomas.[37] They are among our wealthiest and most respectable farmers, possessing good intelligence and education, and none of them ever did anything to bring reproach upon themselves, except it was Thomas. They live in the center of the Eight Mile, on the west side of the county, in a large residence, surrounded by the conveniences of life.

The Sisney family consisted of George W., who first married Panina Brown, and had four children who are now living: Winfield S., John, George W., Jr., and Martha Jane. The latter is now eighteen years old. Mrs. Sisney died in 1863, and Sisney then married Miss Fredonia Williams, who now has four small children. Winfield married Miss Malissa Williams; John, Miss Mollie Higgins; George, Jr., Miss Hannah Tippy. Sisney was a man of more

---

[37] The Illinois Statewide Marriage Index 1763-1900 shows the following data for the Russell marriages in Williamson County:

W. S. Russell married Mary Stansell on Nov. 27, 1856. John R. married Annie Baxter on Oct. 19, 1882; and Thomas J. wasn't found. Harriet married Madison Bolin on Nov. 23, 1854. Nancy W. married Thomas Crenshaw on March 25, 1857. (Thomas was a nephew of John Hart Crenshaw, owner of what is now known as the Old Slave House near Equality — see *Slaves, Salt, Sex & Mr. Crenshaw: The Real Story of the Old Slave House and America's Reverse Underground R.R.* for more information).

Adelade's marriage isn't found and there are too many Mary Russells to determine which one was Jefferson's daughter's marriage. Hope didn't marry until three years after Erwin wrote his book. She married William L. Fain on Nov. 26, 1879.

than ordinary ability; was medium size and compactly built, dark complexion, a very passionate and fearless man, but high-toned, generous and open-hearted. He served as captain in the Eighty-First Illinois Volunteers, and was one of the number who volunteered to run the blockade at Vicksburg.

In 1866 he was elected Sheriff, and again ran in 1874, but was defeated. At his death he had accumulated property to the amount of several thousand dollars. In 1872 he wrote some sensible articles against the stock law, and argued that it would benefit him, but would be a hardship on the poor farmers. The young Sisneys received common school educations, and stand well in this county for honesty and fair dealing.

Of the Hendersons, Joseph Henderson of Kentucky, had three sons who came to this county William, Joseph W., and James. William has seven children: Felix, James, Pad, John, Emma, Margaret and Nancy.[38] Margaret and Nancy are married. Joseph W. has six children: Samuel, William, Thomas, Synoma, Lucy and Dike. James had but one child, Grantie, eleven years old.[39] Joseph W. came to this county in March 1864, and William, March of 1865.

Samuel and James Jr. served four years in the Twentieth Kentucky Union Volunteers. James, Sr., the leader, was born on the head-waters of Blood River, Kentucky, and was forty-four years old when he was killed. He was raised on a farm, but never worked one until he came to this State. When a boy, he drove a team, and one day got drunk, and his father took the team away from him, and from that day until his death he never drank a drop of liquor. He then went to Missouri, and then to Texas, and back to Kentucky, and lived with his brother William. In 1851 he went to California, and remained seven years, and came back to Kentucky with $6,000, and followed buying and selling notes until 1860, when he went to peddling tobacco; — his brother John manufacturing it.

---

[38] Despite the names Erwin provided as children of William Henderson, the 1870 Census of Williamson Co., Illinois, lists a different group. Emma and Nancy aren't found in the census, but 18-year-old Eliza is. Also, William's son James, who is presumed to the James Jr. that Erwin mentions had already married an Emma, who strangely doesn't appear in the 1870 census even though it's two years after the wedding date. The couple is still together in 1880.

[39] Based on the 1870 Census, Grantie must be the Virginia who was listed as five years old that year.

Felix G. traveled with him all over the Southern States.[40] In Guntown they saw seven men hung for opinion's sake. James' indignation was excited, and he declared he would go home and join the Union army. He left his bills uncollected, and went to Paducah, and got permission to raise a company. This company he raised by going around in the bushes at night. The gunboats met him, by agreement, up the river, and took his company to Paducah, and he joined the Twentieth Kentucky Infantry. He then went up the river, and captured the Agnew ferryboat, which he piloted down the river himself. But, not being a pilot, it sometimes took the brush on him. After four months' service, he procured a substitute and started out with five men as a spy. On this raid he captured eleven rebels, and among them, Captain Bolen, who now lives in Paris, Henry county, Tennessee. He next acted as guide, and conducted General Smith's brigade to Fort Henry. After this he left the army, and moved into Massac county, Illinois. Here he remained one year, and then joined the Fifth Iowa Cavalry as guide, in which capacity he served for eight months, and was then guide for General Lowe. He was in a skirmish in Clarksville, and in chasing one man whom he knew, shot at him, and cut a lock of hair from his head, which he picked up and kept. The man came to Marion with Hendricks, from Kentucky, when he had a suit against Henderson, and they had a hearty laugh over it.

While he was with the Fifth Iowa he took a few men and went out from Fort Henry to where a man was harboring five rebels. When Henderson got there they were all in the lot but Captain Ozburn, of Callaway county, Kentucky, who was standing at the gate. Henderson told him to surrender, Ozburn said nothing, but drew his revolver, when Henderson shot him, and walked up to him, and Ozburn fell into his arms. Henderson not thinking he was hurt, again called on him to surrender. Poor Ozburn surrendered his life to his Maker, and sank, and died at his feet. He came to this county February 1864, and in October bought the land, then in the woods, on which he died. Henderson was a large man, weighing over two hundred pounds, and without doubt the most powerful man, physically, in this county. He could not read, but was a coherent thinker: shrewd, cunning, and cautious; a man

---

[40] Felix G. Henderson, who was traveling the South with his uncle James Henderson, Sr., went by the nickname of "Field", a detail Erwin fails to properly introduce at this point before he starts to referring to Felix by his nickname in a few pages.

of but few words, but pleasant and child-like in manners, making him a very safe friend, but a dangerous enemy. Such is the man who was the reputed leader of the Russell side of the Vendetta. Felix always lived with James until within two or three years before his death. Some of the Henderson girls are very handsome, and are excellent school teachers. The men are mostly illiterate, but shrewd and cunning. They have dark skins, coal black eyes and raven hair, and some of them are fine-looking men. They are men of few words, and are not the kind of people that turn over mountains; but a braver set of men don't live on earth. With the exception of Pad, they are considered honest and fair in all their dealings. This comprises the leading families on the Republican side of the Vendetta. Many others are implicated in this bloody feud with them, but I will describe them as they come upon the scene.

The Bulliner family consisted of George Bulliner, his wife and eleven children: Elizabeth, Mary, Nancy Emeline, Rebecca Adeline, David, John, Monroe, George, Emanuel, Amanda Jane and Martha Lane. The youngest is now sixteen years old. Elizabeth married Jordan C. Halstead; Mary, John Gamble; Nancy, W. N. Berkley; Rebecca, Aaron Smith; Amanda, Pierce Crain; Monroe married Miss Josephine Council, a very handsome and accomplished lady; Emanuel, married Miss Mary Tiner, and David, at his death was engaged to Miss Cornelia O'Neal, of Tennessee.

George Bulliner lived in McNairy county, Tennessee, and was a man of considerable means and influence. At the breaking out of the war, he was a loyal man, and in September 1862, raised what was always after known as "Bulliners Company," They first served as State guards, and finally entered the Union Army. Bulliner served without pay. He came to this county on the 28th day of January, 1865, and bought a farm from Arthur Blake, two miles south-east of the Eight Mile, on which stood a two-story brick residence. In 1867 he put up a horse-mill and a cotton-gin. His son David first kept store with F. M. Sparks, a half-mile north of his house, and then put up a store at home. This he kept a few years, and then moved it to Crainville, and went in with Wm. Spence, to whom he afterwards sold out, and with whom he had a little suit, but not one that generated ill-feelings. The other boys worked on the farm, and are young men of fine personal appearance, light complexion, dark hair, social, jovial and very pleasant in their manners and address. George Bulliner was a man of more than ordinary ability, a large, stout-built man, of homely appearance. He was noted for his zeal for what he regarded as right, for his sterling honesty and boldness in asserting and maintaining his opinion, and defending his principles. He was energetic, and a shrewd business man, and was kind and lenient to the poor, buying what ever they had to sell; and in building up the country, and helping his neighbors, he not only became wealthy, but built up a character that was conspicuous and honorable. To a stranger he appeared like a cross, ill-natured man; but that was not his true nature. He was not a religious man, and sometimes resorted to rough sports and amusements. At the time of his death he was sixty-one years old.

The Hinchcliff family consisted of William Hinchcliff, who settled here in an early day, and died in 1858, his wife and three sons: Vincent, Robert, and William. As a family, they are very intellectual, and noted throughout this county for integrity and high social qualities. They live on a farm on the north side of the Eight Mile, a half mile from Russell's. They used to keep store there, and Vince was a physician, a good musician, and a man of fine ability, but of very violent temper. He was agreeable and social to his friends, but unpleasant and offensive to his enemies. Being a leading man, he had some enemies growing out of politics. Robert is a man very different in temper. Educated, refined, a splendid musician, sociable, honest, and a gentleman from the ground up. He is also an artist, and paints with great skill. He lives in a lovely little cottage amid bowers where roses, honeysuckle and jessamines mingle their colors and rich perfumes with the poseys and daisies. A meadow in its green livery, with tall, wild flowers oscillating in the breeze, and fields and forest so blended as to make a landscape of ever varying beauty, surrounds his house, where the song of the little bird is pouring forth, and insects sport playfully in mid-air, which makes their bright hues appear more resplendent by the sun's golden rays. Near the cottage is a flower-garden, containing every thing that can charm the eye or delight the senses. I will not attempt to describe this little floral world, for there is no end to it. This is a picture of his home, and imagination can furnish nothing more delightful than a life gliding away amid a scene like this. Robert and William have never had anything to do or say in the Vendetta, but have both been studiously exonerated from all suspicion by all parties.

The Crain family is a very large one. Spencer and Jasper Crain settled in this county in an early day. Spencer had several children; among them was Jasper U.; Jasper, Sr., had several, among them was William and Spencer, Jr. William Crain had eight children: Nancy Ann, George F., Terry, alias "Big Terry," Noah W., alias "Yaller Bill," William J., alias "Big Jep," Warren,

Marshal T., and Wesley. Jasper U. Crain has seven children: Terry, Samuel R., Lorenzo, Alonzo, Mary, Pierce, and Eva. Spencer Crain, Jr. had three living children, Wm. J. alias "Black Bill," Martha, and Elizabeth.

The other families are too numerous to name. Then, in fact, it would be useless, as only five of those I have mentioned have been implicated in the Vendetta. Most of the Crains are religious, and live honest, upright lives. They are all considered honest, pay their debts, and deal fairly with their neighbors. William and some of his boys would often get into rough-and-tumble fights; but never used weapons. "Big Terry," now dead, was a powerful man. Aside from this, there was nothing to distinguish them from the rest of our citizens. George F. is a Justice of the Peace, and one of the most respectable and honorable citizens of the county. The same could be said of several others of them. They received common school educations, and none of them are very wealthy; but all are good livers, and farmers, and live three miles east of the Eight Mile. They belong to the sanguine temperament (excepting Black Bill who is bilious) and are social and agreeable men to meet. These are the leading families on the Democratic side.

Chapter 3. **The Root Causes**

I WILL GIVE ACCOUNT OF OTHERS as they appear on the scene. The first difficulty in the Vendetta occurred on Saturday, the 4th day of July 1868, in a saloon one and a half miles east of Carbondale; but it is right to say that there is not a drunkard, excepting Samuel Musick, in all the Vendetta. Felix G. Henderson was on his way from Carbondale, about 4 o'clock P. M. It was raining very hard, and he stopped in the saloon, where the Bulliners, for the same reason, had stopped a few minutes before. The Bulliners were playing cards. After a while George Bulliner bantered "Field" for a game. They went to playing. Presently George Bulliner, Jr., (a son of David Bulliner, of Tennessee), commenced by betting on the game, and got to putting in. Field told him to shut up, that it was none of his business. Young George said Bulliner was six and "Field" five. "Field" said he was six and Bulliner five. Bulliner said "Field" was right. "Field" then got up and called young George a dam[n] lying son of a _____.

Young George first got a chair, which was taken from him, and then they clenched. George broke away and got some bottles. "Field" drew his knife, and George Bulliner, Sr., struck him with a bottle, and knocked him six or seven feet. A general fight followed, in which "Field" was badly beaten up. The bar-keeper's wife and James Russell parted them. At this time, "Field" did not know the Bulliners, and asked who they were.

In the fight, "Field" had cut David Stancil on the arm. Next day Stancil sent Eli Farmer to Henderson to apologize for him. When Farmer came James Henderson cursed "Field," and told him that a saloon was no place to be in. After the fight was over, "Field" fearing the Bulliners would follow him, went an unusual route to William Hindman's in this county, where George Sisney washed off the blood. "Field" did not feel satisfied, so next week he went to where young George was plowing in David Stancil's field. They spoke, and Bulliner asked him how he was getting, and if he was hurt. "Field" said "I am badly hurt. I was overpowered the other day, and if you want to try it over I am willing, any way you want to." Bulliner said that he did not want to fight. "Field" told him that he had an equal show now, and that he himself had been mobbed.

Bulliner, fearing that Henderson was going to shoot him, broke for a tree and called for his pistol. Henderson told him that he came to offer him a fair fight, and rode off home.

In the September following, Bulliner had three ricks of hay burned.[41] The tracks of two persons were observed leading in the direction of Cartersville. The next week his cotton-gin was burned and had at the time one hundred thousand pounds of cotton in it, fifteen thousand pounds of which were taken out of the ruins, a week after the fire. Suspicion was thrown by some on Felix, but a large majority at that time supposed it was incendiaries from Tennessee, and it is not known to this day who did commit this arson.

In 1872 Thomas J. Russell and John Bulliner commenced going alternately with Miss Sarah Stocks. They soon became cool rivals. Bulliner finally succeeded in making himself the most acceptable visitor. Envy seized Russell, and they became enemies; but other than a few short words, had no difficulty until the riot at Crainville.

In 1869, a man by the name of Samuel Brethers, who lived at Bulliner's, cultivated a part of Sisney's farm, which joined Bulliner on the east. He raised a crop of oats, and after they were thrashed, he left them on Sisney's farm. He then sold the oats to Sisney to pay the rent, and also sold them to David Bulliner, to pay a debt, and went to Texas. Bulliner claimed the oats, and replevied them from Sisney, but got beat in the suit.[42] On the 26th day of April, 1870, they met at Sisney's blacksmith shop to settle.

They differed about each other's account, and Sisney said, "If we can not agree we will leave it to our betters."

David said "I tried you in law once."

Sisney replied "Yes! and I beat you."

David said "Yes! and you did it by hard swearing;" and Sisney knocked him down with a shovel.

David ran home, got his father, John and Monroe with their pistols, and started back. Sisney, on seeing them coming, retreated out the back way, from his house, with a Henry rifle. John fired on him, near the house, at about 150

---

[41] "Ricks" are large stacks of hay. Usually hay would have been piled high to dry before being baled.

[42] Bulliner had gone to court to claim the oats as his property and that they had been unlawfully taken by Sisney. The legal procedure was called a replevin. To have "replevied" the oats meant that Bulliner had tried to regain possession of them by a court ordered writ of replevin. As Erwin noted, Bulliner lost and Sisney won the case in court.

yards. David fired with a gun, and again at 250 yards, just as Sisney went behind an old tree that stood in the field. Four of the balls took effect in his leg and hip. Sisney then asked for quarters, and George Bulliner stopped his boys. Sisney was carried to his house, and Bulliner waited on him faithfully for several days. They were all indicted in September following, and four of the Bulliners and Sisney each fined $100. This was the only difficulty that occurred between the Sisneys and the Bulliners.

I have now given the three original causes of the Vendetta; first a deck of cards; second a woman; third, oats.

Chapter 4.   **The Crains and the Riots**

THE CRAINS NEXT CAME INTO THE SCENE in a fight against the Sisneys. Marshal T. Crain and John Sisney had had a fight eight years before, but had made it up. Still later, they had another fight, at Mrs. Clements, about some "tales." John was accused of striking Marshal with brass knuckles. They, at this time, agreed never to be friends again, yet not to fight any more; but in November, 1872, they got at it again, with "Big Jep," and Wash (George Jr.) Sisney, thrown in for strikers; but nobody was hurt.

About the 15th day of December, 1872, James Henderson went into the Company store, in Carterville, and bought a pair of boots, and a dog fight occurred at the door, in which the Crain boys had a dog. "Big Terry" was cursing Elijah Peterson for interfering. Henderson thought that they took the other dog to be his, but he said nothing, and started off. "Big Terry" said "I would like to knock that dam black rascal." Henderson, not thinking the remark intended for him, walked on, when Terry added, "That rascal with the boots." James told him it was a good time, to "lam in." A few more words were passed, but no fighting.

This affair threw the Hendersons and Crains into line against each other. The Crains, now being enemies of the Sisneys and Hendersons, became plaint allies to the Bulliners.

On the 25th day of the same month the Carterville riot occurred. John Sisney, Wesley and Marshal Crain were in the Company Store, when Sisney threw out some banter to Marsh, who struck him three times with a weight. Milton Black started towards them, and "Big Terry" told him not to interfere, that they were boys. Black said he would not.

Then Terry said "I am a better man than you, Black."

Black said, "That is untried."

Terry said, "I am going to whip you."

Black replied, "You ain't done it."

Terry started at him, and Black knocked him down three times, and it was supposed with brass knuckles. The other Crain boys started towards Black, and George Sisney cried out "Give Black fair play."

Just then some one knocked him (Sisney) senseless to the floor, and Warren Crain fell on him. They fought around for a while, and then got outside; the fight stopped, and, after a few words, Wesley Council struck Sisney on the forehead with something in his hand, supposed to be a weight. After this the Sisneys and Black went into Blake's grocery, when Terry again come on to Black, but George Bulliner interfered, and said Black should not be imposed upon, and there it had to stop. Sisney and Black went to the hotel to wash, when Terry and posse came in to arrest Black for using knuckles. Black resisted, saying that a private citizen had no right to arrest him. This ended the riot.

Some of the parties were arrested, and their trial set for December 30th, at Crainville. The Hendersons had heard that the Crains had said, if any of them came down on that day they would be to haul home. So, on that day all the Hendersons, Sisneys, Bulliners, Crains, Council, Thomas Russell, some of the Stotlars, and several others, were on hand, and, in place of a trial by law, they had a trial by wager of battle. Russell raised a difficulty with John Bulliner. They commenced fighting on the east side of Wm. Spence's store, and fought around to the south door, John with a little stick, and Tom with his fist. James Henderson told Tom to get a brick, which he did and threw it at Bulliner, who then drew his pistol. Russell then drew his. At this instant David Bulliner came out of the store, and James Henderson drew a revolver about a foot long, and said no man should touch. The Bulliners then went into the house, where some of the Crain boys were. Sam. Henderson struck the house with his fist, and asked:

"Where are those God d--n fighting Crains that were going to whip the Hendersons?"

James H. said: "I can whip any man on the ground."

George Bulliner, standing in the door, said "Henderson, I don't know so much about that, that is hard to take."

Henderson told him to come out and fight like a man.

Bulliner said he had nothing against the Hendersons.

James said: "I have against you; you beat up my nephew."

"Field" spoke up and said: "I am the one; come out and fight a man of your size."

Bulliner started out, but was caught by Wm. Spence, who shoved him back and shut the door. Henderson cursed around for half an hour, calling the Crains traitors, cowards, &c., and then went home, alleging that the

Bulliners and Crains were so thick in Spence's cellar, that when they drew their breath the floor raised. Marshal Crain was indicted for an assault with a deadly weapon on John Sisney, but never had a trial. The State's Attorney filed an information against about twenty of these fellows for riot, and at the February term of the County Court, 1873, they were all in Marion. The information was quashed. Thomas Russell went back to Crainsville, and at Spence's store he met with three of the Bulliner boys. They soon determined on a fight, but Russell ran off to Carterville, a half mile, where he found the Hendersons. He told James to go back with him and see him a fair fight. James started back in a wagon, and they met George Bulliner coming down. James got out of his wagon and said:

"Bulliner, you are the cause of all this trouble; why don't you make your boys behave, and let people alone?"

Bullinger said he could not control them. James said:

"That's a lie; get down and let *us* stop it, for you are heading it; let's fight it out between me and you, and stop it, or, stop it without fighting, just as you want to."

Bulliner said he was for peace. So they agreed to have no more fighting.

Soon after this, Henderson was driving along by Vince Hinchcliff's with a load of rock, when Bulliner overtook him and they had some very hot words, Bulliner threatening to kill him on the spot, and Henderson challenging him to fight. Behind Bulliner was a wagon with five others in it, but they said nothing. Henderson drove on. He always contended from that day that he was waylaid. And it is almost certain that Bulliner had been, before this.

Along in the summer of 1873, Marshal Crain and John Sisney met in Crainville one night, and talked about shooting each other, but put up their pistols without firing.

Jennings, the State's Attorney, had these rioters arrested four times, and the information for riot was as often quashed. On the fifth trial, some of the rioters on the Crain side were convicted; those on the other side changed the venue to Jackson county, where they were acquitted. At one of these attempted trials George Sisney got mad at Jennings, and was cursing him to me, in the County Clerk's office, when Wesley Council stepped in at the door. Sisney called him a "hell cat." Council drew his revolver, and I caught him and told him he should not be hurt. Sisney drew his revolver, but could not shoot without striking me, which he would not do. Wash Sisney was present, and did some talking of a threatening character. Council behaved himself with remarkable coolness to be in the presence of a man of the nerve of Sisney. I got him out of the door, and he went into an adjoining house. After the danger was all over, there were some wonderful exhibitions of bravery among the outsiders.[43]

The next difficulty in the Vendetta was Nov. 6, 1873, at the election in the Eight Mile, when Thomas Russell, David Pleasant and David Bulliner got into a fuss over the old feud, and James Norris, a new actor on the stage, (as was also Pleasant) who worked for the Bulliners, took it up for Bulliner. He went to B's for a gun, and soon returned with one, and Tom drew his revolver, but parties interfered, and prevented any killing. This was a serious affair. It was two desperate young men on each side, facing each other with deadly weapons, and it took the greatest exertion to prevent the death of some of them.

---

[43] The "I" in this chapter is Milo Erwin.

Chapter 5. **First Blood**

ON THE MORNING OF DECEMBER 12, 1873, George Bulliner started to Carbondale, on horseback. The sun was standing against the murky haze of the east, red and sullen, like a great drop of blood, The pearly, vapor-like sails dotted the sky, and covered the more delicate sculptured clouds with their alabaster sides. The great oak-trees lifted their parapets to the morning sky, and spangled the earth with shadows. The voiceless winds swept with sublime resignation lawless through the leafless woods, and a melancholy breeze stirred the dead ferns and drooping rushes. A cold-scented sleuth-hound had followed the tracks of Bulliner remorselessly. This morning two of them, with stealthy movement, took their position near the Jackson county line in an old tree top, on the ground. There, planted on the spot, their ears drank in every sound that broke the air, mouth half open, ears, eyes, soul, all directed up the road to catch, if possible, each passing object. They thought they could tell the thud of Bulliner's horse's feet from all others. They lay down on their breasts, and fixed their eyes on the road winding down the valley. They stuck up brush to shield them from observation, like an Indian watching for his victim, alertly awake to every noise. Bulliner came riding along and one of the assassins fired on him; only two or three of the balls took effect in his hip and leg; but his horse wheeled and threw his back to the assassins, who fired on him again, and forty-four buckshot took effect in his back, and he fell to the earth. The assassins then escaped. Bulliner was soon found and carried to the nearest house, and his sons notified, but after desperate riding John reached the place only in time to hear his father say, "Turn me over and let me die." He did so, and George Bulliner escaped from the cruelties of earth to the charities of heaven. Look here, all you infernal wretches, and contemplate a spectacle which should inflame your hearts with mercy. Right in the face of heaven, and among men, George Bulliner was slain by one of the most sordid mortals that ever disgraced the black catalogue of crime, or befouled the fair fame of civilization, and his death, today, is unexpiated in Williamson County.

On the night of the 27th of March 1874, while Monroe and David Bulliner were on their way home from church, about half a mile westward from home, in a lane, they were fired on by two assassins, who were concealed in the fence corners, about twenty feet apart. The balls went in front of their breasts. David stepped forward a few steps, both drew their revolvers, and commenced firing on the assassins. A perfect hurricane of shots followed. The people going from church knew what it meant, and they stood still. The assassins emptied two double-barrel shot guns and two navy revolvers. David fired three shots, and Monroe six. The last shot from the assassin's gun struck David in the back, and he cried out, "I am shot!" and sank to the ground. Monroe ran to him, and at the same time heard a noise further down the road. He asked who was there; a voice replied, "The Stancils."

Mrs. Stancil, about fifty yards down the road had received a severe wound in the arm and abdomen, from which she afterwards recovered. The assassins retreated southward through the field. It was a scene worthy of the gods to see these two young men facing two concealed assassins, and fighting them like men of iron. At one time, Monroe charged on one of the villains, at the same time firing, and drove him out of the corner, and forced him to take refuge behind a rail, which Monroe struck with a ball. Who can read this without wishing a thousand times that he had shot the life's blood out of his black heart! David was carried home by a host of friends, who had gathered at the scene. At the gate he asked: "Is it a dream? Is it a dream?" and each broken word gurgled up out of the red fountain of his life. His brothers were standing around, their faces sealed with the death seal of inexpressible suffering, and their hearts hushed in the pulsations of woes. His mother lay trembling against the casement, her heart throbbing with its burden of sorrow, while the issues of life or death were being weighed to the soul of her son. His sisters were standing in the vortex of misery, praying for the dreadful slaughter to be stopped, and suing for happiness with the sunny side of life in view. Convulsive sensations of horror and affright, and smothered execrations pervaded the men, and audible sobbings and screams, with tears, were heard among the women.

This was the worst murder of them all. No other equals it in heinousness. You may combine corruption, debauchery and all the forms of degradation known to the inventive genius of man, and cord them together with strings drawn from maidens' hearts, and paint the scene in human blood bespangled with broken vows and seared consciences, and still it will redden Heaven with revengeful blush and leave you to blacken hell to make it equal. It had not been long since the flash of fire from the gun of his father's assassin had sent a blasphemous challenge to his life. The echo from that gun had not ceased to ring, when this deed of barbarity was committed.

David was a gentleman in the fullest sense. There was nothing mean in his appearance or conduct. Twenty-five years of age, tall, and of magnificent appearance, and respected by everybody for his still, quiet manners. But on the morning of the 28th, the twilight shadow of death, cold and gray, came stealing over him. A supernatural lustre lighted up his eye, and illuminated the gathering darkness. At length his eyes closed, and an expression of ineffable placidity settled on his pallid lips, and he was no more. He was taken to Tennessee, where his father had been, and buried.

Chapter 6. **The First Trials**

THE NIGHT DAVID WAS KILLED, the assassins had probably four stands, and there were no less than seven men on the watch for him; but after he was shot, he charged Thomas Russell and David Pleasant of being his murderers.

Jordan Halstead and Samuel R. Crain came to Marion that night, and I wrote out the writs for their arrest; but it was near daylight when the *posse comitatus*, headed by Constable J. V. Grider, surrounded the residence of Jefferson Russell. Thomas was arrested, and a party sent on into Jackson County after Pleasant. They were both brought to Marion, and Russell employed me for his counsel. While he and Pleasant were in my office, Gordon Clifford, alias "Texas Jack," came in, talked a few words with Russell, and soon left town. Pleasant was about twenty-two, tall, awkwardly built, nervous, and seemed badly frightened. The case against him were *nolled*, and he immediately left the country.[44]

Most people believe him to be guilty. One thing I do know, that he was as uneasy as an eel on a hook, and his confused behavior makes it reasonable to suppose him guilty. It is not my business to say who is guilty, and who is not; but, if he is, until repentance composes his mind, he will be a stranger to peace. Russell changed the venue in his case from W. N. Mitchell, J. P., to Geo. W. Young, J. P. All the batteries of the Bulliners were leveled on Russell. They employed three attorneys to assist the State's Attorney. W. W. Clemens was then employed by Russell to assist in his defense. The case went to trial on Thursday, but was *nollied* by The People, who already had another warrant for his arrest issued by George F. Crain, J. P. The State's Attorney, Jennings, had lost confidence in Young. In fact, being a most consummate scoundrel himself, he could see no virtue in anybody.

The object of the prosecution was to get time to hunt up evidence; but it was a source of positive relief to the defense to have the *nolle* entered. I knew, most certainly knew, that Young would send my client to jail; but now I told

---

[44] As a lawyer Erwin often used the verb "nolled" (spelled variously throughout the book) in his writings about the Vendetta. It was the local shorthand for the Latin *nolle prosequi* which literally meant "unwilling to pursue" — the legal motion prosecutors filed when they were dropping charges in a criminal action.

him for the first time that we could clear him. The venue was again changed from Crain, J.P., to William Stover, J.P., of Eight Mile, who came to Marion and heard the case. The trial commenced Friday morning, March 31, 1874. The Bulliners in Tennessee had not only said that "they did not want any more Bulliners brought down there in boxes," but David, Sen., had come up to see that the guilty were prosecuted. Tom's gun was sent for, and the contents extracted. The People proved by two witnesses that Russell was at the window of the church that night, and the wadding picked up from the ground where the shooting was done, was placed to that drawn from the gun, and gave, as they claimed, an unbroken account of the St. Louis tobacco market. Balls and cutwads picked up were similar to those in the gun. They also proved threats. David's dying declaration, saying that it was Russell, was introduced. The defense was an alibi, five witnesses swearing that he retired at eight o'clock, was seen by them at half-past eight, and again at ten, in his room; — the murder having occurred at half-past nine o'clock, two miles away. The tracks were proven to be two numbers too large. The prosecution claimed that defendant's witnesses swore falsely; but I said then, and repeat it now, that they swore the truth. When Russell first employed me, I asked him to call up his witnesses, and let's see if they were going to swear harmoniously, and if there were any of them whose evidence would damage us, we could leave them off. He said:

"Call them as you please; they will swear that I was at home. They know I was at home, and you can call them on the stand without any drilling. I am not afraid for you to do this."

So, I say, if Thomas Russell is guilty, he came out of his window on to the stoop, and down to the ground, and returned the same way.

The prosecution was badly managed. One of defendant's witnesses was Miss Hope Russell, a sister to the defendant, and a lady whose exalted virtues and transcendent beauty claim a consecrated place in this volume.

One of the People's witnesses was Miss Amanda Bulliner, both about sixteen years old.[45] She took the stand with a helpless and confiding look, her

---

[45] Erwin's information on the women's ages appears to be wrong here. The 1870 Census of Williamson Co., Illinois, listed both women as 13 that year which would put their ages closer to 19 at the time of the trial. Amanda was the daughter of George Bulliner. No marriage record has been found for her. *Source*: Illinois Statewide Marriage Index, 1673-1900. Illinois State Archives.

voice was a little softened by emotion, her rose-leaf lips curled delicately, but soon her clear, translucent eye lit up with a brilliant lustre. The shadows of misery seemed to depart. Her soft, round cheek dimpled and dimpled again, like the play of waters in the sun, in a lovely and touching assembly of charms. Her features were of classic regularity. Her presence seemed to hallow the place. So pure, so truthful, so charming her actions, that all pronounced her a most gentle, and most noble creature. Though never a jeweled wreath may span the curls on her beautiful brow, yet happiness may as well erect its shrine around her, for Nature can no further gifts bestow. Monroe Bulliner swore that he was within a few feet of the assassins, but did not recognize them. This was a remarkable exhibition of veracity. He might have identified the parties, and the world believed it true; but, firm as a rock, like a sainted martyr, he stood by the open, bold and honest truth.

One of the witnesses was the famous Sarah Stocks, who swore to threats. Her contour is not as faultless as a Greek goddess, but her form and features had caught some new grace from the times. Her eye was as clear and cold as a stalactite of Capri. She wore a sigh, and there is something in a sigh for everybody. But I will throw no shadow over her, for life in her is as mysterious as in the rich belle; and when the golden chariot of destiny rolls through the skies, she may take her seat among the great.[46]

On Saturday evening, the sun went down behind a fleecy cloud, and kindled a volcano from whose silver-rimmed crater fiery rays of scarlet shot up the clear blue dome of heaven, and the lurid lava streamed downward through vapory cliffs and gorges. Alarm took the place of anxiety. The Russells, Hendersons, Sisneys and their friends were in town, and rumor was rife that they had a load of arms, and that they would rescue Russell if he was committed. The people were scared, and went home. The State's Attorney ran off. The defense thought that the Bulliners were going to assassinate Russell, if he was turned loose. On the contrary, they had no such notion, but thought that they would be killed. The excitement arose from mutual misapprehensions. The Sheriff summoned twenty-five men, with guns, to

---

[46] Apparently Abraham Fozzard drove a more earthly chariot that carried her off in marriage the following year on Sept. 9, 1877, in Williamson County. *Source*: Illinois Statewide Marriage Index, 1673-1900. Illinois State Archives. She was closer to 23 at the time of the trial, based on her age in the 1870 Census of Williamson Co., Illinois. The census shows her likely the daughter of Ben Stocks, a native of England, and likely brother to the Henry Stocks who married into the Russell clan.

hold the prisoner. Calvert closed for the People, amidst the greatest excitement, and the Court said the defendant was not guilty.

The surprised audience looked blank and sad. James Henderson and a dozen others rushed to the defendant, gave him a pistol, and rushed him down stairs, where horses were in waiting. Russell and three others mounted, and left town at full speed. A letter was sent from the State Attorney of Jackson county, by James Conner, to the Sheriff, to hold Russell for the murder of George Bulliner, but, for some reason, was not delivered to the Sheriff until he was gone. The hue and cry was levied immediately, and several days were spent in trying to find him, but he has never been arrested. The Bulliners offered $500 reward for his arrest, and $2,000 for the conviction of him and Pleasant, which they afterward withdrew.

I will relate one incident as an illustration of the excitable foolery of the times. One evening, when all hopes for Russell's recapture were lost, John Russell came into town to see Clemens and myself on business. We had a social meeting appointed at G. L. Owen's that night, for some days before. After Russell was talking to us, we got a buggy and started out. Going on, I told Clemens that the people would think from the fact that Russell was there, that we were going out to see Thomas, and we had better drive rapidly and conceal our buggy, and have some fun: which we did. Sure enough, here they come; on hand cars, horseback, and on foot, with general orders to arrest the "whole boiling," and put them in jail. Several hours were spent by these fellows in fruitless chase after "all three of them." There were several men in that raid, but I have never been able to find one of them.

If Thomas Russell is guilty, it may be that the almighty sovereignty, love, was too strong for him, and envy seized him, and John and not David was the one he wanted to kill. If he could have wrung this lady from John Bulliner, and unstained her life, I doubt not if the shadow of his own would not have again darkened it; and inasmuch as he did not, it may be that the arrowy words wrung by the hand of passion from each of them were destined to hang quivering in memory's core till they festered and bled, making an irremedial wound, shaped in the red-hot forge of jealousy, and cured only by the exultant feelings of gratified revenge. These little bubbles of joy that jet up from the tumultuous waters of passion, soon evaporate, and leave but mingled dross and shame to fester and canker the mind of its possessor, who ever after leads a life of infamy and its accompanying wretchedness. Whoever committed these murders is the guiltiest of them all.

It was he who with death first knocked at our portals, and with buck and ball opened the flood gates of misery, and let murder rush with living tide upon our people. And today his life is ruined, his hopes are blasted, and sooner or later he will come to sorrow, shame and beggary, and have the scorpion thongs of conscience lashing his guilty bosom as he promenades the sidewalks of destiny.

Thomas J. Russell was born February 1st, 1851, is of fine form, dark complexion, black hair, and very intelligent. The charge brought no blush to his cheek, but throughout the trial he sat contented, with but little to say, and kept watching the Bulliners with implacable glance. John Bulliner had his gun. In speaking of these troubles, it looks like repeating the old story, and opening the wounds to bleed afresh; but the cry of murder and bloodshed is of too common occurrence in this county, not to have it recorded. The smoke from one of these bloody acts scarcely settled on the field, when it was renewed. The report started and went the rounds, only to return and be renewed by the slaughter of another victim.

Chapter 7. **Revenge**

I AM BOUND TO RECORD THESE ACTS as they have occurred, for it is a page of history, recorded and sealed by the blood of our fellow-men, that will leave a crimson stain on the county, that will be gazed upon and wondered at by the young, years to come. The Bulliner boys appealed to the law. They appealed to humanity. They and their friends rode night and day, and spent hundreds of dollars in prosecuting the assassins, as they believed. But they were defeated. The law was not supported by a pure public sentiment of the people. The ones that they looked upon as being guilty were turned loose. What could they do? Must they be driven to the bushes by this hard bargain, or be placed for a lifetime at the mercy of assassins, with their hearts enclosed in palisades of sorrow? They saw their father and brother shot down by vandal hands, and their own lives threatened by fiends stalking in midnight darkness. Is it a wonder that the spirit of retaliation seized them, and the stern, old Mosaic law of an eye for an eye and a tooth for a tooth, went into full force among them, and they became aggressors themselves?

Retaliation was taught them by every cord in human nature. They were drawn upon by every principle that calls forth human action. Their lives were a constant appeal to chivalry. What could they do but pick up the gauntlet hurled into their faces, and give vent to an anger long pent up? At this time there were interests more sacred to the Bulliners than those of peace. Justice was more. Honor was more. Fidelity to the memory of a murdered father and brother are considerations for which those who spoke so loud in favor of peace, would have foregone progress and prosperity, and drawn the shotgun in stern resentment and punishment of those who invaded and violated these sacred rights. When can son forget his father? When did passion and crime ever estrange one from the other? When Ocean surrenders up her water, then will the parents of his hopes and tears, and the holy lessons learned on their knees, be alienated from the son's heart. They must, if they are human, esteem revenge for their wrongs as the most sacred inheritance.

The ordinary agents of the law had proven insufficient, and Nature rose up to avenge the injustice. Embassadors were at an end. Words of menace and expostulation were exchanged for the thunders of the shot gun. The quarrels which a hollow peace held in abeyance were to be settled in the bushes. The die was cast. The god of the bushes had been invoked. The red hand of murder was raised. The feuds which had so long fermented among the Vendetta, were relegated to the arbitrament of the murderous shot gun. Already the lurid flames of the midnight gun lit up the fair fields of this county. Already the smoke hung like a wreath over the fairest lands of Egypt, and death stalked with defiant tread over the county. The past was an index to the future. The cries of our future victims had already reached our ears. The Bulliners were not uncomplaining sacrifices. The voice of humanity had issued from the shades of their farm, and it had been unheeded, and one of them has since been convicted of murder. Whether he is guilty or not is not my province to say, but to tell the facts the best I can, and let the world pass its judgment on this slaughtered family.

John Bulliner could have been actuated by but one principle of human action in going into this work of blood, and that was revenge. If any thing could be tolerated to plead in extenuation or palliation of crime, surely it could be urged in his case; but if he is guilty, I would place his crime at nothing less than murder. The assassins of his father were actuated by malice. Their deeds were committed with no ingredients to assuage or cool; — making them the most dastardly acts on record.

The Crain boys were actuated by a very different motive to join in this work. That is, where the power to do wrong with impunity exists, the will is not long wanting. Whenever mankind sees a chance of doing wrong without ever being detected, they do not wait for a provocation. The best of men will do wrong, and nothing but wrong, if you remove the fear or possibility of punishment. It is true that the fear of God restrains a small class. But generally this is but a temporary restraint, and is effective only when protected from strain. But strain, it take away the punishments that men inflict, open the gates to crime, and some of the best men will become the most consummate scoundrels in the land. So it was with the Crains. They did not commence killing from an inherent love of killing, but because it was being done by others, and nobody punished. Hence, men have been heard to say, "I might as well make some money as anybody else."

After Russell's release, several parties formed themselves into fantastic models, and scouted the country. Ready to vie with each other in general follies, they started out by being ridiculous and ended by being vicious and criminal. One of these parties, headed by Vince Hinchcliff, arrested Gordon

Clifford, alias "Texas Jack," down near the bloody grounds, and after treating him very badly, brought him to Marion, and just before daylight, had a mock trial before a J.P., the State's Attorney reading the law out of a patent office report, and probably the drunkest man in the crowd. "Jack" was put in jail without law or evidence, — the only witness being "Smokey Joe," who had never seen "Jack" before. "Texas Jack" was a very mean man, but he ought to have been tried as becomes the ministers of justice in her own sacred temple. He came into this county in 1873, and lived around promiscuously for two years, offering gratuitous meanness for his board. He was about twenty-five years old, tall, slender, fine-looking fellow, and a very fast young man generally, a noisy ladies' man, and horse jockey. He lay in jail until October, when he was indicted for harboring "fugitives from justice," meaning Thomas Russell. He gave bond in the sum of $500, and after having a couple of rows with Hinchcliff for the treatment he received from him he left the country. He said he came from Kansas, and Vince wrote there, and his character was very bad. When he was arrested, the word "hanging" was pretty freely used, and I would suggest that if he ever take a mania for suicide and will come back to this county, he may find somebody who will assist him off in a romantic manner.

Some of their scouting parties talked about hanging men; plans were laid in Marion; meetings were held; names given; the leading men on the Russell-Henderson-Sisney side were to be hung; but they never could get the executioners on the ground.

After the Russell trial, James Henderson was waylaid. He set up many a night all night, watching for the assassins, but his dogs barked and his mules brayed, every time they would come near the house, as if to warn their master that assassins were lurking in the bushes, and they would run off. One night he hitched his mules out in the woods to keep them from making a noise, so that he could kill the assassins, but just before they got up that night in shooting distance of him, the mules broke loose and came running to the house. He worked in his field, surrounded by a dense forest, with Grantie and little Frank Jeffreys acting as guards for him.

On the morning of May 15, 1874, while Frank was on watch, he said he saw somebody behind a pile of logs in the field. James looked and said he guessed it was nothing. In the afternoon, Grantie had to help her mother wash, and Frank was on guard alone. About three o'clock, he said he was lonesome sitting up in the edge of the woods, and wanted to come down to his foster father. James, who had been building fence, told him to come, and he lay down with the boy. Three assassins lay concealed behind a pile of logs, twenty-seven steps away. The dripping drab of a summer sky overhung the scene in pearly sails, and just when our people were looking for light out of darkness, to unmantle the smouldering folds of hatred, they fired on Henderson, who lay on his side, the balls taking effect in his back. He turned over on his face, and put his hand over his eyes while looking at them. One of them walked out from behind the logs and fired at him with a pistol, and struck him in the hand. They then ran off. He said right there, while his agonizing nature was vibrating in horrid suspense between life and death, that he recognized the assassins as James Norris, John Bulliner and Manuel or Monroe Bulliner.

Thomas Wilson, a young man who was near by and saw the men, did not know them. Henderson was carried to the house, and lingered eight days before he died.[47] When the news of the shooting reached Marion, but little concern was manifested. There was a disposition that so long as they kept even down on the "bloody ground" it was all right. One fellow cried out, "Thank God, they have got the old king bee at last." But such a sentiment was too shocking to float unrebuked on the air of Marion. We know what such sentiments have produced in other countries. History tells the fearful tale. The terrible record is written in blood, and the world stands aghast when the book is opened. He was informed that a bunch of bones would be rammed into his face if he repeated that sentence.

There was no high-wrought, inflated tone about Henderson. No straining or twisting of style, but all was plain, simple, easy and natural. He was compelled to toil for the necessaries of life, and bravely bore the frettings and raspings of this cold, dull world. To his friends he was warm-hearted, candid, earnest and honest, and would risk his life for them any time. To his enemies he was cautious, daring and dangerous. He was a man of but few words, but

---

[47] Thus the first of the witnesses who testified against the Klan in the Isaac Vancil trials died. Four months later, the second witness, Milton Stewart Colp was found dead as well. Although there were three James Hendersons in the northwestern part of the county, it's believed that this victim, James, Sr., was the one who testified, as an article on the Norman shooting in 1875 made reference that two of the witnesses had died. If it wasn't James Sr., who testified, then the next likely candidate is James Jr., (the victim's nephew) whose middle initial is listed as "G" in the census just as the witness in the Vancil case.

wore a mild, firm fearless look. He is gone! And the silver-dusted lilies and trailing willows will throw their flickering shadows over his grave, made green by the lichen-fingered touch of time forever.

Soon after his death his wife became a lunatic, and died on the New Year day following. On Saturday, the next day after Henderson was shot, Jason Ditmore was plowing alone in his field, one mile west of Henderson's, and about ten o'clock he was fired on three times in rapid succession, five of the balls striking him, one in the breast, one in each arm, one in the side and thigh; but he soon recovered, and left the county. No reason for this shooting can be given, unless it was that he saw the assassins of Henderson. He was in no known way connected with the Vendetta.[48] When the inquest was held over Henderson, the Coroner issued his warrant for the arrest of John Bulliner and James Norris, but they ran at large until August 25th, 1874, when Deputy Sheriff W. J. Pully arrested Bulliner at Crainville. He was kept under guard at Marion until September 3d, when he was taken before Judge Crawford on a writ of habeas corpus, and was admitted to bail in the sum of $3,000. In October following they were both indicted for murder. Bulliner was put upon his trial, and had four witnesses from Tennessee, who swore that he was there at the time, and he was acquitted by a jury.

Soon after Ditmore was shot, John Rod and one other man were riding beside a field, three miles north-west of Henderson's, and two miles north of the Eight Mile, when they saw a man fall down in the weeds in the field. Thinking something had happened to him, Rod went over to see; when he got within ten feet of the man, he rose and fired on Rod, shooting him through the thigh, and then scampered away. It was rumored that this was Thomas Russell, but rumor had him everywhere, so there is no telling.

On Sunday morning, August 9th, 1874, George W. Sisney went out to his barn lot, and two assassins, who lay concealed in the fence corner near by, snapped their guns at him four times, but being wet with the dew, they did not fire.[49] He was shocked, and called to one of his boys to come to him, when

---

[48] However, Jason may have been a relative to the John Ditmore who testified as a witness for the prosecution in the later trials of "Black Bill" Crain and "Big Jep" Crain as reported in the Feb. 3, 1876, edition of the *Marion Monitor*.

[49] The *Marion Monitor* of Aug. 13, 1874, covered the attack under the headline of "Murderers in the Bush." – "On Sunday morning, just after day light, Mr. George W. Sisney, a well known citizen, living ten miles west of this place in this county, walked out into his lot to care for his stock, when two men with double barreled shot guns snapped

the assassins rose and walked off, and he stood watching them for over two hundred yards. He did not tell who these parties were, but at the October term indicted Timothy Edward Cagle and James Norris, for an assault to murder him, claiming that they were the parties. Cagle is nineteen years old, an orphan boy, slim, awkward built, fair complexion, very pleasant and agreeable. He once had a difficulty with one of the Sisney boys. He worked for David Bulliner thirteen months, with James Norris. After he was indicted he went to New Orleans, but returned, and in March, 1875, gave himself up and lay in jail until September, when he went to trial. I had opened the case for the defense, when it was *nolled* on account of Sisney's death.

About this time rumor was afloat that Dr. Bentley, of Marion, had cut some balls out of John Sisney, supposed to have been received when David Bulliner was killed. On the 17th day of August, W. H. Bentley published an affidavit, stating that he had never cut any ball out of or known of any being in any of the Sisneys, and that the rumor was false. John Sisney was not believed to be guilty, but made a very convenient scape-goat for those who were.[50]

During the month of August, "Field" Henderson and Monroe Bulliner accidentally met in Marion, and had a talk, and agreed to meet at Carterville, and compromise, and have no more trouble. Monroe said he would get John, and "Field" said he would get all the Hendersons, and meet him on a set day. "Field" saw the Henderson's, and they said they had so far nothing to do

---

at him several times at a very short distance – ten or twelve feet. Mr. Sisney was very much frightened, as any reasonable man would be. He called out for one of his boys, and the two villains fled. He saw them distinctly as they ran for more than a hundred yards. He has not told who they are if he knows. We had fervently hoped that these disgraceful scenes had stopped in our county; but these murderous villains are still sneaking around to draw the life blood from some other victim…"

[50] Although the *Marion Monitor* had encouraged the public to adopt "more radical means" to combat the growing violence, in its article following the assassination attempt on Sisney, the former Union officer chose another approach. In September he allowed the *Monitor* to announce his candidacy for sheriff. "In this [Sept. 17, 1874] issue will be found the announcement of G. W. Sisney, as a candidate for sheriff of Williamson county. Mr. Sisney is well known in this county, has served one term as sheriff and his official acts are before the people, therefore we do not consider it necessary for us to say anything further than he is now a candidate for the office, and no doubt would make an efficient sheriff."

with the troubles, and were not going to have; but "Field" went to Carterville by himself on the day, and Monroe, John, and Vincent Hinchcliff met him.

Vince took him out to one side, and said, "'Field,' these boys did not kill your uncle Jim. I know they did not. All they want is to be let alone. The next man that is killed, the last one of the Hendersons will be killed or run out of the county. You fellows, by God, can't kill every body. The people won't stand it."

"Field" said, "Don't say you fellows; I have had nothing to do with it."

Vince replied, "You are the only one of them that has any principle. Old Jim had but d--d few friends; I was one only through fear."

He said he had sent for the boys, two new shot guns, and they had not come, and that is why he knew they did not kill his uncle. Here Monroe and John came out, and John asked "Field" where Sam. Henderson was. "Field" said he did not know, that he was afraid to stay at home and work. John said"

"Sam is in the bushes, and if my enemies do not come out and face me like men, I will go into them myself."

But they all agreed to be friends, and have no further trouble. "Field" was to tell Sam that he could come home and go to work, and that they were not to hurt him; but Sam never came home. This was the first time that "Field" knew that Vince was an enemy to them. He used to deer-drive with his uncle Jim, and he was astonished at his talk.

On Sunday, October 4th, 1874, Vincent Hinchcliff rode out north about a mile, to see a sick man. Coming back about noon, and two hundred and fifty yards from his house, several ruffians had concealed themselves in a skirt of timber, on the east side off the road, which had been fenced in, but had grown up with small bushes. They fired on him sixteen times, four shot guns and twelve pistol shots. He and his horse were both shot dead on the spot. Robert, who started down at the first shot, turned the rise, and what a scene was there to greet his eyes! What a radia of woe surrounded his heart! What a halo of shame! With an agonizing spirit he looked and saw Vince lying face downward on the cold earth, shot to death by the unerring missiles from the murderous shot gun. And the bright sun looked sorrowfully down, a silent witness to this deed of inhuman butchery. And in the woods near by were heard the screams of joy and fiendish yells of these ruffians, holding a regular Kickapoo war dance over his remains, while the smoke from their guns was ascending high up in the dome of day as a signal to the surrounding country that another victim had been offered up. Who does not wish that he could have cut fire-brands from the flames of torment, and with unsparing hand scattered them relentlessly through that forest? Humanity would have directed the stroke, and civilization have countenanced it. Heaven help the assassin whose unsteady aim had left Vince Hinchcliff uncrippled, for he had arms and he would have instantly wielded them with a dexterous hand, and unbarred the gates of perdition for two hell-deserving assassins. At two o'clock of that day two men blacked were seen crossing a field three miles east of Vince's, but were not recognized. At the October term, Fielding G. and Samuel Henderson were indicted for this murder.

On the night of the 12th day of December 1874, Captain Sisney and George Hindman, a young relative, were sitting near a window on the south side of Sisney's house, playing dominoes, when an assassin came on the stoop in his sock feet, and shot through the window at Sisney. About forty shot struck him in the right arm and carried away the muscle. Hindman was badly wounded in the neck and arm, from which he recovered. Sisney's arm withered away. This was a random shot, fired into a family, and the wickedest one ever fired in this county. Marshall Crain said he did this shooting, and that there was no one with him. But the tracks of four persons were seen next day, one at each corner of the yard, and the sock-footed fellow made leaps that would have strained Marshall Crain considerably, At the April Term, 1875, Timothy Cagle was indicted for an assault to murder each of these parties; but on what evidence I am unable to tell. After Sisney's death, both cases were *nolled*. Marshall Crain also said that about this time he tried to kill Milton Black, who had fought "Big Terry," and that he waylaid John Sisney, and came very near killing Worth Tippy, one day, believing it to be Sisney.

On the first day of January 1875, "Field" Henderson was in Carterville, and Monroe Bulliner went up to him and asked him to explain why he had inquired of the chamber-maid at the McNeill House, where he slept. "Field" said he had not done so. Monroe then asked him to go to the girl and see. "Field" said he would not go, for he had not done so. Monroe said that he was satisfied, but a crowd gathered around who took "Field's" refusal to go see the girl as evidence of guilt. Rough words were exchanged, and revolvers drawn, and "Field" commenced backing off. He displayed remarkable coolness and courage. Any other man would have crouched like a spaniel at their feet, or risen like a demon to confront them; but he silently withdrew and boarded the train. The crowd got on also. Monroe came into the same car with him and they talked the matter over, but the crowd was barred up in the baggage car by the conductor, who stood in the door. The train ran a half mile to Crainville, where all the parties got off, and "Field" came on to Marion. It afterwards turned out to be one of Bulliner's friends who inquired for his room, in order to get a pistol he had left there.[51] Monroe Bulliner, Wesley Council, J. M. McCarty, Hugh McCarty, and John Moore, were indicted for a riot, for this affray, and were tried at the November Term of the County Court, 1876, and acquitted.

When "Field" arrived at Marion, he went to the residence of J. D. F. Jennings, State's Attorney, to see if he was indicted for the murder of Hinchcliff. Jennings told him he was, but to keep out of the way until Court. "Field" went home, five miles north of Marion, and Jennings came running up town and told that "Field" had been there with three revolvers, and tried to kill him, and "played thunder" generally. And he had the whole town in the greatest excitement. It was published in the papers, and went the rounds, that "Field" Henderson, the famous outlaw and desperado, had tried to assassinate the State's Attorney for doing his duty. The truth is, he displayed no weapon, but acted as gentlemanly as a man could, to my certain knowledge. I was Henderson's counsel, and we followed Jennings' advice.[52]

In February, the Deputy-Sheriff and another man went out to arrest "Field," who, when he saw them, ran up stairs, and when they came in below he climbed down the stoop and started off through the field. They took after him, and fired on him six times. He returned the fire three times.[53] After his escape he went to Kentucky, where he remained two months, and in April,

---

[51] The Jan. 7, 1875, issue of the *Marion Monitor* summed up the event with far fewer words: "Something of the nature of a riot occurred near Carterville, last week. We cannot give details this week. Pistols shown — no body hurt."

[52] The "I" in this paragraph refers to author Milo Erwin himself.

[53] The Jan. 7, 1875 issue of the *Marion Monitor* ran the following story about the attempted arrest:

"Felix Henderson was indicted at the sitting of our last grand jury, for the murder of Vincent Hinchcliffe. On last Monday, Deputy Sheriff Edrington and posse, having a *capias* for his arrest, went to his place of residence, about 7 miles northwest of here, for the purpose of taking him in charge. He saw them coming, and went up stairs, and when they entered the house, he climbed down one of the posts of the porch, and took to his heels. The officers fired five shots at him, and he in turn fired three shots, all of which took no effect. He escaped and is still at large."

1875, came back and gave himself up, and was admitted to bail on motion, on the 13th day, in the sum of $5,000, which he gave, and at the October Term we went to trial, and proved by fifteen good men that they saw him near a church at the very hour Hinchcliff was killed, twelve miles away. And the State's Attorney, after this evidence was in, entered a *nolle*.

AN ILLINOIS VENDETTA.

The Bulliner-Russell Feud—A Quarrel of Six Years Standing.

[St. Louis Globe-Democrat.]

The Russell-Bulliner feud, which has for six years been a terror to the good citizens of Williamson county, Illinois, and has won for it the sanguinary sobriquet of "Bloody Williamson," has broken out afresh, and promises to be more violent than ever. The gen-

NewspaperArchive.com

IN THE NEWS — These headlines from Aug. 6, 1875 edition of the *Indianapolis Journal* (top) and the Sept. 16, 1875 edition of *The Burlington Daily Hawk-Eye* of Burlington, Iowa, (left) were typical of the wide coverage Southern Illinois' Bloody Vendetta generated around the Midwest. Notice that the Indiana's reprint of the *Globe-Democrat's* story represents one of the first uses of the term, "Bloody Williamson," in connection with Williamson County, a term that would come back to haunt the county during the 1920s.

THE VENDETTA.

A Number of the Williamson County Murderers Arrested.

Interesting Disclosures by One of the Gang of Outlaws.

One Hundred and Sixty Dollars the Price of a Human Life.

The Gang Believed to be Completely Broken Up.

More Horrible Disclosures Expected From One of the Prisoners.

The People Rejoicing over Their Deliverance from Terrorism.

Story of the Capture and Confession of Samuel Music.

The Carbondale correspondent of the Cairo Bulletin furnishes the following interesting particulars concerning the discovery and arrest of the Williamson county outlaws:

Chapter 8.   **The Ku Klux Klan**

DURING THE SUMMER OF 1874, there was an organization of fifteen men, near Carrier's Mills, in Saline county, who extended their operations up into this county. They called themselves "Regulators," and dressed in disguise, and went around to set things in order.

They did not injure any person, but simply notified those whom they thought out of the line of domestic duty, and even in financial affairs, to flank into line again. They generally gave their victim such a scare that he was willing to do anything to be in company by himself. Such a band is a disgrace to any civilized country; but no serious results or disparaging influence came from this one. Rumors were currently circulated of the good they were doing. Lazy, trifling fellows took a scare, and blistered their hands at work; quarrelsome women turned to praying, and brutish husbands became as loving as Adonis, under the potent influence of this country clique.[54] There was probably an organization of a more serious character in this county. Several men were taken out and whipped, and some ten or fifteen notified to leave the county. This was during the years 1874-5.

On the night of the 23d of October, 1874, a party of twenty men in disguise visited the family of Henry D. Carter, in Northern Precinct, and ordered him to leave the county within forty days, whereupon a fight took place, and twenty-two balls were lodged in his house. In a few days, fifty-two men met in arms at the County Line Church, in daylight, and ordered six of the Carters to leave the county.

----

[54] "A body of men calling themselves regulators went to the home of Dick Summers in Saline County, Saturday night … called him out and gave him a lashing, promised him another one if he did not perform such acts they required at his hand … also visited Alex McComb and W. Ginn, lectured them and left without serious violence. They called on Caroline Bell and asked for Mr. Singleton, not finding him they left orders for him to keep clear of that place in the future." All of the persons mentioned were white.

Source: Helen Sutt Lind. 1994. *Events in Egypt: Newspaper Excerpts, Williamson County, Illinois, 1856-1878, Vol. 1*.Privately published. 12; quoting the Oct. 15, 1874 edition of the *Marion Monitor*.

Mr. Carter wrote their names to the Governor, imploring protection. The Governor wrote to Jennings to enforce the law, and of course that ended it. Several anonymous letters were written to editors, threatening them, during these two years; but if there were ever any regular Ku-klux in this county, outside of the band who hung Vancil, it was in 1875, in the west and southwest sides of the county, and a small band which probably included some members of the Vendetta.

■ — ■ — ■ — ■

IT'S AT THIS POINT IN ERWIN'S ACCOUNT of the Vendetta that an interruption is in order. For the most part Erwin considered the activities of the Ku Klux Klan in Williamson and surrounding counties as separate from the crimes of the Bloody Vendetta. Although he may have been technically correct, most people outside the county saw the violence of the deadly feuds and the Klan as all part of the same breakdown of civil society. Upstate and out-of-state newspapers often used "Illinois Ku-Klux" as the headline to introduce stories of both the Klan's outrages as well as the Vendetta trials.

By the highpoint of the Vendetta the Klan was almost a decade old, having its roots in the organization of a half dozen Confederate veterans meeting in a Pulaski, Tennessee, law office on Christmas Eve in 1865. The name Ku Klux came from the Greek word for circle *kuklos*. Former slave trader and Confederate Gen. Nathan Bedford Forrest became commander of the Klan in 1867 and by 1868 the Klan had spread throughout the old Confederacy and beyond.

The *kuklos* reference suggests to many historians both back then as well as today a tie between the Klan and antebellum Knights of the Golden Circle that began to spread out of Cincinnati, Ohio, in 1854, as this *Alton Daily Telegraph* article from 1868 explains.

An Old Order Under a New Name.
The New York Tribune says "the name Ku-Klux is possibly a modification of the infamous title Golden Circle, the Greek word of Circle being Kuklos. A slight variation from the true pronunciation would give the existing popular name. Whether the villains now banded as K.K.K.'s are direct descendants of the Knights of the Golden Circle, we cannot say; but their conduct warrants the

conclusion that they are just the offscourging of that treacherous gang."[55]

Originally, the Golden Circle supported the expansion, forced if necessary, of Southern slave-holding territory to everything within a 1,200 mile radius of Havana, Cuba – basically the American South, Texas, Mexico, parts of Central America, Cuba, Hispaniola and the various Caribbean islands. After a purported invasion of Mexico failed in 1860, the group turned to support the Confederacy following Abraham Lincoln's election that November. During the Civil War the group became a fifth column in the North actively supporting the South and Union anti-war movements. In Southern Illinois the group included thousands of members that harassed Union soldiers home on leave, opposed Union recruitment efforts, and likely assisted Confederate raiders. Erwin himself estimated the Golden Circle included 800 members from Williamson County alone in 1862.[56]

Other than Erwin's account and contemporary newspapers, the published histories of the surrounding counties generally cover up the activities of the Klan in their counties. It took nearly a half century and the organizational efforts of the 20th Century Klan before additional details of the Klan to appear in print as a warning to others about the dangers of the K.K.K. Dr. Andy Hall, a prominent Mount Vernon physician grew up in Franklin County during the 1870s and knew many of the participants. After the Klan held an organizational meeting in Mount Vernon in 1923, he decided to speak out and provide a history of what they had done a half century earlier.

> The headgear of the Franklin County klansmen consisted of a tall white cap with peep holes and a long flowing robe that covered the entire body. And always completely covered their horses with white blankets, even the heads of the animals except for the peep holes through which to see. This was to prevent the possible identity of the animal, disclosing the name of the rider.

---

[55] April 14, 1868. "An Old Order Under a New Name." *Alton Daily Telegraph.* [Alton, Ill.] 1.

[56] Milo Erwin. 1876, reprint 1976. *History of Williamson County, Illinois.* Marion, Ill.: Williamson County Historical Society. 66.

At one time they were so numerous and active in that community that one could seldom start out on the highway without meeting from ten to thirty klansmen. Their principal activities were directed to supervising all the social, moral, and business affairs of the community. Unfortunately they administered punishment to their personal enemies and to those who dared to disobey their orders or warnings.

For several months they carried on unmolested, visiting isolated farm houses in the dead hours of the night, called occupants outside and warned them what they should do or should not do and frequently punishing them in various ways. But they finally woke up the wrong men and after they had suffered several casualties from acute lead poisoning, they suddenly ceased to function as a Klan.[57]

The antebellum night-riders or patrollers organized at the county and township level in slave states to watch the roads for slaves found off their plantation at night served as another antecedent of the Klan. While ostensibly for public safety the patrollers' true objective proved to keep the enslaved population in check through terror and intimidation, a role the Klan is probably best known for attempting, if not achieving. Although Erwin didn't mention it, this early version of the Klan in Williamson County followed its southern predecessors. About a month after the attack on the Carter farm, the Klan began harassing a white teacher at an African-American school east of Marion. In November 1874, J. C. Clark, wrote a letter to the *Marion Monitor* claiming he had received death threats:

[Clark] has had many attacks from enemies swearing that no man shall live in this neighborhood and teach Negroes... some said he would not live to get a month taught...

Needless to add, Clark felt his life in danger. Not much is known about him except that he enlisted in the army at the age of 16, having been born in

---

[57] Andy Hall. July 1923, reprinted April 2002. "Ku Klux Klan in Southern Illinois." *Springhouse*. 19:2. 14. In this article publisher Gary DeNeal introduced the topic for six long paragraphs before reprinting Hall's original 1923 article on the Klan that had been copied in the July 19, 1923, edition of the *Daily Independent* of Murphysboro, Illinois.

White Co., Illinois, and serving four years and nine months. He had "lost health" and was unable to farm so he had moved to Jackson County where due to failures of the fruit crops two years in a row, "he was forced to sell his team and pay his debt." He had a wife and two children and had worked the summer of 1875 for Henry Gray one mile east of Marion. It was Gray and Dr. T. A. Ferguson, a physician with more than 20 years of practice in the county that had helped "him get a colored school."[58]

If the Klan took its white supremacist expansionism from the Golden Circle and its terrorist and racist heritage from the night riders, then the third tradition it followed was that of the Regulators for its purported purpose of promoting law and order. Organizations of Regulators had developed over the first century of American history in a variety of places, usually where organized crime reached a point beyond which frontier courts could handle. Southern Illinois alone provided at least half a dozen major examples of Regulators in action.

Capt. Young and the Exterminators rode against the outlaws and the Harpes in western Kentucky in the late spring and early summer of 1799 reaching as far west as the river pirate nest at Cave-in-Rock. Regulators operating out of Clinton and Washington counties targeted the Goings' Gang of counterfeiters at Walnut Hill in Marion County during the early days of statehood with a major raid in 1821.[59] Another group targeted additional counterfeiters and horse-thieves in Lawrence County also in the early 1820s.[60] Regulators assassinated James Ford, the organized crime lord of southeastern Illinois and western Kentucky at Ford's Ferry, Kentucky, in 1833.[61] Anti-black Regulators attempted to drive out all residents of color from Gallatin County

---

[58] Helen Sutt Lind. 1994. *Events in Egypt: Newspaper Excerpts, Williamson County, Illinois, 1856-1878, Vol. 1.*Privately published. 13; quoting the Nov. 12, 1874 edition of the *Marion Monitor*. See page 42 for Dr. Ferguson's death in January 1875, as reported then in the *Egyptian Press*.

[59] 1881. *History of Marion and Clinton Counties, Illinois*. Philadelphia: Brink, McDonough & Co. 49, 219.

[60] 1883, reprint 1968. *History of Edwards, Lawrence and Wabash Counties, Illinois*. Lawrenceville, Ill.: Lawrence County Historical Society. 109. Online at Ancestry.com.

[61] William D. Snively Jr. and Louanna Furbee. 1968. *Satan's Ferryman: A True Tale of the Old Frontier*. New York: Frederick Unger Publishing Co. 164. Ford's Ferry is just a few miles upriver from Cave-in-Rock on the Kentucky side of the river.

in the spring of 1842 following the burning of John Crenshaw's mill during his trial for kidnapping. Another extra-legal group, the Vigilantes organized by Crenshaw's son-in-law Michael K. Lawler organized to fight them. Regulators fought the outlaw-friendly Flatheads in Pope and Massac counties following a number of kidnappings of black children and assaults on elderly whites in the mid 1840s near Golconda. This grew into what became known as the Flathead-Regulator War or the Massac County Rebellion.[62] Although it's clear that all these groups took the law into their own hands, it's hard looking back at the widespread public corruption during some of these incidents and not sympathize with them to a degree.

All of this begs the question of why did the Klan exist at all in Illinois, unless it was an outgrowth of the Golden Circle and part of a broader Democratic effort to intimidate Republican voters and bring about an end of the military Reconstruction of the old Confederacy. Illinois newspapers were reporting the Klan's organizing efforts in the state and elsewhere in the Midwest as early as 1868.

> The Decatur Republican hears it whispered on the streets that an offshoot of the Ku Klux Klan is to be organized in Decatur. An ex rebel officer, who lately held forth in that city, is said to be the originator.[63]

Erwin didn't write when the Klan organized in Williamson County, but noted that its membership numbered 130 at the time of Vancil's murder in 1872. He claimed it had been broken up the same year, but "did not meet again until 1874, when a few of them formed a Klan in the west side of the county."[64] Note that both 1872 and 1874 were election years.

Vancil's murder on the surface suggests more of a Regulator motive to the Klan's activities rather than racism. Erwin's account reported earlier in the first chapter, "Of Criminals," provided all he wrote on the incident even though it received wide press coverage in the region at the time. Erwin

---

[62] Jon Musgrave. 2005. *Slaves, Salt, Sex & Mr. Crenshaw: The Real Story of the Old Slave House and America's Reverse Underground R.R."* Marion, Ill.: IllinoisHistory.com. 245-251, 269.

[63] April 29, 1868. "News Items." *Alton Daily Telegraph*. [Ill.] 1.

[64] Erwin 66.

mentioned Vancil possessed faults, but didn't explain, though a historian of Union County did a decade later recalling "Lying Ike" Vancil:

> The Vancils were early settlers, and a numerous family in Union County in early days. Jonas Vancil, one of the old members of the family, settled in this precinct.[65] He had a son named Isaac, who, from his able faculty of warping and twisting the truth on convenient occasions, eventually won for him the sobriquet of "Lying Ike" Vancil. He talked recklessly and extravagantly, and was considered, as we are told, the biggest liar in the county. His father was a Dunkard, wore long hair and whiskers, and had a thick growth of hair over his entire face. Ike and his father made a trip to North Carolina — their native State — and during the journey, which in those primitive days was necessarily slow, they run out of money, and in order to "raise the wind," Ike exhibited his father, whom he represented as a wild man from the Rocky Mountains, a fact which his long hair and whiskers seemed to warrant. The "show" was quite successful, and with the funds thus raised they completed their journey.
>
> Ike was full of fun, mischievous as the day was long, and, as an old gentleman said, had the "devil in him as big as a groundhog" He took it into his head once to scatter a camp-meeting (being held in a grove nearby) for some fancied wrong. Having caught a full-grown turkey-buzzard, he made a "turpentine ball," and one night when the meeting had reached its most exciting and interesting point, Ike fastened the ball to the buzzard's leg, set it on fire, and turned the frightened bird loose in the midst of the congregation. A few tallow candles very insufficiently lighted the scene, and when the buzzard commenced flopping around among the people, with the blazing turpentine ball, they thought the devil had burst upon them, and were worse frightened than the poor bird itself was. Such screaming,

---

[65] The precinct was originally called Ridge Precinct, but later after the railroad came through became known as Alto Pass Precinct. Barbara Burr Hubbs in her 1939 *Pioneer Folks and Places of Williamson County, Illinois*, noted that the father "was a confidential friend of George Owl and George Hunter, chiefs of the Indian tribes that lived between Big Muddy River and the Mississippi."

praying and miscellaneous hollering never before, perhaps, had awakened the echoes of the hills around that camp-meeting ground.

There was a cave in the north part of the precinct, near the county line, and Ike finally succeeded in convincing the people that it was haunted by evil spirits, or occupied by thieves and robbers. He rigged a kind of an arrangement in the cave, by which, by some hocus pocus, he could at will produce a most unearthly and horrible sound. The people one day gathered en masse, armed to the teeth, for the purpose of recklessly invading the cavern and capturing a legion of devils, thieves, robbers, bandits, or, Booth Bell-like, taking in a gang of "mooners." But it is needless to say they were themselves "taken in," when they found how beautifully they had been sold. It is not known whether this man of practical jokes is still alive or not. The last heard of him he was in the vicinity of Carbondale. He was naturally intelligent, witty, a good talker, but almost wholly uneducated. Had his intellect been turned to matters of moment instead of things frivolous, he might have made for himself a name long to be remembered among his fellow men.[66]

As it turns out Vancil's unmentioned faults included those of a more amorous nature than Erwin wanted to include. Luckily for history the editor of the Carbondale newspaper didn't share those concerns as he reported the murder in the April 27, 1872, issue of the *New Era*.

WILLIAMSON COUNTY KU KLUX
ISAAC VANCIL HUNG BY MOB ORDERS BY MEN IN DISGUISE
— THE KU KLUX UNIFORM — AN AGED MAN SEIZED IN HIS
OWN HOUSE, TAKEN TO THE WOODS AND HUNG.

During the past twelve years many outrages have been committed in Williamson County, including more than a score of murders, and except in one or two instances, the perpetrators have escaped punishment. Nothing, however, that has occurred of a more startling character, or which shows a more depraved state of society

---

[66] William Henry Perrin. 1883. *History of Alexander, Union and Pulaski Counties, Illinois*. Chicago: O. L. Baskin & Co., Historical Publishers. 412.

than the murder of Isaac Vancil near Herrin's Prairie on Monday night last.

Mr. Vancil was a wealthy farmer, nearly seventy-five years of age, and claimed to be the first white child born in Union County. Except that his reputation for chastity was not the best, little could be brought against him. He engaged in no neighborhood quarrels, had few enemies and was as well liked and as much respected as any rough, ignorant, inoffensive but somewhat overbearing man is apt to be.

For fifty years he lived in adultery with a woman, by whom he had a large number of children, and after her death some four years ago, he made a will bequeathing his property equally among his children. Three years ago he married, but some months since separated from his wife, who, at his request, continued with him in the capacity of housekeeper.

Three or four weeks since a large party of men in Ku Klux disguises, wearing long white robes edged with black, rode up to his door and handed him a paper with the injunction to obey its contents. The paper was an order to do certain things, among which was to dispose of a portion of his property in a given manner, quit visiting his mistresses, and produce a young man who lived with him five or six years ago and who suddenly disappeared, or give a satisfactory account of his absence; disregard of these orders would be followed by death.

Mr. Vancil became much alarmed upon the perusal of the document and took it to Marion and consulted with an old friend, Captain Corder, upon the best course to pursue.[67] The old gentleman finally determined to carry out the behest of his unknown enemies, as the best means of avoiding trouble, and performed the orders to a letter, except producing the body of the young man, that person living in Mississippi; in fact that was known to many of Vancil's neighbors.

For a week or two, Vancil staid away from home, but supposing that the affair had blown over, he ventured to return on Saturday.

---

[67] Capt. Corder would have been Anderson P. Corder, an old veteran of the Mexican War and former state's attorney.

Nothing occurred on Sunday or Monday to excite a suspicion that any further outrage would be attempted, and on Monday night the family retired at their usual hour and soon all were hushed in slumber.

At about eleven o'clock, a knock was heard and fearing no danger, the old man opened the door, when four men disguised in Ku Klux robes entered the house and ordered him to dress himself and accompany them. Outside the door stood six other disguised villains who turned fiercely to the members of the family and bade them keep quiet and not to leave the house till morning on pain of death.

A few rods from the house the party was joined by four more fellows also disguised and the fourteen scoundrels moved rapidly towards a piece of timber half a mile distant. How the poor old feeble white haired victim plead for his life or what appeals he made to his captors to spare him the few remaining years which a kind nature had allotted him; or how all these prayers were answered only by jibes or curses, are only known to the cowardly perpetrators of the dastardly crime.

A neighbor who was returning home heard voices proceeding from the spot where the murder was committed and recognized Vancil's voice but could not understand what he said nor did he dream of the tragedy that was being enacted near him. Despite his prayers and tears and feeble efforts at resistance, Vancil was led into the wood and the party halted beneath the tree that had been selected for the infernal purpose of their meeting. One of the party quickly mounted the tree and to a long projecting limb placed a rope which had been provided for the occasion. The rope was somewhat too long and fearing it might slip and perhaps defeat their hellish design, it was extended over a sapling which grew conveniently nearby.

The sapling was bent over and held in that position until Vancil's arms were pinioned and the fatal noose placed around his neck, when the men who held the sapling let go their hold and the young tree fell back to its original position, jerking Vancil several feet from the ground where, writhing and squirming in his terrible death agony, the fiends left him.

All night long the inmates of that lone farm house listened and waited for the return of the old, feeble white haired owner. But the hours wore on and he came not, nor did the bright morning sun bring even a gleam of hope to the weary watchers. Those sons and daughters whose infancy and youth he had guarded and watched over, what a night of terror it must have been to them. And that gray haired matron who three years before had pledged him her heart, but who had been estranged and again reconciled — none can realize her thoughts as hour after hour passed without bringing back her husband.

At daybreak every member of the household commenced a search for the missing man. The trail of the murderers was soon struck and within half a mile of his own door step the body of poor old "Uncle Ike" was found, stark and cold, hanging from a tree.

This is one of the most cowardly and unprovoked outrages ever perpetuated in the state. Although the people in that neighborhood fear to take active measures for the apprehension of the murderers, the county authorities have taken the matter in hand and are working earnestly to bring the offenders to justice. That an organization of such a character could be formed and parade in their disguises on several occasions without discovery shows a remarkable state of society prevailing in that vicinity. The honor of our state demands that the affair be thoroughly investigated and this band of Ku Klux be broken up.

The Carbondale newspaper's use of the headline "Williamson County Ku-Klux" suggested the Klan was home-grown to Williamson County, but later trials and events would place the leaders of the Franklin County Klan, Aaron Neal, Calvin Moore and Jesse Cavins, at the scene of the murder.[68]

The Klan's order for Vancil to disperse some of his property suggests that the organization's members included either some of his children or their spouses interested in securing their inheritance early. Another family connection in the person of his stepson Pleasant M. Finney also raises questions. Finney's mother was a generation younger than Vancil when they

---

[68] Andy Hall. February 1970. "Ku Klux Klan and the battle at John B. (Jack) Maddox Farm." *Outdoor Illinois*. 15.

married in 1869. The following year Vancil took the additional step of becoming the legal guardian of Pleasant and his two younger siblings while the boy was still 17. Thus despite having separated from his wife, Vancil would have still been the legal guardian for his 19-year-old stepson at the time of his death.[69]

What's troubling about Pleasant are the stories he personally passed down to his descendents as well as his presence in the Klan two years later when that group attacked the Carter residence. The presence of "Ples Finney" as one of the party "in arms" makes him the common link between the two major Klan events in Williamson County. Following the murder Finney's twice-widowed mother moved her family from Vancil's Bend in the northwestern corner of Williamson County for the Corinth area in the northeastern part.

According to Vancil genealogists, descendents of Finney always thought he had been "involved in what happened to Isaac" and that he had been "involved in quite a few things that no one knew including the KKK." Vancil had married Finney's mother, the former Mary (Dillon) Finney in the county in 1869 after Finney's father had died during the Civil War from tuberculosis. Prior to the war authorities had arrested the elder Finney for assault and attempted murder. Father and son had much in common. Family stories also indicated the pair had "always been a radical bunch and very anti black."

> This is the story I got. The Finney's all lived in the general area of County Line Church in Corinth Twp. way back then. Seems all the people in that area were not fond of the few blacks in the area. [Pleasant M. Finney]'s father was killed in the Civil War, and after that it seems he got even more racist. His mother, Mary, seems to have met Isaac Vancil when he was in the area trading or looking for workers and supposedly he hired some of the blacks from "the farm" as they called it.

The descendent assumed that "the farm" meant Fancy Farm, an early settlement and post office located in Franklin County, though the post office

---

[69] Summer 2004. "The Murder of Isaac Vancil." *Footprints in Williamson County, Illinois.* Marion, Ill.: Williamson County Historical Society. 7:2. 14; republishing April 27, 1872. "Williamson County Ku-Klux." *New Era* [Carbondale, Ill.]

often bounced back and forth across the Franklin and Williamson county line depending on the postmaster. This area had seen slavery in territorial days and later an a settlement of free African-Americans known as Skelton Town, though later recalled as either Locust Grove (after their church) or Africa, as it was known by the mid 20th Century.

Liberty Methodist Church stood between County Line Church and Skelton Town. The more tolerant church members provided both a buffer and a shield for the black community that suffered from kidnappings and attempted kidnappings prior to the Civil War and at least one concerted effort to force them all to move out in the early days of the Rebellion.

After Mary & Isaac married, they and Mary's kids all moved to Vancil's Bend. Not far from the house was a ford on the Big Muddy, much later they built a bridge there. PM didn't like the black man working on the farm, he and Isaac had words about it. PM said he would get rid of the man. According to my great grandma, this black man vanished. According to PM's sister, he started going off with this group of men and he said they went to meetings in Corinth Church. One night PM and a few men came across the ford from Franklin Co and Isaac told them they couldn't cut across his land or something to that effect. Seems they wanted to use the ford so they didn't have to go into Blairsville.

At one point some men came and talked to Isaac in a field near the house, he tried to run them off with a hoe or something. Seems this really amused PM, every story had how he would tell of the old man trying to run the gang off with a hoe. I guess a few weeks later, they returned and told him to leave the county or there would be trouble.

Well he didn't and they came back for him. The story PM told his mother was the men had called Isaac outside. I guess he didn't want her to know anything. What he told years later to my grandpa was the girls had just gone to bed and he was out front. He called Isaac outside and said he thought he heard voices in the direction of the river. Isaac got a lantern and walked in the yard.

Once outside Vancil called back inside the house and told Mary to keep herself and the children inside the house until morning.

PM went in the house and watched through the window. The gang of 10 or so men came out of the woods on horses, grabbed Isaac and hung him in the side yard by the house. The next day, Mary and the kids moved back to Corinth.

Sometimes in Finney's story he said he left the house in spite of Vancil's order and watched the hanging. His racism and the stories passed down to his descendents also provide an important clue on the attack on the Carters. They recall that Henry Carter had been working as a teacher in a black school.[70] Finney also proved close to the Raines family which provided five members of the armed party. The following February he married Rachel Caroline Rains, doubtlessly a relative of the clan.[71] Another connection came through Finney's sister Sarah who had previously married William L. Arms who was likely part of the Arnes/Armes/Ames family that lived in Franklin County and provided four members of the raid.[72]

As Erwin noted in his earlier account authorities arrested eight men who won acquittal in 1873 after a change of venue in Franklin County. Following the state's failure, the U.S. Attorney's office indicted Pleasant Veach and others on conspiracy charges in federal court at Springfield, yet they still won acquittals at the January 1874 term. The government's witnesses for the prosecution included Jesse Barnett, Miles A. Colp, Milton S. Colp, James G. Henderson, James Howell, Thomas J. Kelley, Henry B. Norman, Thomas Riddle, and Mary Vancil.[73]

Of the eight men who testified at least two were later shot and killed and another two wounded severely. Erwin reported on the two that died, including Milton Stewart Colp in September 1874. The attacks on Henderson,

---

[70] Jeana Gallagher. Oct. 19, 23, 2005. "Re: Isaac Vancil." E-mails to Jon Musgrave.

[71] The Illinois Statewide Marriage Index, 1673-1900, shows a marriage between the two taking place in Williamson County on February 25, 1875. See also the Bible records of Stella Ann (Ward) Finney at the Williamson County Illinois Trails site at http://iltrails.org/williamson/stellasbible.htm.

[72] Summer 2004. "The Murder of Isaac Vancil." *Footprints in Williamson County, Illinois*. Marion, Ill.: Williamson County Historical Society. 7:2. 14.

[73] Zachariah Owens also served five days as a witness, presumably then for the defense. *Source*: Gallagher. Oct. 23, 2005. "Re: Isaac Vancil."

Norman and Riddle will be covered later in this book. In addition to these four who testified in Springfield, at least one other man, Simon Bishop, had also been shot about the same time as Colp, though whether fatally has not been determined.

In Erwin's account of the Klan raid on the Carter farm he left out a number of details that would have been well-known and fresh for his readers in 1876, but almost entirely lost to modern readers. Luckily, local newspapers at the time covered the incident and reprinted the letter Carter sent to the governor's office and subsequently forwarded to State's Attorney Jennings.

> To his Excellency Governor Beveridge of Illinois — We, the undersigned citizens of Williamson county, State of Illinois, do most ardently beseech you for your protection of our persons and property against a certain number of Williamson and Franklin Counties. On the night of the 23d of October, 1874, the house of Henry D. Carter was visited by a party of fifteen or twenty men in disguise, ordering him and family to leave the county within forty days, or they would crack their necks, whereupon a fight took place, twenty-two balls were lodged in the side of the house. Flying chats were soon prevalent that the house would be burned with the family in it, all this failing to cause the family to abscond. The following men then met in arms in daylight, in County Line church, held a convention among themselves and ordered Henry D. Carter and Henry E. Carter, James M. Carter his sons, and James Carter his brother, to wind up their business in thirty days and leave the county; also that John W. Carter, Seth M. Carter, Dr. D. L. Carter and Geo M. Carter could stay, but would be held responsible for all misdemeanors that might occur in the county around. Signed,
>
> Henry D. x Carter (his mark), Dr. D. L Carter, Seth M. Carter, Henry C. Carter, G. M. Carter and J. M. Carter.

The letter listed the names of the men who constituted, "the party that was in arms." In alphabetical order:

George Ames	T. Ames	Thos. Clarady
John Ames	J. P. Cardwell	J. C. Clemens
Mark Ames	Wm. E. Claraday	James Dearing

John Dearing	A. Henry	R. Parker
John H. Dearing	Jared Jones	Ned Pritchard
Wm. Dearing	Franklin Mark	Wm. Pritchard
D. W. Dunn	David McReynolds	Andrew Raines
E. Dunn	Thos. M'Reynolds	John Raines
J. P. Dunn	W. A. McReynolds	J. W. Raines
J. Eason	W. H. McReynolds	R. Raines
Rich'd Edwards	Seth Moss	Raleigh Raines
Thos. Esry	John W. O'Neal	P. Smith
Ples Finney	E. C. Parker	Wm. Smith
W. J. Fisher	Ed Parker	Wm. Stagrur
W. E. Fletcher	G. W. Parker	James Vaughn
T. A. Foster	Henry Parker	John Vaughn
John Garrison	M. Parker	
David Hayes	R. Parker	

Witnesses to the fact listed by the newspaper included the following:

D. L. Carter	Bedford Eller	Marcus Murray
G. M. Carter	Daniel Hedges	S. Newman
J. W. Carter	J. M. Jourdan	Thomas Riddle
J. W. Carter	John W. Markum	Chas. H. Turner
S. M. Carter	A. C. Martin	Isaac Wilhite
John Crisp	Perry Martin	

With the number of Carters in the second list, it's assumed the witnesses were anti-Klan, which would have made for an interesting meeting at the church house that day[74] Hall's 1923 account provided even more details.

> On one occasion [the Klan] visited Mr. Carter near Thompsonville, Illinois, and left a warning that if he was not out of the country by a certain time they would pay him another visit and that he would be severely punished. Carter had been a soldier in the Civil War and was not in the habit of retreating without a fight. He

---

[74] Lind 1:13-14; quoting the Nov. 12, 1874 edition of the *Marion Monitor*.

and his boys prepared for the promised visit which occurred on the night designated by the Klan and a gun fight was the result. The klansmen retreated in disorder and Carter and his boys held the fort. Several of Carter's neighbors took suddenly ill that night and Dr. Poindexter, who lived nearby was called to treat them. One of the men died. While Dr. Poindexter was rather reticent about disclosing the professional secrets of his patients, yet it was generally understood that they all suffered from acute led poisoning.[75]

Neither the newspaper account, nor Erwin's writings provided any motive for the Klan's objections to the Carters. Two months earlier though the *Marion Monitor* reported that Henry Carter, one of his sons and John Jourdan (of whom there is one by that name on the witness list) had assaulted a Mr. Dunn in a field. Though the newspaper didn't better identify the Dunn allegedly assaulted, there were three by that name mentioned on the list in the party at arms.

As to Vancil's step-son Pleasant, he maintained his violent tendencies. In March 1876, he met his neighbor Thomas Riddle on the road 10 miles northeast of Marion. There, he "fell upon him with a club four feet long and left him for dead." Trouble over a recent survey of their joint property line served as the motive.[76]

Now back to Erwin's account:

---

[75] Hall, 1923.
[76] Lind 1:49; quoting the April 19, 1876 edition of the *Marion Monitor*

Chapter 9.   **Prosecutor Absconds**

AFTER THE DEATH OF HINCHCLIFF, consternation seized every mind; mutual distrust and a want of confidence was felt. The solemn pallor of cholera times hung over our people. Silence pervaded the air.[77]

The responsible men were seen standing around in groups, whispering questions that no man dare answer; while the irresponsible part, and dead-beats were lopping their horses about town, and making wild goose-sallies out to the edge of the bloody ground, quartering on some good farmer for a day and night, eating and drinking with mirth and revelry, and then come back and report some long, airy story of the whereabouts of some noted assassin. Most men had a plan to advise, but the execution of it was generally left to reckless young men, or floating characters, who had nothing to lose and all to gain. Suppressed curses were sometimes whispered against the noted characters, and then the parties would be cautioned, least he brought the killings to Marion.[78]

A low murmur or subdued excitement, would break out in the bloody ground late some evening, and produce the greatest commotion among the neighbors. Pistol shots had been heard at the back of somebody's field, and the sound of hurrying feet or horses running, and out would come five or six

---

[77] And at times the silence could be downright spooky. Over in Carbondale in early January the "great spiritualistic medium of DuQuoin" visited and conducted a number of "satisfactory séances." One of the major accomplishments took place when the spirit of "Dr. Vincent Hinchcliff, who was assassinated at Carterville, Williamson County, some time ago, appeared and talked with Malcolm Stanhouse." Despite the fact that the newspaper's source was present, "we know these things are so because we were there and heard them speak in a horn," no mention was made as to whether Hinchcliff provided any additional clues to his murder. However, he at least shook hands with Stanhouse.

"[N]ot only did they speak and converse, but they went to one and another and of their friends, and shook hands with them — that is to say, the spirit's hand was represented by the big end of the horn, and we shook the horn. There is no use in talking; spirits are spirits in spite of what skeptics say." *Source*: Feb. 4, 1875. *Marion Monitor*, quoting in turn the Jan. 16, 1875, issue of the *Jackson County Era*.

[78] No, we couldn't have that, not the killings in Marion!

men, scared like rabbits, from a thicket. They did not like John Bulliner's movements, or Tom Russell had been seen, or James Norris, a desperate outlaw and daring desperado, armed to the teeth, was lurking in the bushes.

Reporters for city papers would come down here, and go as near the bloody grounds as they felt disposed, find out what they could, (and in those days it was dangerous to seek to know more of the Vendetta than they chose to tell,) and then go back and call us a set of "blood-thirsty barbarians," "Italian brigands," and "Night Riding Ku-klux," and on top of these outrages a series of letters, signed "Big Pete of the Woods," were published by R. F. Brown, in the *Farmer's Advocate*, in Marion, threatening everybody and especially the State's Attorney.

Brown's boy, afterwards, trying to convince me that C. H. Dennison wrote those letters, produced the manuscripts, and I recognized in each of them the hand-writing of J. D. F. Jennings, the State's Attorney. He got terribly scared at his own shadow, and had the sympathy of many people in his great danger. And all the time he was fixing up a plan to steal something and run away, and make the people believe that he had to leave to save his life.

He was so warm that he would burn a man with his kindness, and at the same time lived a life of cold-blooded rascality. He even reported that he saw men around his house, trying to kill him; but the people soon learned to take the square root of what he said for truth.

He was very popular, and the secret of it was his manners, sayings and opinions. He was a professional doctor, lawyer, preacher, fiddler, horn blower and a libertine. When he made music on the square, a crowd would swell around him. When he preached, they all went to hear him, from the talented aristocracy down to the bootblack. He was a rowdy among the rowdies, pious among the pious, Godless among the Godless, and a spooney among the women.

He would get up in a sermon and rattle away until the shrouds and lanyards of conscience must have fairly quacked under the strain, and then go, get on a drunk. He was a clerical blackguard, whose groveling passions assumed full sway at all times. Lost to every Christian restraint, degraded in his tastes, villainous in his nature, corrupt in his principles, how wretched was such an apology for a State's Attorney! He suddenly became wise and learned in the law above his compeers, and found out that all our witnesses were accomplices without veracity, and those who were branded as criminals, looked upon the law with contempt of judgment, and we stultified ourselves trying to enforce the law. "The wickedness of the people is indeed great, when the wickedest men among them are men of renown." And yet we had to look to a man as our leader in this great emergency, who bears the character of being a most consummate scoundrel.

On his face was written legibly, "a liar, a hypocrite." A while before he left, he wrote a letter to Samuel Dunaway and a few other rich men of Marion, threatening to kill them, and signed it "Big Pete." Then he went to these parties and said he knew who it was wanting to kill them, and that if they would give him $5,000 he would hire men to kill them, and even told who he could get to do it. He was awful uneasy for them! But his insinuating toadyism and spaniel-like reverence for his "friends" were but idle and frivolous assertions in this case. They knew his warped and biased soul was steeped in infamy and falsehood.

About the time our people began to see the utter futility of expecting anything like justice in a court where this man was State's Attorney, he had the good sense to defraud the county of $900 and run away and owing everybody.[79] As a prosecutor, he was a regular sarcasm on justice, a great hideous burlesque; free from religious scruples, and ready to sail from any point of the compass. He has gone out to humbug some other people, and will live in our history in an immortality of shame and disgrace. He and Brown, of the *Farmer's Advocate*, did more to injure our county than all the shot guns in it.

In April 1875, the office was declared vacant, and in June J. W. Hartwell was elected to fill the vacancy.

On the 22nd day of January, 1875, B. O. Jones, of Massac, introduced a bill in the Legislature to appropriate $10,000 for the relief of Williamson County. But the speaker appointed a committee against us, with L. F. Plater, of Hardin, as chairman. He wrote to our State's Attorney, Circuit Clerk, and others for information, but none of them ever answered him, and the bill was cut down to $3,000, and passed the House too late to be passed by the Senate. Hon. A. C. Nelson, our Representative, won for himself the illustrious appellation of "Egyptian orator," fighting for this bill.

---

[79] The Sept. 16, 1875, edition of the *Marion Monitor* noted that Jennings owed the county School Fund $927.

Chapter 10. **Third Time's a Charm**

DURING THE SPRING OF 1875, several blinds were found near Bulliner's, and one day John went to Carbondale, and a fresh blind was put up north of his house, about a quarter of a mile, so that they could kill him, as he returned. Monroe found this blind, and told John to look out, and thus saved his life. At one time some men were seen around the house; but they did not get to kill anybody. At this time the people were an entire army of observers. Every man had his eyes riveted on the horizon of crime, and his ears pricked to hear.

On the night of the 4th of July, somebody went to Marshall Crain's house, in Crainville, while he was gone from home, and fired a charge of buck-shot promiscuously around his bed.[80] This gave Marshall such a scare that he determined to go back into the Vendetta, which he had left in January, and he said he hired to John Bulliner to kill Sisney for $300, and got all the money but $5. He wanted to kill John Sisney first, but Bulliner would have him kill the old man. Being afraid to stay at home, he and his wife went to Samuel Musick's to board. On the 7th he asked Sam, if he got into trouble would he help him out. Sam said he would. Again, on the 8th, he asked him, and Sam said he would swear for him, and clear him. Marshall said John Sisney had shot into his house, and he wanted revenge, and he wanted Sam to swear him out of trouble. Sam agreed to do so.

About ten o'clock Wednesday, July the 28th, Marshall started out from Musick's, and went to a neighbor's, and borrowed a gun, saying that he wanted to go a hunting; but in fact he hardly knew what he did want with it. He went down within two miles of Carbondale, and concealed his gun in an old house on the road, near Mrs. Snider's, and went into the field where the Snider boys were thrashing wheat.

Here he met the famous Allen Baker, and had a few words with him privately. This was late in the evening. He then went back to the old house

---

[80] The *Marion Monitor* of July 8, reported it like this, "The residence of Marshal Crain, at Crainville, was fired into on Monday night last, the balls passing through the window and into the head of the bed. The family being absent at the time, no person was injured."

and left his coat and boots, and just after dark, went to Carbondale, where George W. Sisney had moved a few months before for safety.[81] It was raining, and in going up East Main street, he carried a board over his gun, to keep it dry. When he met anybody he would lay his gun under the side-walk, pass on and then go back and get it; and this he did as many as six times. Capt. Sisney lived on the northeast corner of the square, his house extending eastward and facing south, with a porch on the south side. Marshall went up slowly, but Sisney had already retired. He waited around the premises for a while, and when anybody would pass with lanterns, he would go back to an old wood shed in a dark ally, on the east side. The evening train was late that night, and when Marsh, had got tired and almost gave up all hope, it came, and on board was Overton Stanley, a friend of Sisney's, who went directly to Sisney's house to get Sisney to sign a note with him as his security. He called, and about half past nine o'clock, Sisney came down in his parlor, and after lighting a lamp, signed the note and sat down near a window, on the south side; his hands lay folded across his lap. It was a night of rain and clouds.

The wind swept sighingly through the foliage of the trees, with a rustling sound, as of swollen waters. The long, plaintive howl of the watch dog came hurriedly by, and mournfully fell on the ears of Marshall Crain, when the sobs of the gale would subside. He went into the old shed and put fresh caps on his gun, and then went slipping, half stooped, along to the porch, but was so thirsty that he laid his gun down and went out into the street and drank out of a mud-hole with his hands; then taking his gun, he stepped to the window. The curtains were blown about softly in the breeze. All inside wore the sombre gray tint of light. He gently blowed against the curtains, and saw two men, but could not tell which was Sisney. Again he blowed and saw a pair of legs, and was about to shoot, when he saw that the man had on fine boots. That was not Sisney. His breath, assisted by the wind, parted the curtains again, and he saw the black, stiff beard of Sisney. He stepped back, cocked both barrels of his gun, raised it to his shoulder. Just then he heard Sisney say, "I guess it is time to retire."

[81] Sisney had moved to Carbondale by the end of January 1875. The Feb. 4, 1875, issue of the *Marion Monitor* reported a visit by Sisney to the newspaper office. "Mr. George W. Sisney, called on us Tuesday last. Mr. S. has a very bad wound and thinks his arm will likely be a cripple for life. He has moved to Carbondale." He visited the paper office again later in February as the paper reported on Feb. 25, "Capt. G.W. Sisney called on us last Friday. His arm is not altogether well, but much better."

Stanley asked, "What kind of a man is George Moore?"

Sisney replied: "He is a bad one; he is all right, and is a worse man than he looks to be."

Marshall Crain pulled the trigger, and George W. Sisney laid still in death's eternal sleep. Marshall heard Sisney say — "Oh, Lord, I am shot! Lord, have mercy on me!"[82]

It was the only expression of despair that ever came from the brave heart of George Sisney, although he had four times before survived the murderous missiles.

> "Wearied, forsaken and pursued, at last,
>   All safety in despair of safety placed,
>   Courage he thence resumes, resolves to bear
>   All their assaults, since 'tis in vain to fear."

After the murder that night, the winds sallied, and a cold, white fog laid its moist fingers on the heated pulse of Carbondale. The scene in this stricken, smitten and afflicted family was heart rending. Mrs. Sisney, who had raised the window up stairs and cried out for help, was now wringing her hands in agony. Martha Jane, who was sleeping in an adjoining room below, woke up, heard a strangling noise, and asked her father what was the matter; receiving no answer, dressed herself, and went into the parlor. The light, six feet away, had been blown out by the concussion, and all was dark. Stanley said —

"Your pa is shot. Mr. Sisney is killed dead."

He had locked the front door, and she opened it and called for help. The sad and heavyhearted citizens came in droves, their eyes flashing with

---

[82] The murder made the news far and wide. The Aug. 5, 1875, issue of the *Burlington Hawk Eye* of Iowa reprinted a story which provided more information than Erwin about the deadly wound.

Cowardly Murder.

ST. LOUIS, July 29. — George W. Sisney, who was assassinated at Carbondale, Ill., last night, was a prominent business man of that place, and moved there from Williamson county, last fall, where two attempts had been made to kill him, by parties connected with the notorious Bullinger-Russell feud which has cost so many lives in that county. He was shot with a double-barreled shot gun, loaded with buckshot, the charge making a hole in his side three inches in diameter.

resentment, and their spirits rankling in bitter malice. They followed the assassin a piece but could not keep his trail. Sisney remained seated for an hour and a half upright in his chair, shot under the left nipple, which made a hole two inches in diameter. He was buried on the 30th, on his old homestead, with Masonic honors. There we leave him forever. Shall his memory go back to oblivion and shame, or shall it follow those who have gone without blame from intelligence, virtue or Heaven?

I would write for his epitaph, "An honest, brave, true man."[83]

---

[83] Erwin may have written the epitaph but the *Marion Monitor* provided a better obituary in their Aug. 5, issue.

DEATH OF GEO. W. SISNEY.

MURDER MOST FOUL.

The Assassin Still at Work. Is There no Redress?

The Hour is Ripe for Action on the Part of Peaceful and Law Abiding Citizens.

It is a sad and painful duty that we announce this week the death of Capt. Geo. W. Sisney, an old and respected citizen, late of our county. He was brutally assassinated, by some unknown person, at his house in the city of Carbondale, between the hours of 9 and 10 o'clock p.m. on Wednesday, July 28th. This was the third open and bold attempt to assassinate Captain Sisney within the last twelve months. At last they have succeeded; their work, so far as he is concerned, is ended.

The facts, as far as we have been able to gather them, are that on Wednesday evening Mr. Overton Stanley was at Carbondale attending to some business connected with the estate of his brother, William Stanley, deceased, and had went to Capt. Sisney's to get him to go his security on a note, and also settle some little private demand which Sisney held against him. They were sitting in a room on the first floor of Sisney's house, and had about completed their business, when Sisney remarked that it was about time to retire, and almost instantly a shot was fired in at the window which was protected by a wire musquito bar, the contents striking Sisney in the breast near the right nipple, killing him almost instantly. The only words he spoke were, "O, Lord, I am Killed."

An inquest was held over his body by 'Squire Prickett on Thursday the 29th, and the jury returned a verdict that he come to his death by a gunshot wound at the hand of some person to them unknown. He was buried at the Stancil grave yard near his farm in the western part of this county, on Friday the 30th ult., with the honors of the Masonic Fraternity, of which order he was a bright and worthy member, and had been for 12 or 15 years. He leaves a wife and eight children to mourn his tragic and untimely death.

Most of our readers were personally acquainted with Capt. Sisney. He was sheriff of this county from 1866 to 1868, and ran again on the Independent ticket in 1874, but was defeated. He made a good officer, and gave universal satisfaction in the discharge of his public trust. Like most men, who succeed in this world, Capt. Sisney has some

After the murder, Marshall Crain ran down East Main street with his gun, and crossed into the bushes on the north side of the road leading east.[84]

---

enemies. He was a man of indomitable will and courage; yet he was open, frank and generous to a fault.

He was charitable and kind in many respects; yet he did not claim to be a philanthropist in every sense of the work; still no man ever went to him with a meritorious case of charity but what he received recognition and assistance.

He was true to his country, his friends and his home; was too high minded to take a mean advantage of an enemy; was always on the side of law and order, and that a man does not live today who can say that Captain Sisney ever advised or encouraged him to violate or disregard that laws of his county, and it can be truthfully said that he never sought or forced a difficulty with any man. His great misfortune was that he was in the wrong locality. The locality in which he lived was not congenial to his nature, and he did not get along as smoothly as he might have done had he been differently situated. Not but what there are many good people in the vicinity where the Captain lived — in fact it is a good settlement, and some of the best citizens in the State reside there, and Sisney has a host of friends there — but there is an element which no power on earth can control, "their ways are past finding out," and to this element the good people of our county are indebted for the untimely death, not only of Sisney, but many other good and valuable citizens in the western part of the county.

Geo. W. Sisney was Captain of Company "G", 81st Regiment Illinois Infantry Volunteers. He recruited his company, most of them, in this county in July and August, 1862, and was mustered into the service August 26, 1862, many of whom are still living in this and Jackson county. He was severely wounded at the battle of Vicksburg, Miss., in May, 1863, in consequence of which he resigned his position August 3, 1863. He never recovered from the effect of the wounds he received while in the service of this country. But he has "gone to that bourn from whence no traveler ever returns," and to which we are all hastening with the velocity of time. It is a terrible thing to die, even when in old age, emaciated and worn out with disease, with kind friends and loving hearts surrounding the bedside, ready and willing to minister to your every want, to wipe "The cold and sluggish drops From off your peaceful brow." When the solemnity of the occasion makes the transition more serene and hopeful, still with all these surrounding the dying mortal struggles to retain life; he thinks of something he wants to say to the dear ones he leaves behind, but his tongue refuses to serve him and he passes quietly away. How hard it is for a man to be snatched suddenly away from his friends and family without a parting word or moments warning. Ruthlessly murdered like a brute. The very thought of such an act shocks our better nature, and the sober judgment of mankind rises up in condemnation of such an act. One by one our citizens are being taken away by assassination, and it seems like we have no redress, nor way to stop it. There is a way to put a stop to these diabolical outrages if the people of our county will rise up in their might, in solid phalanx, with a determination that murder must

When he got into Mrs. Snider's field, he got lost in the dark. The thunders bellowed over head like the trumpet of the great arch-angel calling sinners to judgment. Crash upon crash, and roar upon roar, till the vast vault of heaven was filled with the giant sound. The lightning, broad and bright, flooded the whole sky with a lurid red, flashing its fire across the field, and illuminating with a dreadful light his solitary form alone amid the wrath of the elements. After wading through swamps and bushes, be arrived at his mother-in-law's, nine miles from Carbondale, just before day, tired, wearied and almost broken down.[85]

Next morning, Colonel D. H. Brush, of Carbondale, offered a reward of $500, which he refused to pay on the conviction of Bulliner and Baker for the murder of Sisney, and suit was brought against him by B. F. Lowe, which is now pending. Samuel Musick, who was teaming for Captain Landrum, was in Carbondale the day Sisney was killed. He saw Marshall Crain there (for he had been in a while that day), who told him that he was there to kill Sisney, and he told Sam where he had left his coat and boots. Sam got them, and wore the boots out. On the morning after the murder, Musick said, he, Marshall, and Allen Baker met in Carterville, and Baker gave as a reason for not coming to help him in the killing, as he had promised at Mrs. Snider's, that it rained. About noon, Marshall, Musick and John Bulliner, met in Crainville, and Marshall told John that Sam was into this thing too, now, and they both told Sam if he told this he would be the next man killed. Marshall then told John how he killed Sisney, and John paid him $15, and told him he would pay him the rest when he sold his wheat. The same day, "Big Jep"

---

cease in this vicinity, no clan or combination can successfully resist the united efforts and determination of the good people of Williamson county. The people must take interest in the matter — collectively and individually. The law is powerless in such cases unless backed and supported by a sound healthy public sentiment of the people.

[84] East Main Street today is still East Main, but is better recognized by readers as the westbound lanes of Route 13.

[85] His mother-in-law appears to have been Angeline Rich Henson. The 1850 Census of Hamilton Co., Illinois, found a Rhoda Rich, 1, daughter of Elias and Angeline Rich. The Illinois Statewide Marriage Index 1673-1900, shows an Angeline Rich marrying Pleasant H. Henson in Williamson County on July 4, 1872. Crain married Rhoda Rich on March 4, 1874, at Mount Carbon near Murphysboro in Jackson County, according to the marriage index, as well as his confession printed in the Jan. 27, 1876, issue of the *Marion Monitor*.

Crain came to Marion. His presence in town created a great deal of talk, and most people believed he was in the Vendetta. He wanted to join a proposed company of militia, and be the captain. He said he could stop the killing; but before this a subscription paper had been circulated to employ detectives, and he signed $25, and after a while he said "he did not like the direction things were taking," and withdrew it.

He went down to Crainville, Friday evening, about four o'clock, and he and Marshal and Musick (according to Musick's statement), went down to Marshal's old house, and after playing cards and drinking awhile, "Big Jep" said: "The next man to kill is Spence," and told Musick to go to John Bulliner's and get a gun for "Black Bill" Crain. Musick said he would not do it; that he would be seen, but he would get one from John Ditmore, in Crainville, if that would do. "Big Jep" said it would do, and that he would go that night and get "Black Bill," who lived four miles south of Crainville, and meet him and Marsh next morning at the back of Mrs. Hampton's field, which is only three miles south. "Big Jep" went off, and at dark, Musick went to John Ditmore's to get his gun, but John would not let it out at night, and told him to come in the morning, which he did very early and got the gun, and put it in Marsh's old house. Then Sam and Marsh got three pints of whiskey, and met in the woods at the back of "Yaller Bill's" field, from where they walked to the back of Mrs. Hampton's field. At the north-west corner a path led up into the woods. They broke weeds and brushes off and threw them in the path as a "sign" and went on up the hill. There they fired three pistol shots as a signal to "Big Jep" and "Black Bill," who came about twelve o'clock, two hours after Marsh and Sam had got there. The object of this meeting was to initiate Sam into the Ku klux, as he said that "Big Jep" thought they had better join them for protection, but they did not do so. They agreed to kill Spence that night. Sam, "Black Bill" and Marsh were to do the killing, and "Big Jep" was to keep them out of trouble. He told them, if they got in jail not to mind staying there two or three months, that the door would be smashed in and they taken out.

They parted, and "Big Jep" went with "Black Bill," and Sam and Marsh went to Wesley Crain's and got dinner. Sam went home and then to Carterville, and got some more whisky, and at dark met "Black Bill" and Marshall at the back of "Yaller Bill's" field, near Crainville. They went up to Marsh's old house, about two hundred yards south of Spence's store, where they waited until ten o'clock, when everything got still. Then Marshall took a gun, which he had got out of a hollow tree in the woods, said to be a Bulliner gun, and they circled around through the woods and came up on the east side of Spence's store.

The rose-flush of day had faded in the West. The sombre-gray of twilight had fallen around them, and the watching stars had taken their stand in the concave up above, like unhappy sentinels, doomed to keep watch over the infinity of the ocean. Spence was asleep up stairs. They were environed by the intense stillness. The thought of murder rolled slowly through their minds, but still they did not relent. The eastern horizon was silvered by the rising moon, and looked like a huge mass of beryl whereon burned ruby flakes of vapor, guarded by the vestal stars above. The sapphire arch overhead burned beautiful and mellow. Marshall went to the door and called out, "Mr. Spence."

Spence asked who was there. Marshall said, "John Sisney; I want to get shrouding for a child." Spence said he would be down in a minute. Soon the tall, august form of William Spence, illuminated by a solitary light, was seen towering grandly between the counters. When he got to the door, Marshall fired both barrels into his abdomen—a charge of sixty buckshot.

Spence said, "Marsh, don't shoot me any more!"

This was an address to humanity. It was a heart-rending cry of distress from a soul in mortal strait. Such a cry ought not to go unheeded by a brother man; but Marsh run his arm through the broken pane in the door, and shot him with a pistol in the face, as he fell. He then punched a pane out of the glass front with his gun, and went into the house, and searched around through trunks and drawers for two or three minutes, when "Big Bill" called him out. He had an old empty pocket-book. They walked off east, along the railroad, half a mile, and then turned south into "Big Terry's" field, and came out into an old road, where Musick asked, "What will I do if I am arrested?"

"Big Bill" said, "Have me and Marsh subpoenaed, and we will swear you clear." After the shooting of Henderson, no man ever understood that it was necessary to fly. They separated and went home. This occurred July 31, 1875.[86]

---

[86] At first even the *Marion Monitor* failed to connect Spence's death with the Vendetta, even as they ran the news account of the murder immediately following the account and obituary of Sisney in their Aug. 5, issue.

William Spence was but little known in this county. He came here a few years ago, but attended to his own business and said but little. He was a good man, strong, firm and dignified to stiffness; but was making money. His death left no orphan or widow to wail at his hearth-stone. Though about forty years of age, he was unmarried. After he was shot he lay in his store all night, and was not found until the holy hush of Sunday morning rested like a benediction on the scene. Sunday morning, Marsh and Musick again met at the back of Mrs. Hampton's field, and Marsh drew his revolver on Sam, and told him he believed he was a traitor, on account of some strange whistling he had heard, and if he did not find the whiskey, which he had concealed the day before, he would kill him. While Sam was preparing a hurried absolution, he found the whiskey, which saved his life. Marshall afterwards said he wished he had shot him; that he thought he was neglecting duty.

On this same day, August 1st, Allen Baker, who lived on the dirt road, at the Crab Orchard Bridge, in Jackson county, was fired on by an assassin, who mistook Baker's shadow on the window-blind for his body, and let in a charge of buck-shot without killing anybody.[87]

Musick was coming back from the meetings at the back of Mrs. Hampton's field, on Sunday afternoon, drunk, as usual, and a mile south of Crainville, he fell in with Carrol Waggoner and his wife, who were going home to Crainville.[88] He got in the wagon with them, and the subject of the murder came up, when Musick said, "Yes, we put the damned old scoundrel out of the way."

"STILL ANOTHER — Wm. Spence, of Crainville, Murdered. Since the above was put in type we have received intelligence that Mr. William Spence was murdered in his storehouse in Crainville, this county, about 9 o'clock on Saturday night, July 31st. He was found by some of the neighbors, Sunday morning, lying in his storeroom with a gunshot wound in the breast. People in the neighborhood heard the shooting, but shooting is so common there it created no alarm. Mr. Spence, as we understand, was a quiet and inoffensive man, and attended strictly to his business. The supposition is that he was killed for his money. We were not personally acquainted with him and know nothing about the situation."

[87] By this point the *Marion Monitor* realized it was probably Vendetta-related, but blamed "some of the murderous gang that infests Jackson County" for the deed rather than Williamson County's own in its edition of Aug. 6. Baker may have also been part of the Ku Klux Klan as a July 19, 1877, article in the same paper described him as "one of the Williamson County Ku Klux." Thus this may have been a retaliatory shooting.

[88] From all appearances this would be the afternoon of August 1.

Mrs. Waggoner of course knew that "we" meant Music, Marshall and "Big Jep."

Late Monday evening following, Music, Marsh and "Yaller Bill" met in Crainville, near Landrum's Mills, and "Yaller Bill" said, "Did either of you boys get any jewelry?"

Marsh said, "No."

Bill said, "If anybody got his watch, it has his name in it, and they will be detected and pull hemp as sure as hell."

He then advised Marsh to take his wife to her mother's, and leave the country, and told Sam to stop drinking, or he would leak it out."

He said, "There is getting too many in this thing anyway."

This conversation is taken from Music's statement, and was denied by all the other boys. This is the only evidence of "Yaller Bill's" connection with the Vendetta. Our people do not believe he is guilty. They say that if he gave Marsh the advice spoken of by Musick, that it is no more than any other brother would have done. Musick went to Carbondale on Tuesday, and remained two weeks. While there, Marsh tried to get him out several times, but Sam was afraid and would not come. Marsh left in about a week after the murder, and went to Missouri, and Sam went to Bird's Point, in the same State.

Never has there been a season of such universal consternation and anxiety among all sexes and ages as was in this county. It threatened us and our posterity with perpetual odium, and the very thought of having our county branded with lasting shame, filled us with living emotions of anger and fire. All felt that it was a time to summon every aid, both human and divine, and with the bayonets save our county. Political prejudices and feelings, which had entered largely into the animus of the Vendetta heretofore, were lost sight of in the duties of the hour. It was an understanding that Republicans sympathized with the Russell side, and the Democrats with the Bulliner side of the Vendetta; but now public considerations of a higher character attracted the attention of our people, and they rose above the trammels of political sympathies, and united as a band of honest freemen. No language that I can command can give adequate utterance to the feelings that it awakened in us, to hear of our friends being shot down like beasts. It was chafing to our hopes and gadding to our spirits. Many believed that we were standing on the threshold of a mighty convulsion, and they watched it with wonder and awe. Others prayed to that

Being who sets liberty up and oppression down, to break the tornado that was hanging over us like a pall.

Our lands went down in value one-third to one-half. The coal fields lay dormant. The fields of grain that were annually garnered on the west side of the county nearly failed. These were stubborn facts, known at home and read by thinking minds throughout the world. The name of Williamson county had become a hiss and by-word. Strangers shunned us like a serpent, and the sting was felt. Affairs were deplorable.

Ruffianism was rampant. Noted assassins were concealed in the thickets of the bloody ground. This was a daily talk, spoken out in thunder tones, that all understood. The air was filled with omens of disaster. Pass the street corners and the breath of murder was whispered in your face. Bold assassins stalked unbridled and unchecked. To bring these outlaws to justice was the universal desire of our people; but how to do it was a point that put to silence the entire country. The people were cursing the officers. Those who knew anything were afraid to tell it. Some were clamorous for public meetings, others for militia, and a few for rewards. Massac county was crying to us from the memory of her dead Vendetta; Missouri was pleading with us with her mangled hundreds, telling us to think of the gallows and the recollections that it suggested; the newspapers were holding a regular matinee over us, and sending a devastating storm of shot at our blood-stained county.[89] There was no relying on internal strength. What was defective within was aggravated by what was bad from without. The abuse from without aggravated the evil influence within, which caused the banks of crime to overflow, and spread ruin and woe over the fairest lands of "Egypt." The minds which needed hardening were relaxed. The hearts which needed fortifying were dissolved. The passions which needed cooling were irritated and disqualified for considerate action.

At this crisis, it was suggested that we meet and pass resolutions that there had never been any crime committed in this county, and straddle the "dark clouds that lowered over our house" on some other county.

During this year the most malignant falsehoods and slanders were hurled over the country about this county, and were received with implicit faith. At any other time they would have returned to pay the inventor with a

---

[89] Massac County's "dead Vendetta" is a reference to the Massac County Rebellion otherwise known as the Flathead-Regulator War of the late 1840s.

vengeance. I raised my voice against these outrages, and claimed that it was steel pens, not shot-guns, that were ruining the business interests of our county. I knew that it was not the falling into crime that would ruin us, but the lying in it. And I did not extenuate crime by apologizing for the inaction of our people. I argued that all collective crimes were conceived in darkness and nursed in secret, and challenged the attention of men only in their effects and results, and that all our people wanted was time. They could not raise vigilance committees, as they were advised by the press, and go out to cutting and shooting their fellow-men, like the cruel Moors. Unexpected as was this deep display of blood-thirsty feelings, the country ought not to be surprised that our people were unprepared to meet it. We live in an age of surprise. The events of 1875 show us that it is impossible to count on what next week will bring. We never can outlive conspiracy until men are taken by the hand instead of the throat. I did not pause to deny that the follies and crimes of individuals in the county had lent plausibility to the maledictions then rife upon us, but insisted that the whole arcana of human ingenuity had been rifled to find a plan to stop it, and that it would be stopped by rewards. The mills of the gods ground slowly in our case, but they ground well. Some of the papers, in speaking of this county, had the skull and cross-bones at the head. I thought that reporters could denounce crime without a criminal and barbarous outrage on a community of honest men. Some of them evinced a reckless disregard for justice, fairness and truth, and spoke of us with a venom and zest that argued the basest kind of demoralization, which called for stern and outspoken rebuke from every honest and virtuous man. They tore down the protection of our reputation – the bulwark of society and left us defenseless in the presence of malevolent villainy.

That anybody should delight in this kind of moral piracy, and leave a community open to the ravages of moral cormorants, is a melancholy subject to think upon. God never gave any man the right to poison the springs of happiness in this way. But it is unjust to charge the journalism of the country indiscriminately with this crime. There were some noble exceptions. The *Jonesboro Gazette* and *Illinois Journal* maintained a dignified course toward us that was as commendable and just as it was prudent and wise. During the years 1874-5 this county had as good and trustworthy a set of Justices and Constables as any in the State, and all offenses, except assassinations, were as effectually punished.

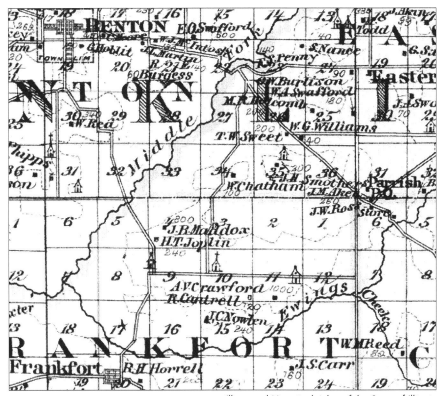

Illustrated Historical Atlas of the State of Illinois

BATTLE OF MADDOX'S LANE — The map above shows the Benton and Frankfort area of Franklin County in 1876. The town of Frankfort in the southwestern corner of the map is now the Franklin Heights section of West Frankfort. The road from Frankfort to Benton in the northwest corner of the map represents what is now Deering Road. Parrish post office can be found in the middle of the map on the right side. The store immediately to the southeast would have been Hiram Summers' establishment where the Klan met. Its liquor sales helped give the crossroads the name of "Sneak Out." J. B. Maddox's farm is identified just east of the Benton and Frankfort Road about in the center of the map. Using current road names, the Klan would have left Parrish by heading south on Baseball Road, turning west on 4 Mile Road, then turning north on Deering, then would have likely hit Maddox's lane in about a half mile.

Chapter 11. **Klan Strikes Again**

SINCE ERWIN WROTE ABOUT THE BLOODY VENDETTA as just part of his larger *History of Williamson County*, he quite understandably left out major events that took place in other counties, such as the Klan's raid on the John B. Maddox farm in Franklin County in the summer of 1875 following the murders of Sisney and Spence. Erwin also didn't find a major connection between the Vendetta and the Klan. Yet it is interesting that just as Marshall Crain and Samuel Musick leave the county until it cools off, the Klan begins its next major offensive.

On Sunday, August 15, 1875, two weeks after Musick confessed to the Waggoners, Twenty-two-year-old John F. Shankton shot Henry B. Norman near Sparta in Randolph Co., Illinois. Norman, had been one of the government's witnesses against the Klan in the federal conspiracy trial following the Isaac Vancil's murder. Colp and Henderson had been killed the year before. Norman made the third victim. Bishop made four when counting the witnesses from the state trials. At first the newspapers reported that Norman had been shot and killed at Blairsville, then another report came that he had not been killed but was "wounded and could not recover." Not until the end of August did the newspapers get the story when they reported the shooting story as incorrect after the editor of the Sparta *Plain Dealer* interviewed the still living Norman who had left the Blairsville area for Randolph County area thinking it would be safer and was living there during the attempt on his life.

Prior to the shooting Norman had brought the 22-year-old Shankton up from Williamson county to work presumably on his farm for about a month. At the end of the money Shankton owed Norman some money so the latter took a bill of sale for some furniture and other goods as security, and Shankton returned to Williamson. On the day of the shooting Shankton arrived at the farm with Norman's brother-in-law James T. King. They drove up in a wagon to the Norman's fence and called him out of his house. Shankton told Norman he had some papers and he wanted his property back. An argument ensued and at some point Shankton picked up a loaded double-barrel shotgun he had thought necessary bring along.

"I ran, he fired, hitting my arm, back and side and took off across the field," Norman told the editor who also learned that both Norman and Davis as well as their families and "two or three other relatives" had left Williamson County under the threat of death.

These two men, along with two others, gave evidence before the U.S. Grand Jury against some of the assassins in that county, lives were threatened, and other two men having since been killed. About 46 shots were lodged in the body of Norman, the greater portion in the right arm. Warm weather may produce mortification and cause amputation of his arm.

Four weeks later John Shanklin, "who shot Henry B. Norman in Randolph County some time since, was 'taken in out of the wet' at Carterville" and placed in the county jail.[90]

The Norman shooting took place Sunday morning, the next big event came just 36 hours later on Monday night two counties to the east in the middle of Franklin County as Hall recalled:

[It was here in August] the Klan met their real Bull Run, Appomattox, and Waterloo... when they visited the home of Jack Maddox, a prominent farmer living in the northwest part of Crawford Prairie, five miles north of Old Frankfort Heights. [91]

Following their success at evading any serious attempt at law enforcement after the Vancil murder and the attack on the Carters, the Klan continued to grow out of control in 1875, particularly in Franklin County.

Their headquarters was located at a little village with a bad name and a bad reputation, known as "Sneak Out." It was located on

---

[90] Lind. 1:32, 35; quoting the Aug. 19 and Aug. 26, 1875 issues of the *Marion Monitor;* and the Sept. 17, 1875 issue of the *Egyptian Press* of Marion.
[91] Hall. July 1923.

the west bank of Ewing Creek where the road between Benton and Thompsonville crosses.[92]

...They traveled over the country in the dead hours of night visiting isolated farm homes calling the occupants out, warning them what they should do and what they should not do, and if orders were not obeyed they would pay them another visit and give them a good beating. Then if orders were not obeyed they would pay them another visit, and hang them. Practically, no efforts whatever had been made by the public officials to suppress this lawless band of night riders.[93]

That all changed in August following the murders of Capt. Sisney and Spence in Jackson County thanks to three men: William W. "Bill" Jacobs., John H. Hogan, and Franklin County Sheriff James F. Mason.

Most of what is known about the events of August 1875 in Franklin County come from the writings of Dr. Hall. Not only did he grow up in Franklin County during that time, he personally knew Jacobs and Hogan. Also, he and his older brother had spent a lot of time on the Maddox farm during that time period.

My older brother, Columbus Hall, was teaching school in Crawford's Prairie in the district in which John Maddox lived and roomed in the Maddox home. I had been in the Maddox home many times. My uncle, Millard McLean, married one of Jack Maddox's daughters; hence, I heard of the activities of the Klan... I also knew that men engaged in any worthwhile endeavor for the good of the community did not need to disguise themselves to hide their

---

[92] Ewing Creek runs along the southern two townships on the east side of Franklin County before entering the Big Muddy River north of West Frankfort. The location of "Sneak Out" roughly corresponds to modern-day Parrish, which was platted in Section 6 of Cave Township for T. J. Eubanks in May 1880. "Sneak Out" seems to have been located on the county road. Parrish is south of the highway and aligned with the railroad that parallels it about a half a mile away from the highway bridge.

[93] Andy Hall. February 1970. "Ku Klux Klan and the battle of John B. (Jack) Maddox Farm." *Outdoor Illinois*. 9-10.

identify, and only those wanting to rob a bank, hold up a train or commit some other unlawful fact need disguise themselves.[94]

On July 29, the day after Sisney's assassination, Jacobs took part in the initiation for Klan membership at Hiram Summers' place at "Sneak Out" where Summers was a whiskey-seller. As he later explained, Jacobs swore the Klan oath for two reasons.

> He joined it for the purpose of exposing and breaking up the organization, and another object he had was to discover the murderer of old man Vancil, who was hung by a band of Ku-Klux for disobedience of their orders about two years ago.

He also told of their passwords and signs.

> The passwords of the Klan were simple. On meeting a supposed member I put my hands in my pants pockets and moved my fingers on the outside. If he was a member he responded by moving his coat by the lapel with his hands, or the lapels of his vest by the same means. Then, taking him by the hand, I would put two fingers on his hand between the thumb and the first finger, and if he was a member he would say something about doing well. The last two words were the passwords, and were sufficient, if used in any sort of phrase.

Shortly after joining Jacobs learned the Klan leadership was planning a call on John B. Maddox and Capt. John Hogan. Both were members of the Masonic Lodge, like Jacobs. As Hall recalled, "as one Mason to another, he was giving them warning in order that they might take due notice and govern themselves accordingly."

As Jacobs later testified, the leadership of the Klan was upset that Maddox "because he had been a little too free with women and with Rice's wife." Hogan had "provoked their hostility" for having the audacity to

---

[94] In addition to his own recollections, Hall also had at his disposal a copy of Erwin's history as well as a scrapbook kept by W. S. Cantrell of Benton, "in which were pasted numerous clippings of the papers published a few days following the battle at Jack Maddox's farm."

prosecute Hiram Summers for "selling his boy whiskey." As Hogan later told a reporter, he had been warned "to pay Summers back the amount of the fine $100 and costs.

> Mr. Maddox at that time was one of the commissioners of Franklin County. He was a most highly respected citizen and one of the outstanding farmers living in Crawford's Prairie, and was perhaps the wealthiest man in that community.[95]
>
> Captain Hogan was another outstanding and highly respect citizen of Franklin County. During the gold rush to California he traveled by wagon to the Golden State where he spent several years. He had served as a soldier in the Union Army during the Civil War.
>
> As an old soldier, Captain Hogan did not propose to take orders and be punished by the Ku-Klux-Klan. Therefore, he called on Governor Beveridge at Springfield, Illinois, explained the activities of the Klan in Franklin County, and told him that he had information that they were to call on Maddox the following Monday night, and at his home at a later date. He suggested measures be taken to suppress and prosecute this lawless band. He also told the governor that if given the authorities and the means, that he would raise a volunteer company and arrest the Klansmen. The governor advised him and Sheriff Mason of Franklin County to organize a volunteer group, go to the Maddox home, and if the Klansmen appeared as they promised to do, arrest and if necessary shoot every man in disguise.[96]

Jacobs told the two men that the Klan wanted to call on Maddox on the 16th and on Hogan on the 20th. Instead the two men beat them to it. Hogan's visit to the governor took place on Friday the 13th. On Saturday the governor wrote to Sheriff Mason.

> Sir: In view of the recent disturbances in Williamson County, and your proximity thereto, I would suggest the propriety of

---

[95] The 1870 Census of Franklin Co., Illinois, shows Maddox owning $14,000 in real estate and $1,500 in personal property. At that point his household included his wife and seven children in ages from 15 down to two.

[96] Hall 1970. 10. These are Hall's own recollections.

organizing an independent military company at Benton. Such an organization without any reference to affairs in Williamson, and composed of good reliable men, would always be ready to aid you in any emergency and would give strength to the civil authorities of the county in preserving order and enforcing the laws. The expense would be small, as uniforms would not be required. Arms, etc. can be furnished by the State. Suppose you confer with some of the prominent citizens of your county and advise me of your determination in the premises.

> Yours very truly,
> Jno. L. Beveridge.

As the sheriff and Hogan worked to organize the group of men who would become the militia company, but more importantly, would become the "reception committee" for Monday night. As Jacobs learned of details in the Klan's planning he passed them along to his lodge brothers including such details as that the Klan would approach Maddox's farm coming from the south and that they would be there "near the house of midnight."

> He also said that he would be with them until they reached a certain position when he would make some excuse and fall out for a moment, and never overtake them.
> The result was that a posse of about forty men, most of whom were Masons, dropped into the Mattox home early the evening of the intended visit. They obstructed the lane running north past the home with threshing machines, mowing machines, wagons and other kinds of farm machinery. Then the posse armed with shot guns secreted themselves south of the house a few hundred yards on either side of a staked and ridered lane and awaited the coming of the Klan.[97]

While the sheriff and the mostly-Masonic posse waited for the Klan, Jacobs was busy just trying to keep up with the riders as they began their rounds that Monday night, August 16, after swearing in "several other persons" into the group, as Jacobs later testified.

---

[97] Hall 1923, 14-15.

[I] was detained till a uniform came and then [we] proceeded toward Crawford's Prairie. When we were within two or three miles of the prairie several men in uniform and mounted dashed up behind us. We then (the initiates) dressed in uniform, and went to Brown's, then to Calvin Moore's, then to James Moore's, then to Rice's, and then to Maddox's.

Aaron Neal who supposedly had been a member of the Southern Klan and been involved in the Southern Illinois Klan since at least the time of Vancil's murder in 1872, led the party that Sunday night and Monday morning. Calvin Moore served as another of the Franklin County bunch and administered the oath to Jacobs that night. No mention was made as to why they visited James Moore's house, but Rice's visit likely was to warn his wife about Maddox.

The visit to James Brown's residence became the first tragedy of the night. As Jacobs' testified, "We went to Brown's to whip him because he had accused people wrongfully." This was the Klan's second visit to Brown. Their first had been on June 24 when four Klan members came in the night and wanted water, a long-established pretense used by the Klan in the South, particularly to scare folks. The press later reported the testimony of Brown's wife Matilda given in the subsequent court hearings.

> They asked about Maddox. They were inside the house, but one only talked. She recognized Neal by his voice. I have known him from his youth and knew his voice. I recognized Calvin Moore by his actions; by a peculiar walk; by a proud, hasty walk. I told my husband they would be back to see him.

Jacobs testified as to what happened on the second visit from the Klan's perspective.

> We were at Brown's at about 11 or 12 o'clock. We inquired at Brown's where he was, and so forth and so on, and about a gun he had. Fourteen of us were at Brown's all disguised. I think Neal professed to act as our captain. He and Calvin Moore gave commands. We went to Brown's to whip him. We had given orders

which he had not complied with, and we were going to whip him, and break a gun he had.

Mrs. Brown recalled the event as well.

> Fourteen called the second time and inquired for Brown. I told them he was in bed, sick. They asked if he had a gun and revolver. I told him no. They told me he was measuring horse-tracks and must stop that in that country. I recognized the voice of Calvin Moore on the second visit. My sick husband was frightened. He didn't appear like the same man and died the next day. I think fright hastened his death.

Dr. Thomas David Ray also testified that he had been "waiting on Brown at the visit by the Ku Klux" and agreed that the visit had hastened Brown's death. Mrs. Brown's testimony took place about two weeks after her husband's death and her reaction to the Klan's visit appears much calmer than reported immediately after the event.[98]

One local paper reported that when the Klan called for her husband who was sick in bed, she went outside to face them, telling them "he was sick" and "begged them to kill her if they must kill someone." They backed off, but "told her they would call again."[99]

Based on Jacobs' timeline and other news accounts, the group must have visited Rice's around midnight for they arrived at Maddox's at about 2 o'clock in the morning of the 17th.

> We went then to Maddox's to give him orders. When we left the main road, we debated whether we should go to Maddox's. We decided to do so, and when we got into Maddox's lane, I thought I saw someone run across it, near the house. As we came up in front of the house, I heard the command "Halt," and the order to surrender, in the name of the people of the State of Illinois.

---

[98] Hall 1973, 15; quoting an unnamed article datelined August 28, 1875 at Centralia, Illinois.

[99] Lind 1:31; quoting the Aug. 19, 1875 edition of the *Marion Monitor*.

I next heard a cap bursted: next a pistol shot. All of us wheeled and the firing commenced. I saw Neal's mule run past me. I heard that it was the intention to give Maddox orders first, whip him, if disobeyed, and hang him if he persisted in disobedience.

John Duckworth also testified about the events of that night as a member of the Klan.

Mr. John Duckworth, the wounded Ku-Klux, then took the stand as a witness for the prosecution. His evidence was a little confused. He testified that he had been a member of the Golden Ring about three months... [and] was initiated at Eli Sommers' lot.

... Neal acted as captain, or as the members designated him, grand master. He was at Maddox's and rode a mule. I had a pistol. Calvin Moore had a gun, and George Proctor a gun. The object of the organization was to make fellows do as we wanted them to.

The law could not get at us. We gave a man orders, and if he did not obey we whipped him, and would hang him if he did not then obey. Neal was along at the time of the Maddox affair. He was in front. I was in front, too. I was shot and did not know anything more.

The trial testimonies summarized provides only the driest possible version of what happened at Maddox's lane.

At the appointed hour [the Klan] came up from the south and passed the sheriff's posse going on to the house where they ran into the obstructed lane. They then turned and started to make a quick get away. The sheriff attempted to arrest them when they reached where he and his men were located. A shot was fired at Mr. Mason by a Klansman and they attempted to get away. But the posse opened up with their old shotguns and many of the riders and horses were wounded. In the confusion and darkness most of the Klansmen shed their white robes and escaped.

Bloodstained robes were found all over the fields and along the lane leading from the Maddox home the next morning.

Yet, even Dr. Hall's account isn't nearly as tantalizing as the newspaper accounts the next day such as the clipping from the Benton paper Hall found.

> The Ku-Klux, disguised in long-white robes, high white hats and wearing masks, appeared armed with shotguns and pistols, fourteen strong, looking, in the grim darkness, in the language of one of the boys, "they came up through narrow lane, silently, two abreast and looking truly grand and majestic, and enough to frighten the devil."
>
> When they had come near the house the sheriff stepped out and commanded them to "Halt — in the name of the People of the State of Illinois, and by the authority invested in me as Sheriff, I command you to surrender."
>
> The leader answered the command by firing off his pistol at the sheriff and at the same instant, the bursting of a cap fortunately, without harming either, the band wheeled their horses, and attempted to escape.

A few days later the *Franklin County Courier* provided additional details.

> … When the sheriff ordered them to surrender he was fired upon and a battle ensued in which the Ku-Klux met a disastrous defeat.
>
> When the smoke of the battle was lifted, John Duckworth was found severely wounded in the lane, a dead horse belonging to Rev. Proctor, another horse and mule belonging to Maddox's neighbor, and Ku-Klux robes were scattered up and down the lane and through the fields that had been discarded by members of the Ku-Klux Klan. The reconnaissance, captures, etc., made since Tuesday noon, is given by our own special reporter, in a much more clear and lucid manner than we could have given.
>
> LATEST FROM THE KU-KLUX
> Since last Tuesday, I have been continually in pursuit of the facts connected with the battle with the Ku-Klux at the residence of J. B. Maddox, which occurred last Monday night. Our of the 14 Ku-Klux that went there that night, there was only one escaped unhurt – most of them seriously; and it is now known that there is but few, if any, of

them that have fled the country, but are hiding in the woods, and being cared for by their friends. They were so terribly demoralized that few of the Ku-Klux reached their homes until after day light on Tuesday morning. There is one of them that has not been seen or heard of since the fight, by any of his friends, but on yesterday (Wednesday) evening, there was a stranger passing down the McLeansboro and Frankfort road who discovered a boy bareheaded and in his shirtsleeves, walking through the woods.

The traveler then rode up to him and found that he was badly shot – two shots having stuck him about the left eye, which he things was out, and a heavy load of shot had struck him on the right side of the face and neck and in the right shoulder. He asked him what was the matter? The wounded man gave a blank stare at him, but never spoke. The traveler says that he did not know whether he could speak or not."[100]

The Marion paper reported additional, if not contradictory, details.

Shortly after 2, a body of men arrived in white coats and hats and dark masks… ordered to halt, the reply was, "No, by God, we will not surrender." … they fired upon the sheriff and turned to escape… 20 guns were discharged… one man named Duckworth was fatally wounded and now lies at the point of death in Benton… He told who the others were… next morning masks and coats were found scattered along the lane at Maddox's… Thirteen were picked up, six were badly riddled with bullets, and bloody. A. Neal and Captain G. M. Cantrell (formerly of the 110th Illinois Volunteers) were arrested, the latter badly wounded.

The paper also noted that there were over "100 of these characters" in Williamson County and that they had names "of 40 of them and are in pursuit of them."[101]

---

[100] Hall 1970, 11-12; quoting the Aug. 21, 1875, edition of the *Franklin County Courier*.

[101] Lind 1:31; quoting the Aug. 19, 1875 edition of the *Marion Monitor*.

Local papers weren't the only ones interested in the case. Big city papers covered the atrocities as well almost on a blow-by-blow basis, particularly the St. Louis *Globe-Democrat*. Even a reporter for the *Chicago Tribune* had been in the area the week before the battle on Maddox's lane.[102]

The *Burlington Hawk-Eye* especially followed the stories, usually reprinting ones from the St. Louis and Chicago papers.

TERRIBLE FIGHT BETWEEN VOLUNTEERS AND THE OUTLAWS.

CHICAGO, August 17. — A Times special from Benton, Franklin county, Illinois, says a terrible fight occurred yesterday in that county. The circumstances are that of late a band of ku klux has been marauding in that section, killing and plundering innocent inhabitants. Recently a gentlemen there obtained from Governor Beveridge permission to organize a band of militia for the purpose of wiping the miscreants out. Yesterday they met a party of the ku klux, and after considerable fighting killed one and dangerously injured five others. No further details can be obtained at this writing.

In Jackson county a similar band of men are running about the country devoting their time to plundering alone. Trouble is anticipated in that county also.

THE PARTICULARS.

DUQUOIN, Illinois, August 17. — A bloody fight occurred, last night, in the vicinity of Benton, Franklin county, between the Sheriff of the above named county, with a posse of about twenty men under his command, and a band of Ku-Klux…

About two o'clock at night, fourteen in number, the Ku Klux … appeared… the Sheriff slipped out and commanded them to halt. The answer was a pistol shot fired by the leader of the band, which fortunately took no effect.

The sheriff and posse returned this fire with a better result. Several men were wounded, one mortally, but all succeeded in

---

[102] On August 12, 1875, the *Marion Monitor* reported the following: "LOCAL MATTERS — H. W. Thomson, reporter for the *Chicago Tribune*, was in this county on Tuesday last. He was writing up the history of the bloody deeds of this county."

getting away, except the one mortally wounded. This one, fearing death from his wounds, confessed and revealed the names of thirty or forty more of his companions. From the quantity of bloody clothes found near the fight, it is supposed that several must have been hit. [103]

When the smoke cleared from the battle and the posse found Duckworth in the road, they truly expected him not to live through the night.

> The wounded Duckworth was carried into Mr. Maddox's home where was examined by Dr. Thomas David Ray, a member of the posse and at that time practicing medicine in Frankfort Heights. Dr. Ray thought Duckworth mortally wounded and so informed him. Duckworth made what he thought was a death-bed confession and gave them all the information he could concerning the Klansmen[104]

Besides the wounded Klansman's testimony, the sheriff's posse found good evidence in the animals remaining. A dead horse they recognized as belonging to the Rev. Proctor which as it turns out had been ridden by his son who was shot in the foot. They also found a horse that belonged to one of Maddox's neighbors Green Cantrell with a saddle full of shot. They arrested Cantrell who swore he wasn't injured at all even though Dr. Zachariah Hickman removed 42 pieces of lead shot from his backside.

Another easy break came from Aaron Neal, one of the Klansman who had ridden a mule to the encounter sitting on a saddle he'd borrowed from Maddox's son a few days earlier.

Following the battle at Maddox's lane the citizens in the county seat held a public meeting in Benton to discuss the Klan's activities. W. W. Barr, John McFall, C. Moore, F. M. Youngblood and John Hogan all offered remarks and suggestions. The citizens then appointed Moore and Youngblood along with J. J. St. Clair and C. Payne as a committee on resolutions, which reported back the following:

---

[103] Aug. 19, 1875. "Terrible Fight Between Volunteers and the Outlaws." *Burlington* [Iowa] *Hawk-Eye*. 1.

[104] Hall 1970, 11-12.

WHEREAS, a secret band of outlaws are now in existence in the county, calling themselves Ku-Klux, who are bound together by oaths, and traverse the county in complete disguise and in the night time, take peaceable citizens from their beds, whip them, and order them to perform actions under penalty of life, which are inconsistent with the rights and privileges of free men and citizens of the county.

AND WHEREAS, James F. Mason, the Sheriff of this county, having heard that a body of these Ku-Klux, disguised and armed, would visit John B. Maddox upon last night, for the purpose of terrifying him into the performance of certain things which they were desirous he should do, summoned a posse of men, with arms, secreted themselves at the residence of John B. Maddox – and when the Ku-Klux, 14 in number, armed and disguised made their appearance about 2 o'clock, the Sheriff, in the name of the People of the State of Illinois, and by virtue of the office as Sheriff of Franklin County demanded their surrender; to which they responded by firing upon the Sheriff and attempting to flee, whereupon the Sheriff and posse immediately fired upon the disguised men, fatally wounding one man and seriously injuring others.

THEREFORE, BE IT RESOLVED, That we, as law-abiding and peaceable citizens of Franklin County, determined to uphold the laws of our country, and protect our citizens from outrage, do hereby cordially endorse the action of the Sheriff and this posse in their conduct last night; and that we condemn in the strongest manner, these armed and disguised marauders, and that to their suppression and the maintenance of the laws and liberties of our citizens, we do hereby pledge our lives and money.

The crowd unanimously adopted the resolution. Almost immediately about 60 men organized into a military company designed to assist the sheriff. The company elected John B. Hogan, captain; G. S. Hubbard, 1st Lt.; J. L. Harrell, 2nd Lt.; B. H. Flannigan, 3rd Lt.; and William Drummons, orderly sergeant.

By that Friday Sheriff Mason and Captain Hogan, who also served as a deputy U.S. Marshal, along with a number of guards, arrived in Centralia, Illinois, at 7 p.m. with a number of the Klan suspects. The defendants included Aaron Neal, the reputed grand master, Green M. Cantrell, John Duckworth, Williamson Briley, James Lannlus, James Abshear and Frank Fleming.

> The raised platform was densely crowded with people, all anxious to catch a glimpse of the live Ku-Klux, and the only thing necessary to make the reception an ovation was a brass band.

The men then went before U.S. Commissioner Zabadee Curlee of Tamaroa, who assisted by William Stoker of Centralia, organized into a United States Commissioner's Court under the federal statute entitled, "Crimes against the elective franchise and civil rights of citizens."

Despite the evidence and testimony Curlee required relatively low bails to be given for the men's freedom. During Curlee's absence for sickness, Stoker even dismissed a second count against Neal for conspiracy.[105]

> The preliminary examination of the marauders took place before United States Commissioner Curlee. The prosecution was made under the United States Ku-klux law. The government was represented by District Attorney Van Dorston, assisted by Hon. W. W. Barr, of Franklin county. The defense by Messrs. Payne and Williams, of Benton.
>
> The principal witnesses examined were John B. Maddox, W. W. Jacobs, Mrs. James Brown, Dr. Ray and John Duckworth. Duckworth testified that he was at the fight in Maddox Lane, and on that night Aaron Neal was the leader of the band. He gave the names of fourteen men as being then with the gang; Calvin Moore, George Proctor, George Herd, Wilson Sommers, Thos. Sommers, Mardona Sommers. Henderson Sommers, Rufus Stripling, W. W. Briley, Wm. Plasters, Green Cantrell, W. W. Jacobs, himself and Aaron Neal. He testified that on the night of the 29th of July the band met at the house of Hiram Sommers, and resolved to give a visitation to Maddox and Brown. The latter was supposed to have some improper women about his place; the former was charged with

---

[105] Hall 1970, 13-15.

having measured their horses' tracks. When they came to Brown's house they found him in a dying condition.

The testimony of W. W. Jacobs, another of the band, confirmed that of young Duckworth. Aaron Neal was the leader that night, and Calvin Moore administered the oath. The Franklin county band was only part of a regular organization that existed in Williamson, Saline and Jackson counties, and its object was to do what they pleased, regardless of law. They visited James Brown that night to make him break a gun with which he had threatened to shoot any Ku-klux who visited him.

Dr. Ray, of Franklin county, testified that the death of Mr. James Brown was hastened by the Ku-klux visitation that night, but could now swear that it was the immediate cause. The testimony was contradicted by that of the succeeding witness, without any new point being developed.

The result of the examination was that Aaron Neal was held over. Two charges had been preferred against him: first, for conspiracy to injure the public; and second, for conspiracy against the liberty and property of Mr. Maddox. The first charge was dismissed. On the second, he was held over in $2,000 bail. He gave bond, with his brothers Jeremiah Neal and Thomas Neal, as securities. The others, R. Poindexter, James Abshier, Frank Fleming and William Nolan, were held over in $1,000.

Great indignation is felt that Neal should have been allowed to go free on so small a bond. At the conclusion of the preliminary examination, Aaron Neal went home, under a guard, to Franklin county, where he is charged under State law, before the County Court, with riot and unlawful assembly.[106]

Despite the federal prosecution, the Klan members eventually got off and their activities somewhat died off for a time, or were at least overshadowed by the events taking place to the south in Williamson County.

Now back to Erwin's account:

---

[106] Sept. 2, 1875. "The Illinois Ku Klux." *Burlington* [Iowa] *Hawk Eye*. 1.

Chapter 12. **Light at the Tunnel's End**

ON THE FOURTH DAY OF AUGUST, 1875, Governor Beveridge wrote to our Sheriff, offering to do all in his power to relieve the county whenever the Sheriff thought proper to call on him. At the August Special Term, 1875, the County Commissioners offered a reward of $1,000 for each of the murderers of David Bulliner, James Henderson, Vincent Hinchcliff and William Spence, and on the 9th of August, the Governor, issued a proclamation offering $400 reward for the arrest and conviction of each of the criminals referred to, and also for the murderers of George W. Sisney and George Bulliner. And on the 22d of August, the Jackson County Court offered $400 reward for the murderers of Sisney and Bulliner.[107]

This was a gloomy period, but it was that gloom which preceded the dawn. It was the dark hour which ushered in the bright morning. Criminals leave gates open for detection. There are certain weak meshes in the network of devilish texture. We were just looking forward to the no distant day, when the dark veil that concealed the festering crimes of the county should be rent asunder by a daring and skillful hand. It came. Mrs. Waggoner told her brother, James H. Duncan, of Marion, who the guilty parties were. Mr. Duncan is a man about thirty-six years old, very intelligent, firm as a rock, and a man of remarkable courage. He could not withhold his efforts in behalf of his suffering countrymen, while they were bleeding at every vein. In him, the people felt that they had a leader in whom they could trust. A man of discretion and nerve, and though for a long time he was not publicly known in the work, yet he was backing all the efforts and laid all the plans. A woman told who were guilty, but it took a man of iron to arrest and bring them to justice. Mr. Duncan stood up firmly on the side of the people throughout the prosecutions, and but for his discretion and assistance, we might today be suffering the calamities of a Vendetta. He went to a "friend" and told him he knew who killed Spence, and he intended to have them brought to justice, and he wanted some man to execute his plans. His "friend" advised him to get Benjamin F. Lowe, of Marion. Lowe agreed to go into it. Sam Musick was

---

[107] Although Erwin doesn't mention it, August also saw the successful ambush of the Klan in Franklin County by the sheriff at the Maddox farm.

the first man to be arrested. Lowe went to Cairo and inquired at the post office for a letter for Samuel Musick; being told that there was one, he told the postmaster not to let anybody have it but Musick in person. Lowe then got the Deputy Sheriff, and in about an hour Samuel called for his letter and was arrested. Lowe brought him to Marion on the 10th day of September. No confidence was put in this move by the people, and consequently no stir was made until Musick was taken before Young, J. P. and asked time for trial. His case was set down for hearing September 20th and he sent to jail. Two hours afterwards, through the influence of Captain Landrum, who promised him protection, he sent for the Sheriff and Circuit Clerk, and made a complete confession of killing Spence and Sisney, and implicated "Big Jep," "Black Bill," "Yaller Bill," Samuel R. Crain, Marshall Crain, John Bulliner and Allen Baker.[108]

---

[108] A Carbondale reporter with the initial B. provided the details as to how authorities lubricated a confession out of Music in a story headlined, "The Illinois Bandits – Story of the Capture and Confession of Samuel Musick."

The Carbondale correspondent of the *Cairo Bulletin* furnishes the following interesting particulars concerning the discovery and arrest of the Williamson county outlaws:

CARBONDALE, Ill., Sept. 11, 1875, Our whole town was in a whirl of excitement last night when I sent you the dispatch concerning the arrests of the Williamson county assassins. I tried to give you a brief but correct report, and succeeded as well as possible under the circumstances. I will now go more into the detail.

Samuel Musick was arrested in Cairo, and had been recently at work across the river in Missouri. Sam is a man about 28 years of age. He has made Carbondale his home for six or eight years. He is what might be properly termed a "hard case," drinking and carousing frequently. He has a bad eye in his head, and is altogether a man for whom the people at large had little use, though it is not known that he had, previous to this, been engaged in any really criminal business. For a year and a half past he has been working for Mr. J. W. Landrum, whose farm is near Carterville. His associations were entirely among the Bulliners and their friends. He was just the man to be made their tool, and how well and yet how badly has performed their work the results show. That your readers may see clearly the starting point, I will say that the killing of Spence, at Crainville, was witnessed by a resident of that neighborhood. This gentleman, whose name for wise purposes is withheld from the public, told his story to several persons in whom he had implicit confidence. He initiated to Officer Lower that if he would arrest Sam Musick and ply him plentifully with whisky he could get a clue that would expose the whole business. Accordingly the arrest was made. Lowe and his prisoner passed through here yesterday morning. Musick was bountifully supplied with

Lowe then swore out writs against these parties for murder, and the Sheriff summoned a posse of twenty-five men and boarded the train for Crainville, seven miles west. Here "Big Jep," "Yaller Bill" and Samuel R. were arrested. The Sheriff then went with a few men to "Black Bill's," and arrested him, and another party went after and got John Bulliner, and they were all brought to Marion that night and put under guard.

Lowe went on to Carbondale and got Cain Brush, and went to DuQuoin after Allen Baker, who had moved up there awhile before.

They found Baker at home, and Lowe said: "We want you to go to Marion for killing Spence."

Baker made fun of the charge; he got very mad, and Lowe took down a revolver which was sticking in the wall.

Baker said, "You damned thief, put that back, or steal something else."

Lowe said he would when it became necessary; that he would look around — that he thought he could find a Bulliner gun, — this was their pistol. Lowe said, "I have been told that you are a brave man and a powerful man, and that you just eat men whole; so don't be surprised if I act a little curious in your presence."

Baker demanded their authority.

Lowe told him to look at Brush and himself; they were the papers in the case. Lowe arrived in Marion with him next morning.

On Monday, the 13th, their case was called before John H. Reynolds, J. P., but by agreement was set down for hearing on the 16th. The prisoners were loosely guarded around town for a few days, and the people became indignant, and the Sheriff put them in jail. Musick accused Bulliner, Baker and Samuel R. Crain with the murder of Sisney, in Jackson county.[109] Lowe

---

whisky, seemed happy as a lord, and generously treated some of his acquaintances. On arriving at Marion he was just in the proper mood to "squeal," and a clever advantage was taken to draw from him everything he knew. *Source*: B. Sept. 16, 1875. "The Illinois Bandits." *Decatur Daily Republican* (Decatur, Ill.). 6.

[109] The public hoped Baker would confess quickly like Musick as Mr. B. outlined:

"Officer Lowe came on to this place. He secured the assistance of City Marshal Brush, and proceeded to DuQuoin, there they arrested Allen Baker. They brought him down on the midnight train, and took him to Marion this morning. Baker said but little about his arrest, but it is believed that he will join Musick in making a confession, for this reason: Some four weeks ago Baker was working for Mr. Purdy at a sawmill two or three miles east of the place. I believe Baker was notified to leave, but paid no attention

went before Murphy, J.P., in Murphysboro, and swore out a writ for them there, and Sheriff Kimball came over on the 15th, and took them over to the Jackson jail, where they were tried on the 22d, Musick testifying against them, and Samuel R. released for want of evidence against him, and the others committed.[110]

The greatest excitement prevailed. A special term of the County Court was convened, and the State Attorney empowered to employ counsel to assist him. He employed the Hon. W. J. Allen and A. D. Duff, of Carbondale. The employment of these men produced a revolution in public sentiment. The rich men stepped to the front, and the bummers stepped aside. Landrum, Ogden, Nelson, Washburn, Ferrell, Herring, Harrison, Goodall, Campbell,

---

to the notice. At any rate, a fearful charge of shot was fired at him through the window, but missed him. He then left and went to DuQuoin. Musick says that Marshall Crain also fired this shot — that Crain was getting fearful that Baker would expose the gang, and thought it best to put him out of the way. From what I know of Baker, when he is informed of the treachery of Crain he will make a clean breast of all he knows." *Source*: B. Sept. 16, 1875. "The Illinois Bandits." *Decatur Daily Republican* (Decatur, Ill.). 6.

[110] The *Marion Monitor* issue of Aug. 6, 1875, reported the attack at the time confirming that Baker had been living and working at Purdy's Mill:

"Some of the murderous gang that infests Jackson County fired a heavy charge of buckshot into Allen Baker's house Sunday night… all that saved his life was the would-be assassins thought his shadow on the window was his body."

This attack came just four days after Capt. Sisney's killing and a day after Spence's. Later in August following the Klan raids in Franklin County unknown parties launched another attack on Purdy's Mill which stood on Crab Orchard Creek near Carbondale. The *Monitor* issue of Aug. 26, reported the recent attack on a Mrs. Williams, which they blamed on members of the Ku Klux Klan:

"MORE KU-KLUXISM — We are informed that a few days ago as Mrs. George Williams, whose husband had been in the employ of Mr. Purdy, at the mill on Crab Orchard, was returning to her home after a brief absence, she was stopped by a man disguised and masked, who asked her where her husband was — saying "we" have been watching the house for some time without seeing him; and now he came to tell her to tell her husband to get away as soon as possible, "or we will kill him." She asked the fellow what her husband had done that they should want to kill him; the fellow, with several oaths, told her to shut her mouth, it was none of her business — only to tell her husband to leave, and if she didn't "we will kill you." Mr. Williams left home immediately. We learn that Governor Beveridge has authorized our Mayor to organize a company to hunt up such scoundrels as the fellow who met Mrs. Williams, and we hope it will be done, and that speedily, too. — Carbondale Observer."

Grider, Mitchell, Young, and a host of others, who have stood up for the right and breasted the world's dark tide for the good of the county, came on the stage, holding up one hand to save the innocent, and the other to crush the guilty. And our imagination which had been so used to scenes of blood, was now playing over the rope and gallows; and our ears, which had heard the shrieks of agonizing victims and the fierce yells of their savage slayers, were now saluted by the slogan of returning justice.

On Friday, September 16th, the case was called, the People proving the facts above detailed of the murder. The defense was an alibi, W. W. Clemens and J. B. Calvert appearing for the defendants. Two of the Jacks and two Craigs swore that "Big Bill" was eight miles away that fatal night. "Big Jep" proved his whereabouts by a dozen witnesses. Other minor facts were proven, and after a tedious examination of two days the Court committed all the defendants to jail, except Musick, who never had any examination.

Chapter 13. **Capturing Marshall**

MUSICK SAID THAT MARSHALL HAD GONE to his wife's aunt, in Missouri. Lowe then, in order to find out where his wife's aunt lived in Missouri, had his mother-in-law subpoenaed as a witness against the boys before Reynolds. State's Attorney Hartwell then told Mrs. Rich that he believed they were going to impeach her, as she had to swear for the People, and it would be necessary for him to know where her people lived, so as to be able to meet them. She said her sister lived in Butler county, Mo., and was married to Ben. Lewis. She was not used as a witness.

Lowe left Marion after the trial and went to Makanda, Jackson county, and at ten o'clock in the night started out to the Smiths, in this county who were relatives of the Crains. He found where Marshall's folks lived, so that he could shun them, but it being nearly daylight, he went back to Makanda, and laid up all day. Starting out again at night, he soon found where Marshall and his wife had staid all night the night they left the country. It was a half mile east of Makanda. Marshall counted his money here, and said he had enough to go by St. Louis, and then to his uncle, Thomas Crain, in Boone county, Ark. They left here two weeks before for St. Louis, from where he went to Springfield, and then to Boone county, Ark., but returned to Butler county, Mo. He left his wife here with Dr. Adams, and started on foot to the Cherokee Bend to pick cotton, and had got sixty-five miles when he was arrested.

From Makanda, Lowe came to Marion, and on September 20th left for Butler county, Mo. On arriving there, he hired A. Thomas to go out to Dr. Adams and make a survey. He found that Marshall had left on foot for the Bend, carrying a pistol, a budget, and wearing velvet pants. The County Attorney wanted Lowe to remain there until Marshall returned, saying that Dr. Adams would report the fact; but Lowe left Thomas to arrest him if he returned, and took the train for Corning, Ark., thirty-three miles. Here he hired a constable, and left for the Cherokee Bend. Fifteen miles from here he struck Marshall's trail. He had traveled through a wild, sunburnt, arid waste, whose solemn silence is rarely ever broken by the tread of a white man, and his tracks were plainly to be seen in the sand, where the thirsty earth gaped under the merciless sun. Marshall had given his name as "Crain," from

Missouri, and had tried to hire at every place he came to. For fifteen miles Lowe followed his trail. Marshall was inquiring for Jacksonport, and Lowe, when asked what he wanted with him, would say, "he stole a watch up in Missouri."

They came to a river, when the ferryman told them that Crain was at Mr. Gray's, a half mile ahead. They rode on up to the house, and a woman was standing at the gate, and when asked, said Marshall was in the house, with a chill on him. It was a double log house, with a bed-room between. Lowe went in, and Marshall was lying fast asleep on the bed. Lowe gave him a shake, and he awoke very suddenly, raised up and reached for his pistol over his head. Lowe pushed him back with a Derringer, and asked him his name. He said "Marshall Crain," and asked, "who are you?" Lowe said, "You know me." Marsh said, "Yes, how are you, Frank Lowe?" The constable was at the foot of the bed. Lowe told him he had a warrant for his arrest, and asked him if he should read it. Marsh said, "No." Lowe then tied him, and took his pistol, and put him on horse back behind himself. At this juncture Gray came out of the field, and Lowe apologized for the liberty he had taken. Gray said it was all right.

The sun was half-an hour high, and it was twelve miles to William Gossett's, the next house, where they arrived at 10 o'clock. There they got supper. Frank then made a bed on the floor for Marsh, and hired a school teacher for $2.00, to guard him, and lay down himself. He saw Marsh untying the rope from his legs; he got it off. Frank rose and stopped him. Marsh said he would have jumped through the window and been gone in fifteen minutes. They started on, then, and arrived at Corning that evening. Marsh had a chill, and was put to bed in the hotel. Frank also had a chill. Marsh got something to eat, and then Frank called the jailer, and asked Marsh if he would go without a requisition; if he would not, he would put him in jail and get one. Marsh said he wanted the men to understand that he was going to Illinois of his own free will. He was then handcuffed, and wanted Frank to write to his wife, who was ten miles in the country, that he was under arrest, going to Illinois, and that she must not try to come through on foot, but wait until she got money from him. He said she would come through on foot, if he did not tell her. He said she was too good for him, and he cared for nobody else on earth. Within four miles of Cairo, Frank told him about the boys being in jail. He did not believe it. Frank produced a *Globe-Democrat* containing the proceedings at their trial, which satisfied him. Frank said, "Bulliner, Baker and Musick have employed me to catch you, so they could swear it onto you, and then come clear; that was the arrangement."

Marsh said, "I don't know so damned well; they are as guilty as I am in the thing."

They landed at Cairo Saturday, Sept. 28th, at 4 o'clock, A.M., and took a freight train for Carbondale. While going up, Marsh told Frank the whole story that he afterwards swore to. On the train he was very noisy, hallooing for Jeff. Davis, and talked freely of killing men. He was mad at everybody, and wanted to be unhandcuffed to fight men who asked him questions. At one place, ten or twelve men stood looking at him.

He said, "If your eyes were in dogs' heads there would be sheep killed tonight." Well might he be excited, for he was in the hands of a powerful, shrewd, ingenious man, who brought every cunning contrivance, and subtle influence to bear on him, to get a confession out of him. It was a wonderful achievement, on the part of Lowe, to get a full confession out of a great criminal like Marshall Crain in so short a time. He was afraid of a mob, at Carbondale, and seemed anxious and reckless. When the whistle blowed at Carbondale he was frightened. Frank told him that the good people and officers of Carbondale would assist him against a mob, and if he had thought of danger he would have telegraphed to Marion for twenty men. He wanted to know if the people were very bitter against him. Frank told him they would only hang him, that was all. He said he did not care for his life.

At Carbondale the people did not know him, but presently John Crain came in and settled the matter. Frank took him out to the old house where he had concealed his gun the night he killed Sisney, to get some powder and shot which he said Allen Baker had put there for him to kill Sisney with. They found the powder. Frank left him at Carbondale, where he received medical attention until Monday, when he was taken to the Murphysboro jail.

On the 17th day of September, Sheriff Norris wrote the Governor for arms and ammunition for a company of militia. On the 19th, the Governor promptly responded that he had sent 100 rifles by express. The Sheriff also sent the names of Z. Hudgens for Captain, W. J. Pully first, and Wm. Hendrickson, for second Lieutenants, but these men were not commissioned. The guns arrived Saturday, the 21st, and an effort was made to raise a company of militia by the Sheriff which ended in a "big laugh." But on the 15th previous, W. N. Mitchell and J. W. Landrum returned from Springfield with power to raise two companies, which they did; one at Marion and one at

Carterville. The company at Marion was raised on the 25th, and the guns opened. J. V. Grider was elected Captain, Wm. Hendrickson first and W. J. Pully, second Lieutenants. There was some opposition to the militia, but these officers were responsible, brave, cautious men, and did nothing to irritate the public, and went quietly along, doing their whole duty. The Carterville company elected Landrum Captain, Wm. Dowell first, and Wilshire Bandy second Lieutenants. A kind of local pride seized the surrounding counties at this time, and they were continually holding up the misfortunes of each other, and justifying themselves.

John Bulliner and Allen Baker were indicted at the October term of the Jackson Circuit Court, and went to trial at the same term, defended by F. E. Albright, of Murphysboro. Marshal Crain, who was taken from his cell one night, made a desperate effort to escape by running from his guard and falling on the ground, but was recaptured. He had been before the grand-jury and swore against Bulliner and Baker, but now formed the design of going back on what he had stated there, and clearing the boys; and wrote the following letter to them in jail, which he was probably persuaded to write

"Allen, I want you and John to post-man Jack, Sam, Jack, and Tedford, Johnny Rich, Jeff, "Yaller Bill," Wesley and Sarah Rich that they were to have a surprise party at Sarah Rich's, and I came in eight or nine o'clock, on the night George Sisney was shot and that I was barefooted. I know I sent my boots and coat by Sam Musick, but that won't convict me. Now, boys, do all you can for me and I will do all in my power for you. Employ the same lawyer for me that you and Allen have got. All is right; if I hang, I fear I will hang. John lecture for me in this case and clear me. When Spence was killed I was at Cal. Craig's. Prove this by him and other witnesses, tell to them that I was there about half after nine o'clock, on the night Sisney was killed. Allen, you and John and all the boys will come clear. I shall swear that I was forced to swear what I did; if I hang, it is all right. I shall swear that Sam Musick told me that he killed Mr. Spence, and he told me that he was going to put ammunition in that house, so when he turned State's evidence he could make some proof. He told me this. Can you and John state too that he told you that he put it there when he was hauling for Landrum. If you and John come clear, go and post Mrs. Rich and Johnny, and Wesley and Anderson Thedford; tell Ant. Thedford to swear he seen me close to his daddy's, at about nine o'clock, as he came from his daddy's. He said he would swear anything for me. Post James Craig and prove by these, and tell mother not to go back on me, and clear me; they can do it. Have they swore against me? Tell Jim Craig I want to prove I was at his house by him and other witnesses when Spence was killed. Give information how I will move my trial to Marion."

This letter was to be destroyed by the boys; but when Marsh went on the stand and denied as he was to, any knowledge of the killing of Sisney, Albright produced this letter, and asked him if he wrote it. Marsh saw the point to this, that he was to be made the guilty party, and he turned like a furious lion and swore them both to prison. Musick also swore the facts heretofore detailed. The case closed on the 12th of October, after lasting a week. On the next day the jury brought in a verdict of guilty, with the penalty of twenty-five years in the State prison. The case was prosecuted by State's Attorney Pugh, and Duff and Allen, the latter of whom made the finest law speech probably ever made in the West. The prisoners were jovial and noisy until the verdict came in, when a sad, heavy, forlorn expression settled on the brow of Bulliner, never to be removed. Baker was evidently at his father's house, in Carbondale, the night that Sisney was killed. He lived about two miles east of there, and went home about ten o'clock that night, and when arrested told Mrs. Hill, with whom he and his wife boarded, that his life depended on what she swore, and suggested that he came home about nine o'clock, but did not ask her to swear falsely. She swore to this conversation, and it ruined him. The powder and shot which they proved he bought, was probably left at Purdy's mill. He had had a difficulty with Purdy a while before. $200.00 worth of belts were cut to pieces, and some powder, shot and caps found lying there.

Baker is about thirty-three years old, fair complexion, long black hair, thin build, and has a desperate-looking gray eye; raised in this county. He was considered a wild reckless, uncertain fellow. He once killed a man near Pine Bluff, Arkansas, while a soldier, and was sentenced to six months' imprisonment in the military prison. He had been married for some months. Marshall Crain once said to me, "Milo, I have got religion as to all my sins but one, and I want to ask you about that." "What is it?" I asked. He answered, "You know I swore a lie against Allen Baker; it was me that killed Sisney, and I swore that it was him." I asked him why he did it. He said, "To save my own neck." I told him that I was no preacher, but that if he acted in good faith to save his own neck, it was no sin, but I thought self-defense; that a man had a right to exert all the powers which God had given him, to save his neck, either to swear a lie or take life. He said that was looking at it in a new light. I said, "Then, Marsh, Baker is not guilty?" He replied, "Well-yes-God d— him; he got nothing but justice. He was always agreeing, promising and contracting, but I never could get him on the grounds."

It was a heart-rending scene to see John Bulliner parting from his aged mother. He went to the penitentiary, and she returned home, to live through black days and nights, with the clumsy and crude condolence this world gives, and now lives in a little cottage, a half-mile north of the Bulliner homestead. Her life speaks, and her children read in it, "No ray of light for the future." Henceforth she can say, "I'll bear affliction till it do cry out itself enough, enough, and die." The scene of beauty and delight is changed. No roses bloom upon her faded cheeks. No laughing graces, wanton in her eyes; but grief, lean-looking, sallow care and pining discontent; a rueful train dwells on her brow, all forlorn."

At the October session of the Williamson Circuit Court, Music, "Big Jep," "Black Bill," "Yaller Bill," and Marshall, were all indicted for the murder of Spence. Musick's case was continued; Noah W. Crain alias "Yaller Bill," was admitted to bail on motion; William J. Crain alias "Big Jep," and William J. Crain alias "Black Bill" prayed for a change of venue, and their case was sent to Alexander county. The indictment against "Yaller Bill" was *nolled* at the April term, 1876.

On Tuesday, October 19, 1875, Marshall T. Crain was arraigned and plead not guilty. He had no attorney, and the Court appointed W. W. Clemens, who filed an affidavit for a continuance, which the Judge said was not sufficient. On Wednesday, October 20th the defendant again renewed his motion for a continuance. The Judge said he could not entertain two motions for a continuance, but that every witness, mentioned in the affidavit, should be here to-morrow. The defendant then in person withdrew his plea of not guilty, and entered one of guilty to the crime of murder, as charged. To this the State's Attorney objected, saying that he could not withdraw his plea of not guilty. The defendant insisted by himself and counsel that be had a right to plead guilty, and throw himself upon the mercy of the Court. The Court then fully explained to the defendant all his rights, and the consequence of entering a plea of guilty; when the defendant again, after a full knowledge of all his rights, entered a plea of guilty. The Court then had the indictment again read to the defendant, and then again asked him if he was guilty or not, and the defendant again pleaded guilty to murder. The Court then ordered a jury called, when Crain said he did not want a jury, that he threw himself on the mercy of the Court. Then Judge Crawford ordered the plea of guilty to be entered, and the case continued until Thursday. On that day witnesses were called and examined, and from the evidence it appeared beyond all doubt that Marshall Crain was guilty of murder.

During the examination of witnesses the court room became crowded with ladies and gentlemen. Marshall's wife came in and took a seat by him. She is a small, sallow, serene, calm-looking woman, with a half-closed, glassy, soulless eye. She seemed perfectly indifferent to the battery of eyes upon her. At the close of the evidence, Marshall, who had set like a statue, only occasionally laughing, seemed nervous and excited. After a few minutes of awful suspense, Judge M. C. Crawford said;

"It is not often that we are called to decide a question of so great importance as this. Marshall Crain has been indicted, arraigned and now acknowledges himself guilty of the highest crime known to the law." Here he rehearsed the manner of his pleading guilty, and said, "It is natural for all men to avoid serious responsibility, and I would much rather his case had been tried by a jury; but the defendant persisted in his plea of guilty, and threw himself on the mercy of the Court; and that I might act advisedly, I had the witnesses summoned and brought to court to see if the plea was really true, as pleaded in this case; and it clearly appears; not only by the plea, but by the mouths of witnesses, that the defendant is guilty of murder. A murder that seldom occurs in any country, and among any people, a murder without passion. Out in the still woods, God's first temple, they coolly and deliberately planned to take the life of their fellow-man." Here the Judge and the whole audience were bathed in tears. He then went over the circumstances of the killing in a feeling and touching manner, and continued, "The Legislature, in making the death penalty, clearly contemplated that there would cases arise which would deserve this penalty." Again he rehearsed the facts to see if they met the requirements of the highest penalty. "By the law we stand or fall. No other crime equals this in coolness, and by all the laws of God and man, this man has forfeited his life to the people of the State. The responsibility is a great one. I hope to God that never again will a court in a civilized country have this duty to do." Here Judge Crawford burst out in a flood of tears, and after a short pause, dashed the tears from his eyes, his face lighted up with an unearthly radiance, he said, "The People and my position make it my duty to administer the law and pronounce its judgment, and before my God and my fellow-man, I must do my duty. What have you to say, Marshall Crain, why sentence of death shall not be pronounced against you?"

Marshall, with a chilled and torpid color, a cold moisture gleaming on his forehead, a severe and majestic expression in his eye, notably intensified by the strong language of Judge Crawford, rose, and in a clear voice said, "I have had no time to prepare for trial. I have been forced into trial. I have been indicted and tried (two-and-a-half days) without time to consult a lawyer. I was dragged into this work by other parties. I had a higher power and influence over me. I could not resist. I don't think I have done enough to be hung for. Spence was harboring parties that were trying to kill me. I don't think I deserve hanging. I was influenced by John Bulliner, a man of good mind and education, and I am not a man of good mind, and no education."

Crawford said: "I am now about to pronounce against you the highest penalty of the law, and in all probability the sentence will be executed, and you will have to appear before a bar transcendently greater than this. There remains but few powers that can give you relief. The Chief Executive may interfere and commute your sentence or pardon you, and the Supreme Court may reverse your judgment; but it is my duty to tell you that neither of these will likely be done. Therefore, I warn you to make your peace with God. "Here he spoke of the consolation of the Christian Religion, and said: "I will call upon you, Marshall Crain, as a living witness, that I have warned you to prepare to meet your God," and continued "The sentence of the Court is that the defendant be hanged by the neck until he is dead, within the walls of the prison in the town of Marion, County of Williamson and State of Illinois, on the 21st day of January, A.D. 1876, between the hours of ten o'clock in the morning and two o'clock in the afternoon of the same day. May God have mercy upon you."

As Crain was taken to the jail he boasted to the guards that he would never shed a tear. The next day, he asked permission to come before Judge Crawford and tell all he knew about the bloody Vendetta. But he was sent to the grand jury and confessed the facts detailed by Musick, as to himself; but was taken from there, screaming at the top of his voice, and his atoning lamentations were heard around the jail for several days. The same day he wrote a letter to Crawford, telling him he had done his duty, and he hoped he would continue to do it, and that the people would forgive him for his crimes, and that the county might be restored to its original peace and prosperity.

At the same term of Court, Calvin Craig, Robert Craig, Monroe Jack and John Jack were indicted for perjury for swearing the alibi for "Black Bill," before Reynolds, J.P.

After the sentence of Crain, a guard of ten men were detailed from the militia to guard the jail by night and two by day. This guard did its duty faithfully until after the execution. Nightly attacks were expected from the "Ku-klux," which were supposed to exist in the county. The guards were often summoned to fall into line at some apparent alarm.

Noah E. Norris, the Sheriff, is about thirty-five years old, a quiet, honest man, and a cousin to the Crains, and on this account there was considerable feeling against him. He was often threatened, and violent outbreaks of passion were sometimes expected, and it was talked "that some man had to hang on the 21st." But it is true that he performed his duty, and that under the most trying circumstances and greatest disadvantages that ever a Sheriff did. When the feeling against him was at its ebb, he removed Charles Robinson, the jailer, a man that the people had confidence in, and put in David Coke, a comparative stranger. But it so happened that Coke was a man from the ground up, and made one of the best and most reliable jailers in the State.

On the 27th day of October, George W. Sisney, Jr., came to the cell, and Marshall said, "Wash, I am ruined, I murdered your father, and ask you to forgive me," and fell weeping on his knees. Wash said: "You murdered him without cause, and I will never forgive you," and walked away with the excitement of gratified vanity lighting with radiance on the vestal roses of his cheeks. Some said that Wash ought to have forgiven him, "that forgiveness is the odor that flowers breathe when trampled upon." Others said he did right.

Marshall spent his time reading the Bible until, by the 21st of November, he was ready for baptism, according to the rites of the Christian Church. He was dressed in a long, white robe, and taken out, under a heavy guard, to the millpond of Mann & Edwards, and after a sermon by W. H. Boles, was baptized *into* the Church.

November 27th, another militia company was organized in the east end of the county, with J. T. Cunningham as Captain, and George Burnett, first and John Davis second Lieutenants.

December 21st, when the night guards went on duty they went into Marshall's cell, where "Big Bill" and "Big Jep" also stayed, and Marsh was gone. The jail was instantly surrounded by the guards, who cocked their guns to shoot him off the roof. The Captain again went into the cell, and found that a hole had been sawed and burnt through the ceiling. A boy was sent up in the garret but could not find Marshall. The Captain then found him rolled up in a mattress, in the cell, having come down from the garret, when the alarm was given. He had commenced sawing the shingles out of the roof, and had his blankets torn up for a rope to let him down. How the saw got into the cell is not known. The other boys said they had nothing to do with the attempted escape ; that they "aimed to saw out with the statute." After this Marshall was chained down, as he said, "for the slaughter."

On the 25th of December, James H. Duncan, assisted by W. M. Davis and J. V. Grider, the plans having been previously arranged by Duncan — ran in on James Norris at Mr. Poteete's, at a ball, five miles southwest of Marion. This man is the most notorious and dreaded of all the assassins. Sisney tried for a year to have him arrested. He was brought to Marion and put in the same cell with Marshall.

"Big Jep" and "Big Bill" remained in jail until the 31st day of December, when they were taken to Cairo for trial. The case was called January 28th, and lasted until the 8th day of February. In addition to the facts detailed heretofore of the killing, two witnesses swore to seeing "Black Bill" going up to Crainville that fatal evening, another that he was at home in bed next morning, facts inconsistent with his alibi. Threats were sworn to by Narcissa Waggoner on "Big Jep" of a bad character. Musick was corroborated by many other circumstances, such as the bringing in of the weed broken at the back of Mrs. Hampton's field. Several other witnesses swore to the alibi of both boys. A great many swore they would not believe Musick on his oath, and they proved good characters. In all, there were about one hundred witnesses. Clemens, Calvert and Linegar appeared for defendants, Allen and Duff for the People. The jury found a verdict of guilty, and ten of them being for hanging and two for acquitting, they compromised on a term of twenty years. When the verdict was read, "Big Jep" cried; but "Big Bill" remained unmoved.

On the 18th of February, a motion for a new trial was overruled, and the prisoners were taken to Joliet.

"Black Bill" stands six feet three inches in height, dark skin, sharp features, gray eyes, black hair and mustache, and very neat in his dress, about thirty years old, and unmarried. "Big Jep" is thirty-five years old, stands six feet one inch in height, a full, round face, large head, light blue eyes, brown hair, fair complexion, and, like Bill, dresses neat.

Musick said of "Big Jep:" "He did all the planning, but he is a coward, and whenever anything was to happen he would skulk to some relative, and lay concealed like a cut-throat until the crime was over, and then, like a bird of ill-omen, his death-screech was again heard."

Narcissa Waggoner, who swore against "Big Jep," (she having boarded him and Spence at the same time they had their difficulty) is a daughter of George Duncan, a respectable citizen of this county, and the wife of Carroll Waggoner. She is about thirty years of age, and is a woman of strong intellect. Her testimony was clear, consistent and conclusive. Before the trial at Cairo it was whispered around that her character for truth would be assailed. But persecuted, wounded, bleeding, hunted-down Williamson county rose like a furious lion at the mention of this, and insinuated that it would be considered an assault on honor, an attempt at justice: and the noise silenced. She is the lady who unlocked the archives of secrecy and let the light shine in. For a time she kept the signet sealed in her own heart, but her spirit chafed and her divine form wasted beneath the load. It came to her in her dreams that she ought to tell it. Honor was beating at her bosom. The lives of future victims were pleading with her. The wild winds wafted begging from suffering women to her. All social life demanded it. The moral sense of the civilized world called on her to tell. Our lands had depreciated three millions of dollars, and the people were hopeless; but she put her finger on the guilty party, and the fountains of blood dried up; and the breast of every law-loving citizen swelled with joy and pride at the action of this heroic lady. Humanity will not forget the generous woman who, though living among the criminals, dared to take the proud rank of dignified resistance to subordination, and spend the unbought grace of her life saving her country, where men had failed. She lives in this emancipated, disenthralled county to-day, an illustration of exalted womanhood, with the gratitude of her county.

Chapter 14. **The Trial of the Crains**

ANOTHER INTERRUPTION IS REQUIRED HERE. Although Erwin wrote in great detail about the other trials, he provided little about this one. In fact, he wrote more about the attacks on Narcissa Waggoner's virtues. He gave no reason, but his readers in 1876 had already read about the trial in minute detail. The *Marion Monitor* all but ran the transcripts of it over two issues in February beginning on the third. Since 21st Century readers didn't have that chance, here are the accounts straight from the 19th Century press.

■ — ■ — ■ — ■

THE CRAIN TRIAL
MUSICK REHEARSES HIS PART!
He Tells the Story of the Murder of Spence and Sisney
And Who Did It.

On the assembling of court, Judge Baker announced that one of the jurors, Mr. S. P. Bennett, having been taken ill the night previous, would not be able to sit on the jury, and asked the attorneys what they proposed to do about it. The juror was discharged and another juror selected to serve in his place. The following Witnesses for the people were then called and sworn: Samuel Musick, John Ditmore, H. V. Ferrell, J. W. Landrum, Mary C. Tippy, Wm. Hendrickson, Martin Davis, Leonard Fuller, Narcissa Waggoner, Newman Grimes, H. W. Johnson, Monroe Rolan, Ann Impsen, John Craig, William Rollan, Thomas Duncan, James Hampton alias Joseph Hostetter. Judge Allen for the prosecution then addressed the jury for about thirty minutes marking out the line the prosecution would follow. At the conclusion of Judge Allen's remarks, court adjourned until 1:30 o'clock, p.m.

AFTERNOON SESSION. — On the opening of court after dinner, Mr. W. W. Clemens for the defendants presented the case for the defense, occupying the time of the court for nearly two hours. The first witness called was:

DR. H. V. FERRELL, of Carterville, who testified as follows: — I know the defendants. I have known Jep. Crain for about four years, and it will be six years in March since I became acquainted with William Crain — I speak of him as Black Bill. I knew William Spence for about two years, becoming acquainted with him in 1873. On Saturday morning, the first day of August last, Mr. Dowell told me that Mr. Spence was murdered in his store. I was on my way over Crab Orchard. On my way home I went by and saw Mr. Spence, and saw he was dead. It appeared as if there had been a chair near the door, and as if he had sat down in it and then fallen out of it. There was a number of wounds on his person. Shortly after I was summoned by the coroner to make the examination, and found quite a number of wounds in the region of the stomach and bowels; one shot had entered the right eye and came out the ear. If I remember right he was laying against the door when I first saw him – in his store. The wounds I thought were produced by a shot gun, judging from other wounds I had seen produced by a similar weapon. I probed the wounds but did not extract any shot. I made a written report of the examination and furnished it to the coroner. There were no wounds in his hands. I think Mr. Spence died from the effects of the wounds. The killing occurred in July last, in Williamson county, State of Illinois. My attention was called to a bruise that appeared to have been made by the muzzle of a shot gun. I do not remember how many shot entered the body, (at this point the doctor spoke in such a low voice that the reporter lost a part of the testimony) Continuing, Dr. Ferrell said: The front doors to the store are glass above the locks, and the glass was knocked out. The house has what is called a glass front, the glass coming down lower than the panels of the doors. I think there was one pane of glass in the front broken out. I think there was a counter on each side of the store room. The house fronts to the North, but the counters do not come all the way up to the front of the building – there is room to pass between the window and the end of the counter. Mr. Spence had fallen down and his left leg was thrown across the chair; his head was to the North. It seems to me that someone said there was a box between the end of the counter and the window, but I don't remember if this was the case. I think Mr. Spence had one slipper on. The house is a two story building with stairs in the back end of the store room. Mr. Spence's bed was in the north end of the building. I can't say how many windows there are in the building above the door. Mr. Spence told me he was a Scotchman. He had no family there, and roomed alone; he took his meals at Call Waggoner's, some distance north of his store. On cross examination Dr. Ferrell stated that in his opinion Spence was shot with some small shot, some large shot and some slugs, judging from the character of the wounds, which were similar to wounds he had seen on Hinchcliff, Ditmore, and others. The doctor also testified that to the best of his recollection there was some fifty odd wounds on Spence's person. The cross examination elicited nothing new from the doctor, and hence we omit it.

SAM MUSICK – was the next witness called. Musick is an ordinary looking individual, about five feet seven inches high, and heavy set. He is thirty three years of age, and his countenance indicates that he is by no means a teetotaler, and would not make a good member of Father Lame's temperance society. He has ruddy complexion, light gray or blue eyes, long curly hair and light moustache. While his clothing is by no means expensive, he was neatly and cleanly dressed. So far he has given his testimony in a clear, straightforward manner, and without the least apparent excitement. He detailed the circumstances attending the

MURDER OF WM. SPENCE AS FOLLOWS: — My name is Samuel Musick; I am thirty-three years of age; I lived at Crainville, in Williamson county, last summer I lived there about twelve months. I was living at Carbondale and Murphysboro before that. I was working for Mr. Landrum at Crainville, and drove a team for him. I think I went there in August, and quit his services in 1875 – probably in July. I worked for Mr. Hodges about two years, and drove a team. I was at Carbondale and Murphysboro for about seven or eight years. I am married; was married in Missouri. I know the defendants. I have known Jep. Crain for five or six years, and I have known Black Bill for pretty near a year. I got acquainted with Jep. in Murphysboro. Mr. Landrum's mill is right in town in Crainville, and the house I lived in is right close to the mill. Marshall Crain lived close to the mill, and about fifty yards from me. I have no children; Marshall Crain had no children. I knew Mr. Spence about one year. Marshall Crain lived about two hundred yards northeast of Mr. Spence's store. I lived south of Marshall Crain's. Mr. Landrum lived fifty yards east of me. One of the defendants is a brother and the other a cousin of Marshall Crain – Jep being his brother. He is known as "Big Jep" and lived in Crainville. He is not married. I think I quit work for Mr. Landrum in July last, we were not doing much, teaming got dull, and I quit work. I did not go direct from Hodges to Landrum; I think I quit Hodges in the winter, and went to Landrum's the next August. I was living at Crainville the last days of last July, and Marshall Crain lived there then. He moved a part of his things sometime in July, towards the last of the month and no one occupied the house after he left it. There was a bedstead and some other things left in the house. There was no family that I know of lived in the house after he left; I have seen men in the house after he moved. It was a box house, and stood about twenty steps form the road; the road was only a country road running north and south-called the Marion and Carbondale road.

The funeral of Capt. Sisney was on a Friday, towards the last of the month. They said they buried him at Bulliner's. The remains were brought to Crainville, and I saw some of the procession in town – on Friday. Me and Marshall and Jep met in town that evening and went to Marshall's house, and Jep said Spence was the next man he wanted killed, and wanted me to go to John Bulliner's and get a gun. I told him I d did not want to do that, for I would be seen; but I said I would go to Ditmore's and get his, and he said that would do. We were to meet back of Mrs. Hampton's field on Saturday morning, and if we got there first we were to break some weeds and bushes to let them know we were there, and go on the hill and shoot. The place where we broke the weeds there was a path that turned out of the road. There was two paths at this place, one turned north and the other south; the road was not a public one, and there was no house in sight. I had been along the road but not back of the field before that. Where we met was two and a half or three miles south of Crainville, and about one mile from Black Bill's house. We got there about eight or nine o'clock and waited until they come. They came about 10 o'clock I reckon. We had some whisky, and talked it over and agreed to KILL HIM THAT NIGHT. Me and Black Bill and Marshall Crain were to do it. Marshall and me took the whisky out, we had three pints; we got it at Carterville; I took two pints and Marshall one-it was in pint bottles. Marshall and I started pretty early, and walked to the place together. We got together in the woods close to "Yaller" Bill's, and there was two men overtook us – Al. Robinson and Joe Bullard; they were walking and we went to the end of the lane together, and they went one way and we went the other. We broke the weeds and went on the hill and waited.

I don't remember what kind of weeds they were; we broke bushes, too; some of the weeds we broke clear off and put them in the path, and we fired a pistol two or three times. We didn't have a watch, and I don't know what time it was. I am only guessing at the time. I don't remember if it was cloudy or not. We both broke weeds and threw them down in the path; there is only one path there and that is fifteen or twenty feet from the fence. The road is a dim country road on the edge of the hill. We went just on top of the hill when we fired the pistol-it was in the road and two or three shots were fired before the other boys came. I don't remember how near they came before we saw them. We drank some of the whisky while there were there. It was agreed that I was to go home, get some whisky, and meet them in the woods back of "Yaller" Bill's; I don't know who selected the place where we were to meet, but were to meet at dark. There is a ticket where we were to meet. We had dinner that day at Wes. Crain's – Jep told us we had better go up there and get dinner. Wes. Crain is a brother to Jep. It is one quarter of a mile or more from where the meeting was to Wes. Crain's. We went up and found no one at home, but we went in and eat a cold snack, and went back to where we met. Jep. and Black Bill started to Black Bill's, but I don't know what they went there for. I left Marshall at - - - - - and went home, and then to Crainville and got some whisky, and came back and met him where I had agreed to. I don't remember what kind of clothing the others wore, only Black Bill's. He had on a sharp topped cap, and socks over his shoes or was in his stocking feet. I don't know if anything was said about his cap. We staid there till it was dark and then went to Marshall's where the guns were. We had no guns when we were in the woods. Marshall had a pistol. There was two shot guns in the house-Marshall took one and me the other – I took Ditmore's. I went after it Friday night and Ditmore did not want his gun to be away from home at night, and I went in the morning, got it and put it in Marshall's house. I was talking to Marshall about the gun, and he gave me the key that night, so if he didn't get there I could put it in the house. I saw him the next morning before I put the gun in the house, and then I went in and put the gun on the bedstead. I think there was something on the bed stead, which stood in the northeast corner of the house. The other gun was put in the house after dark the night before Marshall. We got it out of a hollow tree out in the woods. It was John Bulliner's gun. We had no light in the house, and staid there until nine or ten o'clock; both the doors shut, and we talked very low. I don't remember what we talked about. We had the guns but I don't remember if anything was said about what we were going to do. When we left Black Bill took the gun. I got from Ditmore, and Marshall took the other one. It was nine or ten o'clock, and we had been waiting for it to get still and quiet before we went out. We went out the gate and across the road, east till we got to the store. When we got there, Marshall called to Mr. Spence, and said: "Mr. Spence," (he called twice) and said John Sisney wanted to get some shrouding for a child. Mr. Spence said he would come as soon as he got his shoes. Black Bill and I was back about ten steps out east of the door, while Marshall was in front of the door. When Spence came down Marshall shot him with the shot gun he reached in and shot him with the pistol. Spence made a noise – a groan, which was the only noise I heard. When Marshall shot we stepped up to the corner of the house, and just about that time Marshall lobbed a light out of the window on the east side of the house and went in. He broke the light out with the muzzle of his gun I think. He was not in the store [missing words] than two or three minutes, though I did not see him in the store; he took his gun in through the window. When he came out we started east, and he had a picket book and dropped it, and said there was nothing in it. This was on the railroad track. We went east till we came to Terry Crain's lane, and I went to Landrum's and then home. Marshall and Bill carried the guns. I said to them, "What shall I do if I am arrested," when Bill said have us subpoenaed and we will swear you clear. When we were in the woods back of Mrs. Hampton's field Black Bill said he belonged to the Ku Klux, and Jep asked him if he couldn't initiate us, and he said that he could. Jep named that day that if any of us got in jail and remained in one month or three months, we needn't be uneasy for we would be taken out. Some one said something about getting the keys from "Old Charley," Jep said, "never mind the keys, mash the door in;" – Old Charley was the jailor at Marion – this was at the field Jep used this language; I don't know if it was Bill or Marshall talked about the keys; don't remember Jep saying where he was going to stay that night; I don't know which one said it but the reason they wanted Spence killed was because they thought he was a spy for the Sisneys. I have not seen the gun since that night; Black Bill had it last I knowed anything about it; Ditmore lived two hundred and fifty yards from where I lived, in the same village. We met on the evening Sisney was killed in Crainville, about thirty yards from the drug store; don't know who mentioned about meeting at the house; I remember before we got there Marshall Crain [missing words] to shoot Spence himself; I don't remember if Black Bill had the socks on his feet when he went up to kill Spence; it was not a very light night, but was not raining; I did not see any lights on the way up to the store. When we went from the store I didn't think it was over a quarter of a mile till I parted from them and went to bed; did not seem them any more that night; I don't remember seeing any light up stairs before he was shot; did not hear any alarm, as if any was coming. While Marshall was in the house Black Bill called and said to him, "come on they are coming." Bill changed his voice; Marshall came out right away.

At six o'clock court adjourned until eight thirty this evening, when Sam Musick will continue his evidence.

EVENING SESSION — Jep wanted me to go to John Bulliner's and get a gun, but said I didn't want to do that for I would be seen; and I told him I would get Ditmore's gun, and he said that would do; we told him we had the guns, and where they were; I don't remember what Jep said; I knew Marshall Crain about a year before this occurrence; I don't know how long we had lived neighbors?; he came there after I moved to [missing words]; he made me a confident from about the first of July – it was between the fifth and the tenth when I found it out; there was a lane back of Mrs. Hampton's field where we broke the weeds; it was near the north end; it run north and south; I don't know if it was traveled by wagons or not; I think it was wide enough; Wes Crain's was southeast, and we went through a cornfield to his house; I don't know the given name of Mrs. Hampton; it was about three o'clock when Jep and I and Marshall went down to the old house; I was drinking at that time and don't remember correctly; I first told about this thing to Mr. Landrum at Marion, Williamson county. There was no house in sight where we met in the woods back of Mrs. Hampton's house was southwest, but don't know what distance from the place; the farm on the cast of the lane was near a quarter of a mile long; I was at the same place the next Sunday evening after Spence was killed on Saturday night; I was never there after that time; Spence was killed in July, in the last of the month, and I was arrested about the 13th of September, and taken to Marion and put in jail.

Q — State if you made any statements soon after you were put in jail to persons about the breaking of the weeds you have spoken of near Mrs. Hampton's field? Question objected to; objection overruled, and exceptions taken. I did the evening after I was put in jail, to Mr. Landrum, Mr. Hartwell and Mr. Norris; I told it to Mr. Landrum first, when there was no one present but me and him; that was after I was in jail; it was in the evening I spoke to Landrum about it; I told it to Landrum first; the cap Black Bill wore was speckled, white and blue I think; the spots were small; I did not have my hands on it; I don't know if he had it on in the old house; we had whisky back of the field; when we met nothing was said about how Jep and Black Bill came; they were there when I got there; I don't know how Black Bill got to Crainville, I did not hear him say; Marshall stood not far from the door at Spence's when he shot-probably not more than three or four steps; I don't know if he fired both shots a one both barrels went off at once if he did; I did not examine Ditmore's gun when I got it and don't remember if anything was said in the house about the guns being loaded; going out I did not go on the railroad track; in going to Spence's some times we were together and sometimes one behind the other.

H. W. JOHNSON testified as follows: My name is H. W. Johnson; I reside in DuQuoin, which has been my home for seventeen years; I am a millwright; I was at Crainville, Williamson county, in July last; I knew Wm. Spence, I went to Crainville the first of June, and was putting in mill machinery for Mr. Landrum; the mill was three hundred yards or more from Spence's store; I remember Spence's death. I think about dark, after supper, (I boarded with Mr. Landrum) I went to the Crainville post office, and when I left the post office it was dark; I left the railroad west of Spence's store to shun a mud hole; when I got west of the store I heard something that attracted my attention, some one said I want to get some article of goods; I heard a reply that they should be waited on; the calling seemed to be by Spence's drug store or in that direction; when I got near my boarding house I heard the discharge of a double barreled gun, and I went about ten steps further and heard a single report; the first shot was undoubtedly a double barreled gun, the barrels pulled off simultaneously; I should think it was between nine and ten o'clock; it was a pretty dark, cloudy night; what attracted me attention when I stopped I don't remember, but when I had stopped I heard a voice "we want to get," and gathered from the reply they would be waited on; I suppose I was three hundred yards away when I heard the report; I don't think there was any lights burning when the shots were fired; it is nearly north from my boarding house to the store, in going up and down the railroad track; I saw the remains the next day before they were removed and after they were laid out; Spence's was a store house with a counter on each side; he was lying on the east side of the house, apparently as if he had fallen out of a chair; I wouldn't be positive if his head was against the end of the building; he had his pants on and his vest was unbuttoned; I think there was on shoe on one foot and a shoe lying in the middle of the floor; the glass in the door, on the side where he was laying, one light was broken out; the glass in the door are ten inches wide by fourteen inches long; one side light east of the door was broken out; Crainville is in Williamson county, Illinois.

JOHN DITMORE testified as follows: I live one half or three quarters of a mile from Carterville; last July I lived in Crainville, and worked at Landrum's mill; I know Sam Musick; I have known him pretty near a year; I knew Mr.

Spence; I heard of his death next morning, but I can't tell at exactly what hour, probably at five or six o'clock; I owned a heavy double barreled shot gun at the time; had had it about a year; the gun was not at my house the night Spence was killed; the night before Spence was killed, on Friday evening, just before dark, Sam Musick came there and wanted the gun, but I didn't let him have her; I told him that I never loaned her at night, but would let him have her in the morning; it was just good day light when I let him have her; he said he was going turkey hunting; there was a young man at my house that used the gun, and my boy would go with him; I was at home the night Spence was killed; I heard the reports of two guns that night; I suppose I lived nearly one hundred yards from the store – north of west from the store; I live south of the railroad; as well as I remember a few minutes after nine the shots were fired; there was a lady at our house that night, and just as I was getting ready to go to bed the shots were fired; I was not up to the store till Kirt Brown came up and told me Spence was killed; he was laying close to the door, a double door with panels and top glass; the panels came down even with the lock; the distance from the floor to the lock is about three feet; the floor is about a foot from the natural elevation of the ground; I was not on the inquest but was present part of the time; the door had not been opened when I got there; I was not in the store till after the body had been moved; I didn't notice anything about the lights he had in the store; I was the third or fourth one to get there; we just went to the door and looked in and could see his feet, and by putting our heads in could see the body; there was a light on the left of the door, broken out, I got my gun back Saturday morning, eight days after the murder; found it in Jep Crain's old grocery house, nobody told me it was there; I first stumbled on it; Jep owns, or did own, the property; I didn't go inside then, but could see through the windows; I don't know how the gun came there; both barrels were loaded and capped; I drawed the loads; it was loaded with shot larger than bird shot, I call them rabbit shot; the shot were all the same size.

THOS. DUNCAN testified as follows: I have lived in Williamson county all my life; I live four miles from Crainville. I have known the defendants as long as I have known anybody; I was acquainted with Mr. Spence, and heard of his death I heard Jep Crain say in February last that he and Spence had had a quarrel, and some one asked him why he did not hit him; that if he ever did hurt him he would kill him. This conversation was on a Sunday in February last; at Carroll Waggoner's house. I never heard him say anything else. He said Spence had ordered him out of his store.

MRS. CARROLL WAGGONER testified as follows: I live in Crain city, Williamson county, Illinois; I was born and raised in that county; I am the wife of Call Waggoner; I will have lived in Crainville three years in March next; we went there to keep a boarding house, and are still in that business. I was acquainted with Wm. Spence; he boarded with us for about two years; he was boarding with me at the time of his death; Mr. Spence's store was about three hundred yards from the house; Mr. Spence never slept at the store until about two weeks before he was killed; he said what was to be, and went there to sleep; I know the defendants; I went to school with Black Bill. George Duncan is my father; Big Jep Crain boarded with us about two years. I know the day Jep and Spence had a difficulty at the table in my house, it was on the fourth Sunday in February last. They were quarreling a good many times from October to February. I was not present at the difficulty in the store, but I heard Jep say at the breakfast table that he intended to go into the store and "naturally massacre" Spence if he did not take back what he had said. I don't know what the trouble was. Sam, Yellow Bill and Jep Crain came to the house, and Sam and Yellow Bill were delving Jep about Spence, and Jep said they might laugh about it now, but he intended to kill Spence when he could a little dark between him and Spence, and that he would kill him for five dollars. Jep said I won't take his slurs any longer. This conversation was on the fourth Sunday in February last. Jep left my on the 23d of April last. After that Jep made some remarks at my table and wanted me to turn Spence away, and I told him I could not do it. He then wanted me to put off supper late so that he could catch Spence between the house and the store; he said he would shoot him and LAUGH TO SEE HIM KICK. I told him I could not put off supper, and he then said he would not come in until ten o'clock; I told him to let Spence alone, that he was not troubling any one. Jep said Spence felt himself better than he was. I told Jep I was going to tell my husband what he had said, and he replied there was no use in it; he didn't mean any harm, and there was no use to tell about it. After leaving my house Jep never came about it again, and I have never had any conversation with him since; Mr. Spence went to his store for sleep only the Thursday night before the Saturday night on which he was killed. I saw Big Jep on Tuesday morning of that week. Spence told me on Wednesday morning that he was going back to the store to lodge.

WORTH TIPPY testified: I was born and raised in Williamson county. I knew Wm. Spence; I knew the defendant since I have known anybody. In February or March, me and Wash Sisney and Black Bill were coming from Marion, and some one said lets go by Crainville and get some whiskey, when Black Bill said lets go by, "I wants to whip Spence;" I think he was owing Spence some and he was cutting up about it. Bill said he would knock his d--d old Scotch head off his shoulders. I was a witness before the coroner's inquest, and said I had never [heard any] threats. These are the only threats I ever heard. I never heard Jep. say anything.

WASHINGTON SISNEY testified: I am the son of Capt. Sisney, who was killed at Carbondale; I know W. J. Crain, "Black Bill;" I knew Mr. Spence; I heard Black Bill say, as we were coming from Marion, that he owed Spence some and he was making a fuss about it, and if he made much more fuss about it he would knock his head off his shoulders; this was in February, near Bainbridge, on the way from Marion, and was considerably out of my way to go to Crainville from where I was then living. I never heard any other threats.

MARTIN DAVIS testified: I have lived in Williamson county, in this State, for twenty years, and was there last August; I was not personally acquainted with Mr. Spence; I heard of his death about 9 o'clock the next morning after the killing; I know the defendants – have been acquainted with Jep a good many years, and have seen Black Bill, but am not well acquainted with him. I was in Marion the morning Musick was put in jail there, but can't tell the exact date. I think it was sometime about the first of September. Shortly after, probably the 13th, Mr. Hartwell, Mr. Fuller, and Mr. Hendrickson and I went out some ten miles west of town to the widow Hampton's farm. At the west end of the farm we found a lane, but it was so small we did not drive the team through it. Mr. Hartwell, Hendrickson, and Mr. Fuller went down the lane, and shortly Mr. Hartwell called and I went down. We found a lot of weeds broken off, and others bent over, I picked up some hazel bushes and went and compared with the stumps and they fit exactly. From their appearance I would judge the weeds had been broken off a month. From the description given us the place was not hard to find; it was a desolate looking place, and there was not much travel that way; I found one bunch, about a handful, consisting of weeds and hazel brush, thrown on the ground in the road. I was along when Black Bill was arrested. He was arrested before we made the trip to the place where the weeds were broken. Sheriff Norris, Mr. Grider, Mr. Calvert and myself, made the arrest. It was at night, about eleven o'clock, and about two miles from the place where the weeds were broken; Bill was arrested at his house in bed, by Sheriff Norris and Mr. Calvert. Bill said in a jesting and laughing way that he and Big Jep would make a jail full themselves. When Bill got his clothes on we went to Crainville and then Carterville, but did not go to Marion that night. We staid at Crainville all night. I had a double barreled shot gun; I don't know anything about his saying he would get away if I didn't have a shot gun; he said in a laughing manner that when he got to the hollow he had a good horse, and he was going to leave us; I told him I had a good shot gun with sixteen slugs in each barrel, and they would follow him. This was the evening after Musick was put in jail in Marion.

At five o'clock court adjourned.

WILLIAM HENDRICKSON testified as follows: I live in Marion, Williamson county; I was born and raised there; was there last August and September; was not personally acquainted with Spence; I knew him when I saw him; I think it was about the 10th of September when Musick was brought there; I was one of a party that made a search for the broken weeds and bushes; Mr. Hartwell, county attorney, Mr. Fuller and Mr. Davis were with me; we went to the northwest corner of Mrs. Hampton's field; we went along the south side of the farm till we struck a lane, and went down that lane one-fourth of a mile till we struck the corner of Mrs. Hampton's field; it was a dark, out of the way place; there may have been some wagons went down the lane, but it was not traveled much; there was a kind of a hill to the right and then to the left was another knoll; it is a quarter of a mile from any house; we found some hazel bushes and some weeds broken off and laid along the road; some of the weeds were broken over, but not clear off; some of the hazel bushes were broken off and laid on one side of the road; (here a lot of weeds and bushes were produced by Mr. Hendrickson.) These were found in different places; this was the bunch (producing some hazel bushes) that was found on the east of the road; these are the weeds that were broken over (producing another bunch) the broken weeds that were bent over were on the east side of the road; I was raised on a farm in Williamson county, and I think from the appearance of the weeds they were broke two months; the sun would shine on them a part of the time; I had never heard any statement before about these things; going to the place along the lane we found some weeds broken off but were not satisfied until we got where these weeds were found; I think this was Monday afternoon, September 13, last.

L. C. FULLER testified as follows: I live in Marion, Williamson county; I am the City Marshal; was there last September, and remember Musick being brought there and put in jail; I think it was Friday the 10th of September; me and Mr. Hartwell went to a place-the widow Hampton's. At the south end of the field we got out of the hack and went on to the northwest corner of the lane; it did not look like a public road, or was much traveled; we found some weeds broken right at the corner of the field, there was a lane at the north of the field, thought east; (witness made a diagram explaining the locality where the weeds were found); the weeds were broken off and laid down at the side of the road; there was some bushes with them, and some weeds were bent over; the handful was right at the side of the road; we took up the tops of the bushes and compared them with the stumps. Stock could not have broken these weeds. I would not say for certain but would think the weeds and bushes might have been broken for a month. We found some near the fence and others eight or ten steps from the fence on the west side of the road. This search was made I think on Monday afternoon Musick was put in jail. I heard no statements where these weeds would be found only from Mr. Hartwell. I think the nearest house to this place was between a quarter and a half mile away.

JAMES W. LANDRUM testified as follows: I have resided in Crainville, Williamson county since 1868, and I am acquainted with the defendants; I became acquainted with Black Bill in 1866, perhaps, and have known Jep since the year 1860. I was well acquainted with William Spence, and know where the assassination occurred; as I remember on the night of the 31st of July between nine and ten o'clock, I heard the report of a gun and got out of bed and went to the door to see if I could hear any excitement, but I could hear none. The report seemed to be a very heavy, dull report. My house was about two hundred and fifty or three hundred yards from Spence's store in a nearly due north direction. I saw Mr. Spence early in the morning, about sun up. He was laying close to the door of his store room, as I remember back against the counter or a box, with one slipper on and the other off; I saw a bloody spot and a hole as if the ball had gone in the right eye, and came out near the ear. I did not make an examination of the body; examined the front part of the house and through the store, and found quite a tumbling of valises, trunks and paper cases. All these things seemed to have been opened as if there had been a search. I did not find any other wounds on the body, only those made by the shot. The store was what might be called a glass front;

the first pane of glass nearest where Mr. Spence lay was entirely out. The glass in the door were smaller than on the side of the house; where the large pane was knocked out there was evidence of some one having crawled through into the store; that was the condition of the store early in the morning; I did not examine the stomach and breast of Mr. Spence after he was shot; Spence had a store and done a general neighborhood furnishing business; I was in the saw mill business and putting up a flouring mill; I was told of the death of Spence early in the morning by Mr. William Crain, "Yellow Bill;" I went on up as soon as I could get on my boots; the doors of the store were not opened; there was some people there; there was no other business relations between us than this; I deposited my money with Mr. Spence, and when I bought a load of cotton I would give an order and he would pay it; I am pretty well satisfied he had only a small amount of money at that time; there was no expectation of his receiving money just at that time; I deposited my money with Mr. Spence and payed my hands through him; I was expecting five thousand dollars at that time, and told my hands that fact; I had put off some that I was owing and told them about it; Judge Lemma, of Carbondale, was to get the money for me and came down on the Friday previous and stayed at my house, and then went to Spence's store and stayed till the train come, and went home; that is a very independent railroad and not very regular; it's time was about ten o'clock but it varied sometimes three fourths of an hour; the Saturday in the forenoon I was at home and after breakfast went over to my farm, about four miles; from my place Mrs. Hampton's is near due east; I have several hundred acres of land; I passed within about one half of a mile of the place spoken of, where the meeting was to be held; I would suppose it was eight or nine o'clock when I passed this place; I was riding; when I was passing, going to my farm, at the end of the lane. I was due north to the place; before I got to my place I heard a gun, and before I got to my farm I heard another; the sounds were in the direction of the widow Hampton's from me, but it was a distinct sound; I saw a pocket-book in the hands of one Hill and examined it; knew it was Spence's hand writing in it; I saw it as they came into the crowd around the store; I knew Jep staid with his brother Marshall, within two hundred yards of my house; Marshall lived between fifty and two hundred yards of Musick; I don't know how long he staid about there; when he came back from the north I saw him once or twice passing back and forth; don't remember of seeing him that Sunday or the next day, Monday; don't remember the day Spence was buried, but it was Tuesday or Wednesday; on Saturday I staid on my farm till pretty late in the evening; persons had told me my cattle were breaking into people's fields and that is what attracted my attention when I heard the shooting; saw Black Bill that evening as I was going around my farm; was going angling south, and met him coming up the hill; thought he was a little excited; he said he was going down to Warren Crain's to get his nag; he was walking; this was something near one o'clock.

At the conclusion of Mr. Landrum's testimony, the prosecution closed their case; and the evidence for the defense was heard. Something over twenty witnesses were examined during the day and it is probable as many more will be called before the case is closed. The first witness for the defense is:

HENRY BOWLES, who testified as follows: I heard of the killing of Mr. Spence, and suppose he was killed on Saturday night, the last of the month; I was in Marion the Friday before the Saturday on which Spence was killed; I knew Jep for twenty or twenty five years. I saw him in Marion on that Friday. The sun was probably an hour high when I saw him; I did not see him on Thursday. I don't know anything about the trains on that day. Old Man Ward was in town that day and we went out together. I was detained while Ward was finishing up a game of cards with Crain and others. I had no watch and am only guessing at the time.

JAMES SAMUELS testified: I have known Jep Crain since 1855; heard of the death of Spence on Sunday after he was killed; saw Jep Crain on Thursday before that at the depot. Saw him get off the train; asked Jep if he knew the particulars of the killing of Sisney. On Friday morning I saw Eke Norris and Jep together. Saw him again about ten o'clock, but can't say with any certainty that I saw him after that. The train from Marion to Carbondale leaves about nine o'clock a.m., and I saw Jep after the train had left. This was on the Friday before the Saturday on which Spence was killed. Think the second train from Marion to Carbondale leaves about three p.m., but can't say whether the train was late that day. Wesley Crain, a brother of Big Jep, D. B. Ward and James Hampton, all testified to that they had seen Jep in Marion on the Friday afternoon before the Saturday on which Spence was killed. This evidence was introduced to refute the statement made by Musick that he (Musick), Jep and Marshall Crain had had a meeting at Marshall's house on that same Friday afternoon.

COLUMBUS WAGGONER testified: I live at Crainville; am in the dry goods business; have known Jep Crain for three or four years; know the time of the Carbondale and Shawneetown railroad; the train goes down about ten in the morning and 4 P.M. Crainville is west of Marion; I heard of the death of Spence; was at Crainville on the Friday before the killing, also on Thursday; don't remember of seeing Jep the Thursday before the killing; he made his home at Crainville, but had been away; don't think he had been back but a few days before the killing of Spence; saw him the Friday afternoon before the killing, coming from the train; he got off the train; I don't remember if the train was late that evening; I think this was the day that Sisney was buried; there was a number of persons came back to Crainville to get on the train to go home. I saw Jep after he got off the train two or three different times at the drug store, and outside near the door; the times were not far apart that I saw him; I think he was not there more than half an hour or an hour; I don't remember the latest time I saw him; the times I saw him were not more than or fifteen minutes apart. I think there was some parties going away and he said to them hold on, that he would go with them; I don't think I saw them start off; I think it was some of the Craig boys he went with; I don't know that I know Bransen; I think Jim Craig was one of the parties; Jep came in the store after a coat; I don't think it was over half an hour after he got off the train that he came after the coat; I think I saw him about ten minutes, maybe a longer time, after that; I think he came after the coat before he harked the parties; I don't remember the time that elapsed between the time; the regular time for the train to go down at that time was four o'clock.

L. D. CRAIN testified: I live one half mile east of Crainville; I have known the defendants since we were boys; we are somewhere from one-third to one-fifth cousins; I heard of the death of Spence about 8 o'clock the morning after he was killed; went to Crainville on Friday, the day before, and staid there till the corpse of Sisney came up; then went to the burying, and came back and staid till sun down; saw Jep get off the train; the time of the train was then four o'clock; I think the train was late that day; took out my watch and it was ten minutes after four o'clock; saw Jep for a few minutes after he got off the train; don't think he was out of my sight till he left town, only when he went into the back room of the drug store; I think the drug store is forty or fifty feet north of Spence's store; Jep spoke about going across Crab Orchard creek that evening. It is three miles to the creek; when I saw him last he was going off with James Craig and some one else. He has two brothers living over the creek – Warren and Wesley Crain; he would have to cross the creek going to Warren's; I don't think Jep was out of my sight five minutes from the time he got off the train till he left town; I am sure this was on Friday afternoon, the day before Spence was killed; I know where Marshall Crain's house is, right south of the drug store, perhaps one hundred fifty yards; think Yellow Bill was there that evening; don't remember their going off together; Yellow Bill was around there all evening; their nicknames, "Yellow Bill," "Big Bill" and "Big Jep", originated because there are so many of us of the same name; the evening Jep was there I was in the drug store; I did not see Sam Musick, Marshall Crain and Jep together; Sam Musick was at the depot drunk, and was most of the time in the house; I saw Marshall there; did not see Musick, Marshall and Jep Crain together that day; their nick names were given to them by other parties for the purpose of designating them; Jep may have lived in Murphysboro for a year or so; Black Bill was in the army, but I can't say how long, perhaps two or three years; think he was in the 81st regiment. During harvest times Jep would go North to harvest- he went north during this season.

N. J. CRAIN testified: I have known Jep Crain since he was a child; he is my brother; I have heard of the death of Spence; Dr. Brown and I found him; I went to Dr. Brown's early in the morning to get some whisky for Sam Musick, and as I came back my cow was across the track and I said to the doctor I would drive her up; when I went by the store I saw the lights broken out, and I went up and saw Spence dead; I told Ditmore, Mr. Landrum and others; I was in Crainville on the Friday before from eight or nine o'clock in the morning; I went to Sisney's funeral, and when I got back I was in Crainville all the balance of the evening; I saw Jep Crain that evening get off the train down from Marion; I think the train was on time; I saw Jep get off, and after he was off he stopped and shook hands with a good many boys, probably Judge Lemma; halloaed to me about mule; he spoke to Bransen, and said wait till he got a coat; he went to Cal Waggoner's, got his coat and came back and stood around the drug store; Jep, Bransen and Craig went with me to get the mule; I might have seen Musick, but don't remember; I don't remember that I saw Musick about the depot; my house is south of the drug store about three hundred yards; me and Jep started from the store together and met Bransen and Craig at the blacksmith shop, and went from there to the stable and got the mule; I told Craig to ride the mule and let Jep ride his horse; the Marshall Crain house is over 100 yards north from my house, and we passed it going down; the house is about 70 feet west of the road and we were in company when we passed the house; I did not see Marshall Crain or Sam Musick or any one else at the house; Jep said he was going to Warren Crain's and started South; it is something near three miles to the Crab Orchard; I don't think Jep was out of my sight exceeding ten minutes after he got off the train; when we went to my house he only staid long enough for me to catch the mile; it had been raining; I was at home Friday night; these nicknames were given to us by other persons; when we went into the war there was three Bill Crains in one company, and they nicknamed us; these name were applied to us in the army; I was in the army with Black Bill pretty near two years when I was captured; we were in the Eighty-first regiment – Black Bill was never absent from Williamson county long at any other time; Jep was away just before Spence was killed; had been gone better than six months, and come back on Tuesday before the night Spence was killed, and staid till Thursday morning; he said he was going to Marion; did not see him anymore on Thursday; I don't remember anything about halloaing anything to Marshall the morning of the Saturday Spence was killed; I don't remember halloaing to him the [day] Musick had gone; Jep had relatives in the direction he was going that Friday evening before Spence was killed; Jep and Black Bill are cousins; Black Bill and his two sisters keep house and farm; I don't remember the date of his father's death; Black Bill run the farm after his father's death; Mr. Craig would cross the creek going home; I don't know exactly where Bransen lived.

J. U. CRAIN testified as follows: I reside in Williamson county; lived there about sixty-one years; lived on the same farm forty years; I know defendants ever since they sucked; Jep lived at Crainville, and the other one lived over on Grassy; I heard of the death of Spence the evening after he was killed; I was in Crainville on Friday before the killing; I was to the burying of Captain Sisney; the body came on the cars to Crainville I saw Jep Crain get off of the train; I staid at Smither's till after sundown, and this day I staid pretty late; there are two stores at Crainville, one a drug store and the other a dry goods store; the buildings are about eighty feet apart, with no buildings between them; one door opens to east, and the other to the north; I saw Jep around after he got off the train; I heard Jep call Jim Craig to hold on he would go with him; there was another man with Craig, they called Bransen; I don't recollect the time, but I heard him call to Craig hold on, he would go with them; I saw him about there all the time; I couldn't set any particular time that he was out of my sight; I don't think there was a half hour that he was out of sight; I heard him say hold on he was going to get something; I did not see Jep, Marshall Crain and Sam Musick together at all; I don't think they could have got together and been out of sight half an hour. The train is sometimes there a little after and sometimes a little before four o'clock; I know the Marsh Crain house; it is some two hundred yards from the drug store; don't know whether Musick was there that day or not; might have seen him, but don't remember; saw Jep because I knew he had gone to Marion.

JAMES CRAIG testified: I know Jep Crain; I heard of the death of Spence: he was killed on Saturday night; I was in Crainville the Friday before. I went there between two and three o'clock, and was there two or three hours. I saw Jep, the defendant, there that day. I saw him coming from the train. I did not see him get off. He came up to where the crowd was, and we were around there, and when I got ready to go he said wait, he would go with me. He got a mile and I rode it, and he rode the nag I had. The mule was very small, and I rode it and he rode my horse. We had been about the store there together. I saw him between the time. I saw him coming from the train and when we left, around among the crowd; I don't think I missed him over fifteen or twenty minutes at any time; he said he was going to get his coat, and think he went back to the drug store; I don't know if the train was late that afternoon; from the first I saw of Jep till we started was sometime, maybe an hour and maybe two hours; I had no watch; Mr. Crain and myself, Yellow Bill and Billy Bransen went to Yellow Bill's stable and got the mule; Bransen and myself went home, and Jep went to Warren's; we had some difficulty in crossing the creek was very full; I swam the stock over and the other two went across on a foot log. I am sure this was on the Friday night before Spence was killed; I did not see Jep and Marshall and Musick in consultation that afternoon; when we went by the Marshall Crain home we did not go in nor did not see any one; the Marsh Crain homes is in sight of the drug store in an old field, with no woods between them.

MARY A. CRAIN testified: I know Jep Crain; I heard of the death of Spence on Sunday; I saw Jep on Friday night at our house, and he left there Saturday morning. It was dusky – dark when he got there and he staid all night. It was about seven o'clock in the morning, and Warren and Jep said they were going to Black Bill's and they went in that direction; it's a mile and a half south of west from our house to Black Bill's; my husband got back sometime between twelve and one o'clock; I am sure this was on Friday night before the Saturday on which Mr. Spence was killed. My sister told me Jep had got back, and this was the first I had seen him. I live three or four miles from Crainville, in Williamson county.

MRS. ANNA CRAIN testified: I live about ten miles from Marion; I know both the defendants; I live about a quarter of a mile from Black Bill; I remember the death of Mr. Spence; I remember where I was the day he was killed; I was at home; Jep and Bill came to my house, I should think between eleven and twelve o'clock; they did not stop long; I had not seen Jep for some time; when they left Jep went to Black Bill's; and Bill went to get some cattle out of my field; he went right west; he never came in; I did not see him come he went in that direction; I am step mother of Black Bill, and am aunt by marriage to Jep; the field where the cattle were in was close to the house; the house was right on the coroner of the field; only divided by a fence about the house; Martha Crain, sister of Bill, left with Jep; I can't tell, but took it to be between eleven and twelve o'clock when they came; this was the Saturday before Spence was killed; it is called four or five miles from our home to Crainville.

MARTHA CRAIN testified as follows: I know the defendant; Black Bill is my brother; I live with him; there are three in the family; Bill and myself and sister; my brother died last winter; Bill is a farmer and follows it for a living; I have known Jep all my life; I heard of the death of Spence the next day, on Sunday evening; I was at home, and at step-mother's twice the day before; I saw Jep and Bill that day; Jep came to our house that day; Warren Crain was with him; Bill was at home but not at the house when Jep came; he came in in a little while; they staid there about an hour, and then went to look over Warren Crain's corn; saw them again at step-mother's; about twelve, one or two when me and Jep got home; we went from step-mother's; Bill went around the field; there was some breeding cattle there of Mr. Landrum's; was quarter of an hour when Bill came; we were still at the table when the clock struck two; Bill and Jep were both there; Jep left our house at nearly three o'clock to go to Phil Smith's, in southwest direction; Bill was still at home when Jep left; Bill said when he went away that he was going to catch a horse and see if he couldn't sell him; did not see Jep any more that day; I staid at Widow Craig's that night well between eleven and twelve o'clock, sitting up with a sick child; went home next morning about nine o'clock; Bill was there when I got home; he was not at home on Saturday evening when I left.

SARAH HAMPTON testified as follows: My mother's name is Louisa Hampton; I know the defendants, Black Bill don't live far from us; I heard of the death of Mr. Spence on Sunday; I saw Black Bill, Jep and Warren Crain the day before the murder; they came up and looked at the cattle; I was out in the pasture with Caroline Payne and Benny Payne; when I came back I found Warren, Black Bill and Jep there; they asked which one had been shot, and I showed them; that was about ten o'clock.

PHILLIP T. SMITH testified as follows: I know the defendants; I live west of Crainville. I heard of the death of Mr. Spence on the Sunday evening after he was killed; I was at Forney Tunster's hauling hay; it is southwest of Black Bill's about a mile; I saw Jep Crain that evening, and he said he was going to Phil Smith's; I was unloading hay; I wanted a drink and him and I went to the well and sat down on some rocks and talked awhile; it was between twelve and three o'clock; he was afoot; in going from Black Bill's to Bill Smith's that would be the way to go; it was about two miles from where I was at work to Phil Smith's; Phil Smith's wife passes for his sister; it was about a mile from where I was unloading hay to Black Bill's; it was on Saturday, the last day of July.

JOHN SMITH testified as follows: I know the defendants; I live at home with my father, about nine miles from Crainville, a little east of north; I heard of the death of Spence on Sunday; I saw Jep at night on Saturday just about good dark; I had been at John and Dave Baker's threshing wheat; when I got home I found Jep there; he staid at our house till Wednesday morning; he went to church next day at New Hope meeting house.

PHILIP D. SMITH testified as follows: I live about 8 or 9 miles south of Crainville; I know the defendants; I heard of the death of Mr. Spence on Sunday evening after was killed on Saturday; I saw Jep Crain the Saturday evening before, passing by a neighbor's house to my house and I found him there when I got home; I think he staid there till Tuesday about noon; we went to church the next day at the Tedford meeting house, about three quarters of a mile from my house; he was going about three hours; I think it was about an hour by sun when I first saw him; he was afoot. I saw Jep in Carbondale going home, he said, from the north where he had been harvesting; this I think was on Monday or Tuesday; I did not see him get off the train; I wanted him to go out home with me.

SAMUEL CRAIN testified: I live near Crainville, Williamson county; I know the defendants; I was not present at the preliminary examination before Squire Reynolds, and only a part of the time before Judge Crawford; I expect I was present on the day you allude, but can't fix the day or date; I was there when Jep and Spence had a fuss, but don't remember this date; Thomas Duncan was there, but I don't remember whether it was in the morning or afternoon. I was at the store when Jep and Spence had some words; at Mrs. Waggoner's I can't tell, for the fact that we were all joking and rigging Jep about his and Spence's quarrel; I don't believe I can tell what was said, for we were all laughing and joking and I could not have told in an hour after what was said; I don't remember hearing Jep say anything about massacring or killing Spence; I think if anything of that kind had been said I would have remembered it; I did not hear it; we were joking Jep about having a quarrel with Spence and abusing each other so and not fighting; it was in the morning; and in the evening we were talking about it again, and Jep was a little angry of course, for he had just come out of a quarrel, and we were teasing him about it; I don't remember that I heard him make any dangerous threats, and if he did I did not hear them. I did not have any knowledge that there was going to be a difficulty between Spence and Jep; they got to talking about the affairs of Williamson county, and Spence said the people were not capable of electing their officers, and they ought to be appointed.

N. E. NORRIS testified: I know the defendants; I arrested Black Bill, and it was a part of my posse that arrested Big Jep at Crainville; we made the arrest at night; there was Mart Davis, Jim Grider, Mr. Calvert and myself in the party that arrested Black Bill; some fifty or sixty yards from the house we divided. Mr. Grider and Davis going around on the west side of the house, and Mr. Calvert and I went in the front way; it was further for Davis and Grider to go around; Bill was in bed and Grider and Davis came up in five or ten minutes after: I did not right immediately make known my business; before going in I halloared at the gate and one of the girls came out and caught one of the dogs; Bill told them that it was me and told them to take off the dogs; I think I had told Bill what my business was, and named the parties we had got and sent on; I remember mentioning Jep's before Davis came up; Bill said "if me and Jep get in the same cell we will about fill it up;" I was present at the trials before Squire Reynolds and Judge Crawford, but don't think I was present when Mrs. Waggoner gave her evidence. I think she was nearly through when I got there; Judges Allen and Duff and Mr. Hartwell were there; I don't know that I paid much attention and could not be positive what she said; After arresting Black Bill we went to Crainville and then to

Carterville, where we staid all night; the next morning Bill went to Dock McCarty's house, fifty or sixty steps away, and presently came back by himself, he was only gone a few minutes. I don't know that I heard any of Mrs. Waggoner's testimony before Judge Crawford.

CHAS. H. DENNISON testified as follows: I know about the time, but not the exact date that Musick was put in jail at Marion and I was at the jail shortly after in company with Mr. Landrum and Sheriff Norris. Mr. Landrum came to me and wanted me to get some one else to go to the jail with him. He said Musick was going to make a statement. We started to Mr. Hartwell's office, and on the way met Sheriff Norris, and asked him to go with us. We then went to his cell and Landrum said: "Now Sam, we have come, and want you to make a statement." Landrum remarked that Musick was not a murderer, but that he had been drawn into the affair through bad company and whisky. He said he had been acquainted with Musick for a long time, that he was a good friend of Musick's and would put his hand in his pocket and let him have his last dollar. Landrum said he wanted Musick to tell the truth and not to implicate an innocent man in the murders. Musick said if he told all he knew he would have to implicate some of Norris' relatives. Norris said go on don't shield anybody – let the truth come out. Musick then said if he told the truth they would kill him or mob him. Landrum replied that Musick should never see the parties, that he should have money enough to take him out of their reach. I think Landrum had just come from the jail when he come to me. Musick asked me to come back, and I went back in the evening, and the jailer brought in a light. Musick asked me if "they had gone after the boys." and asked me if they were going to "bring them in here." I told him I guessed they would, when he said, "I can't see them – I want the money promised me. I want to leave here before they come in." I replied "Sam, you will have to stay. They will not put the boys in with you; but you will have to go before the grand jury and tell what you know about this matter." He said "By God, I can't do that; I want to leave." I replied that he couldn't think of leaving, that he would have to stay, that he would not be harmed.

LANDRUM'S PROMISE AGAIN. Sheriff Norris was put on the stand again, and testified as to what occurred in the jail when Landrum, Dennison and Norris went to hear Musick's statement. Sheriff Norris' version of what took place at the interview is substantially the same as sworn to by Mr. Dennison.

WHERE WAS BLACK BILL ON THAT SATURDAY NIGHT? – John Rollen was the next witness, and was introduced to swear that Black Bill was seven or eight miles from Crainville the night that Spence was killed. Rollen saw Black Bill and spoke to him one half hour before sundown on that Saturday night.

HE SLEPT WITH CALVIN? — Calvin Craig testified as follows: I knew Mr. Spence; I heard of his death on Sunday after it occurred; Sunday was the 1st of August; in the morning of the day before we loaded up the threshing machine and went to Phillip Turnage's and threshed some wheat; we left there just at dusk, and I had a couple of horses going home, and Munn Jack had a yoke of Oxen and came up behind me; it was probably eight o'clock when we got to John Jack's, and we stopped there; John Jack was there, and so was Wm. Crain (Black Bill) there. Monroe Jack came up while I was there and passed by; I was there and passed by; I was sitting on my horse and John Jack was in the yard; I think Black Bill was in the act of getting on his horse; when I got ready to go, I asked Mr. Crain to go home with me and stay all night, and he said he would go, that he wanted to swap horses with me anyhow; he went off with me to my house; my wife was not at home, she was at High Craig's to set up. Black Bill staid all night with me, and left about sun up the next morning. Robt. Craig came to my house just about the time he left. I got breakfast myself; it must have been nine o'clock in the evening, probably a little later, when we went to bed. I think it must be close to nine or ten miles from my house to Crainville, the direction being a little west of north. I have known Black Bill since we were boys.

ROBERT CRAIG deposed that he ate breakfast at Calvin Craig's on Sunday morning, and that Black Bill ate at the table with them; also that he had seen him at John Jack's the night previous. Monroe Jack swore that he saw Black Bill at his brother John Jack's gate on Saturday evening an hour after dark. Other witnesses corroborated the above statement.

THEN CAME "MACKADO." — Mr. William J. Mackado was next called. Mr. Mackado has lived in Jefferson county since 1849, and was well acquainted with same Musick when that individual lived at Spring Garden. After telling all about Musick, from his boyhood up to the time he went into the rebel army, Mr. Mackado wound up saying he would not believe him under oath.

A LITTLE MORE MUSICK. — Sam Musick was brought from his cell and put on the stand again. He was asked whether he had ever been in Jail in

Marion county. Sam said he was, and told what got him into prison. He went out walking with another man's wife and she forgot to go home that night, and the next day her husband had him arrested and they put him jail and kept him there three weeks. He was asked whether he was ever under arrest and made his escape by jumping off a train of cars. He said he was not.

WOULDN'T BELIEVE HIM. — David Crawford, an old man in soldier clothes, testified that he knew Sam Musick when he lived at Spring Garden, and from his reputation in that community he would not believe him under oath.

JACK THE SON OF SAMUEL. — John Jack said that he had lived in Williamson county all his life, and that his father's name was Samuel. Mr. Jack swore that on the night of the 31st of July last-the night on which Spence was killed – he was in his stable yard unhitching his horses when Black Bill Crain rode up and spoke to him. Jack told Crain to go to the house, and when he got done he would come. Mr. Jack also testified that Black Bill staid and ate supper with him; at about eight o'clock left his house in company with Calvin Craig, who had asked Bill to go home and stay all night with him.

With this witness the defense closed their case, when the prosecution introduced some

EVIDENCE IN REBUTTAL. — It would be a tedious task to go over all the evidence, and we shall not undertake it. The main points are all we shall attempt to give. Mr. County Attorney Hartwell, of Williamson county, was called to the stand, and testified that on the preliminary examination of the prisoners and Yellow Bill Crain, Black Bill testified that he had taken a certain route in going from Crainville to John Jack's on that fatal Saturday night.

THEY SAW BILL — Several witnesses, among them Mrs. Mary Ann Tippy and Mrs. Ann Impson, testified that they saw Black Bill on the afternoon or evening of the night on which Spence was killed, going towards Crainville.[111] One witness said it was about three or four o'clock she saw him pass her house, and the other said it was as late as five. These witnesses lived apart, and saw Bill at different points on the road.

---

[111] Mary Ann was the former Mary A. Impson who married W. W. Tippy on Feb. 12, 1871, in Williamson Co., Illinois. W. W. was likely the same as the Worth Tippy mentioned else as no Worth Tippy appears in the census, but W. W. does. Mrs. Ann Impson is likely her mother, though Mary Ann is not found in Ann's household in the 1870 Census (or anywhere else for that matter). Ann is definitely the right generation to be Mary Ann's mother.

MORE ABOUT MUSICK — Mr. James W. Landrum was recalled and testified as follows, concerning the interview with Musick when he was about to make his statement concerning the matter. Mr. Landrum said: I can only state what took place at the interview with Musick when Mr. Dennison and Mr. Norris were present. Their statements are in the main correct. I went to Musick and appealed to him in this way, that he had been in my employ; that he had had my confidence, and I did not believe him a bad man. I said to him for God's sake don't implicate any innocent man. He said if he told all he would have to implicate some of Norris' friends. Mr. Norris said if that is so let it come out; Musick said that he was afraid that that they would kill him or mob him, that they were 100 strong. I told him not to be afraid; that if he came clear, he should have money to go away. I know Sam Musick, but I can't tell just how long I have known him. He came to me in 1874, and worked for me until the next July. I was acquainted with his character for truth and veracity; I think it is good, and if he was sober I would believe him on oath.

SOME PERSONS WHO WOULD BELIEVE MUSICK. — Laban Carter, a Justice of the Peace at Carterville; Mr. J. C. Hodges and Paul W. Willis, of Murphysboro; Mr. Burton, of Carbondale; Mr. Wm. A. Weaver, of Grand Tower; Mr. A. R. Warders, of Williamson county; Mr. E. H. Brush, of Carbondale, all testified that they would believe Musick on oath, and Samuel's character was made whole again.

BLACK BILL AGAIN. — Tutt Hampton and John Craig testified that they went to Black Bill's house on the Sunday morning after the Saturday night on which Spence was killed, and found Black Bill laying on the bed, and that he got up and ate breakfast with them. This was some time between six and nine o'clock.

The prosecution then closed their case. The defense presented several witnesses in rebuttal, but the evidence would be of no importance to the reader. Judge Allen made the closing speech in the trial. It is said by competent Judges that his speech in this case was one of the ablest of his life. It was full of sound reasoning; and the manner in which he dealt with some of the witnesses for the defense was by no means flattering to them. His argument lasted for about five hours. The court then read the instructions to the jury, after which the case was given to them to decide.

THE VERDICT. — At seven o'clock, yesterday (Wednesday) morning, after being out eighteen hours, the jury returned a verdict of guilty, fixing the term of imprisonment of the prisoners at twenty years in the penitentiary. This ends another chapter of the bloody vendetta of our county. Men too mean to live and not fit to die, raised in our county, proved guilty of crimes of a character dark enough to put to shame the vilest fiend of the dark beyond. Surely the time has come when all honest men should labor together for the strict enforcement of the law, and let the wrath of an offended people be revenged by bringing to the bar of justice all those who are yet in the back ground whose hands are stained with the blood of their fellow man and their hearts darkened with perjury and their time and talent employed in devising plans which leads to the darkening of our reputation draining the treasury and will, if not checked, drive us into bankruptcy and total wreck.

Illustrated Historical Atlas of the State of Illinois

CARTERVILLE COUNTRYSIDE — The peaceful tranquility of this illustration belies the violence area residents experienced during the Vendetta. Published in 1876 the sketch shows the residence next to James W. Landrum's mill where Samuel Musick worked. Landrum's mill is shown later on in this volume as well as the front cover.

Chapter 15. **Marshall's Last Days**

ON THE 12TH OF JANUARY, 1876, Marshall constructed him a gun out of an old tin can, by rolling the tin round a stick and wrapping it with wire. He then took a large cartridge which Norris had, and when he was turned loose to exercise, went to the provision door and called Music, and told him he wanted him to look at that, as he wanted to show him a sign. He put the gun in the door and struck the cartridge three times with a poker, but it did not fire. One of the guards told Sam he was going to shoot him, and Sam got away. Marshall said he did not expect to shoot Sam, but to shoot above his head and make him break his neck jerking back. On the 14th, when he lost all hopes of killing Music, he threw his gun out of the window. On the 15th, the following conversation took place between him and Robert Wallace, day guard. Marshall, looking out into the hall, asked:

"Is that the place?"

W.—"Yes."

"Where will I stand?" said Marsh.

W.—"On a trap door."

M.—"I thought I would stand above it; will I fall through to the floor?"

W.—"You will drop four feet."

M.—"I want to drop six."

W.—"That would jerk your head off."

M.—"How will the gallows be fixed; will the post come up from below?"

W.—"No; it will be a frame fixed on the floor above."

M.—"Do you think God will pardon a man calling on him in the last moments?"

W.—"I can not tell."

M.—"I heard Sisney say when I shot him, 'Oh, Lord, have mercy on me.' The Bible says, 'He that calleth upon the Lord, he will pardon.' Do you think Sisney is in Heaven?"

W.—"I hope so."

M.—"So do I, and I wish he was."

Up to this time he had been jovial and funny, but now he said he had troubled the guards enough; he had something else to think about; that he would do no more to get out, and he hoped none of them thought hard of him.

On the 25th day of October he wrote to his cousin, Jesse Ragsdale, of Missouri, giving an account of his melancholy condition, and on the 16th he tried writing again. He wrote a letter to an abandoned woman in the south cell of the jail, advising her to live a life of virtue. This was a sensible letter. He was now daily attended by ministers and religious people, and by his faithful wife. On the 18th and 19th, the gallows was erected by Samuel S. Ireland, by cutting a hole in the upper floor, three feet ten inches square, in which he made a trap door, and erected two posts with a cross beam, six and a half feet from the trap door. On the morning of the 19th, Marshall awoke and screamed out, "Oh, Lord, let me die easy!" and then prayed for a while audibly. On the morning of the 21st, he yearned to pour the balm of forgiveness into the goaded bosom of Musick. The strife was over, and the battle lost, and the scars of a wounded spirit were imprinted on his face, as the lightning leaves its scathings, and the storms of passion leave their deep and blasted traces on the soul. He asked for Sam to be brought into his cell; but Sam would not go. Marsh told them to get me, that I could bring him in. Sam said if I advised him, he would go in. I did not, but offered him protection; he did not go. Marsh said, "Tell Sam to forgive me." I did so, but Sam would not, saying that Marsh had told things on him that were not true. Marsh said that was so, and now to ask him again. I did so, and Sam forgave him for all wrongs. It was a sad scene—two desperate men tamed to child-like softness, and weeping bitterly. They then went over their troubles together, and I carried the words from one cell to the other. Soon after, Marsh's wife entered his cell, and he took her on his knees and embraced her. It was a scene which should be sacred from all intrusion. Even the eye of friendship should not invade its hallowed bounds. Her eyes glittered with a metallic gleam, and the soft curl of her lips was lost in a quiver of despair. Her's was a deadly pallor. It was the incandescence, and not the flame of passion, that was burning in her inmost being. She would burst out into shrieks of great anguish, and then subside into sobs. She dreaded the heaving of her own bosom – dreaded the future and the world. If she could have died she would have been happy and holy in the hope of mercy. To be torn from a love made holier by past sorrows, was an insult to the attribute of Heaven. Marsh was in his sock feet, with a pair of jeans pants on, and a ragged jeans coat. He looked care-worn, and shed a few tears. Twenty-seven years old, spare made, weight 120 pounds, light hair, fair skin, light-gray eyes, with a bashful expression. He was married to Miss Rhoda Rich, March 4th, 1874. In speaking of the murder of James Henderson, Marshall said that John Bulliner gave Jonas G. Ellett and Mart. Dyal $300 to do it.[112]

By ten o'clock an anxious and expectant crowd was swaying to and fro in front of the jail. He bade farewell to his friends, and told them to bury him in the Hampton Cemetery. At eleven o'clock the militia formed on the Square, and marched to the jail and surrounded it. At least 3,000 people were present. The jail is situated a little south-east of the Square, and is a brick building, two stories high, with the cells up stairs. At twelve o'clock he was dressed in a white suit, with his robe over it. At twelve o'clock and ten minutes he took leave of his wife.

At twelve o'clock and twenty minutes, with a firm step, he walked out of the cell and stood before a window on the east side, and in a strong voice said. "Gentlemen, I must make a statement in regard to this matter. I feel it my duty to God and man to make it. I am guilty of killing the two men. My punishment is just. I hope all of you will forgive me. I pray God will Judge and prosper this country. Good-bye to all."

He then read a poem of twenty-four verses, which he composed for the occasion. Then, with a firm, steady step, he walked on to the trap-door. At 12:34 Sanford W. Gee read a few passages of Scripture from John, and then sung, "There is a fountain filled with blood," Crain and all the rest joining in the singing, and then Gee prayed, Crain getting on his knees. The jury was then called and answered. About thirty persons were in the hall. At 12:46 his legs and arms were bound; at 12:52 the white cap was put on his head, by John B. Edrington, Deputy Sheriff, who told him that he held a death-warrant, saying, at this hour and at this place he was ordered to hang him. At 12:54 the rope was put on his neck, and the front part of the cap pulled down by J. L. Kelly. When he was asked if he had anything to say, said, "I am the murderer of William Spence and George Sisney; that is all I have got to say." He was asked if he was ready to receive the execution, and said, "I am." He

---

[112] Ellett's role is also suggested in stories passed down by a descendent of Pleasant M. Finney, a Klan member (if not at that time, then later) who was living in Isaac Vancil's house at the time of the murder and a friend of Ellett's. Henderson had served as a witness in the Vancil murder trial in which a grand jury had indicted Ellett. *Source:* Gallagher. Oct. 18.

was then told that he had four minutes to live, and said, "That was all." At 12:56 the Deputy said, "Time up," and Brice Holland severed the rope which held the trap-door, and Marshall Thomas Crain swung between Heaven and earth.

After the jerking of the rope he swung around and then was still; he did not struggle. At 1:06 his pulse beat twenty; at 1:18 no pulsation at his wrist; at 1:22 pulsation ceased, and life was pronounced extinct by Drs. S. H. Bundy and John O'Hara. After hanging thirty minutes the body was cut down, and his neck was found partially dislocated; the eyes and countenance looked natural, Sheriff Norris mournfully did his duty up to the time of the execution and then left, saying the law should take its course. At 1:30 his body was put in a coffin and taken outside the jail and exhibited to the people, and then given to his brother Warren, who started, at 3:00, for home. He was buried next day. And the wild winds of Heaven will sing their hoarse lullaby over his grave until the mighty angel Gabriel writes the solemn legend, "Finis," on the hoary page of time.

No polished stela points to his rest. He left to his wife as a legacy, the memory of a sad and unhappy man. He had nothing to plead in extenuation of his crime against the laws of his country; but he has the frailty of human nature to plead for him at the bar of God. This is a plea that has ever opened the chambers of mercy to the sorrowing children of men. Crain was hung, "and yet men whose guilt has wearied Heaven for vengeance, are left to cumber earth." Marshall was not a man of genius; but when he came to this work of blood his skill was displayed in a wonderful manner. So ingeniously were his plans laid, and so dexterously executed that nothing but treachery itself could unravel them.

Part of Marshall's poem was discovered by Cyrus Oberly to have been taken from one by William Delaney, a New York desperado.

James Norris is twenty-five years old, a large, fine-looking man, very intelligent and pleasant, but was a wild, reckless boy-loved all kinds of amusements, and got into some difficulties, and was several times indicted. His father is a respectable citizen of this county. James worked for Bulliner in 1874, when he got into the trouble with Russell and Pleasant. At the April Term 1876, he was indicted for the murder of James Henderson, and went to trial defended by Clemens and myself—Allen and Duff prosecuting. Henderson's dying declaration was introduced, saying that he saw and knew Norris; also, Jacob Beard testified that he met Norris in Cairo, five days after the shooting, and Norris was armed, and said he was on the scout, and asked if Henderson was dead, saying he knew who killed him. The defense was an alibi, four witnesses swearing that he was in Tennessee that very day. The jury found him guilty, and fixed his time at eighteen years. In overruling the motion for a new trial, the Court said he could not let the verdict stand, only on the fact that Beard's testimony made him an accessory to the crime. He was carried to Joliet, April 27. Since then Clemens went to McNairy county, Tennessee, and got fifteen other affidavits that he was there at the time.

It had been reported in Tennessee that some of the Hendersons were seen there, trying to kill Norris and Bulliner, and a company of one hundred men were raised and scouted the country there, in which Norris took part; but the Governor refused to pardon him. The people said "This 'alibi' business is getting 'too thin'," and there was a strong prejudice existing here against the Bulliner family in Tennessee. They thought David Bulliner, Sr., was running the whole Bulliner side of the Vendetta, and any one coming from McNairy County was looked upon as a scoundrel. This was all wrong. David Bulliner is a good man, and his son George is as polished a gentleman as lives in Tennessee. Those other men are common, sober, honest men. James Norris was not proven guilty.

Samuel Musick stands five feet ten inches high, thirty-four years old, spare built, light complexion, high cheek bones, pale blue eyes, moustache, and a low, broad forehead, with black, curling hair, and has an honest, open countenance. He was born in 1842, in Jefferson County, Illinois. He had three sisters and four brothers. His father was a poor farmer, and at ten years of age Sam lost his mother. In 1854, his father moved to Union County, Ky. When the war carne up, he and two of his brothers joined the 13th Kentucky (rebel) Cavalry, and served one year. Was in the battles of Fort Donelson, Uniontown and Rollington. He deserted the rebels and took the oath. In 1863, his father moved back to this State. Sam came back and was arrested and taken to Louisville, where he remained three months, and was tried for being a guerrilla, and turned over as a prisoner of war, and sent to Camp Chase. In 1865, he was turned loose and came to Illinois. He subsequently lived at Centralia, and for the last eight years lived around Carbondale, working, teaming generally, and drove a hack to Marion for six months, in 1869. In 1872, he hired to drive a log team at Mt. Carbon, and, while at this business, in the edge of Missouri, was married to Miss Mary A. Griffin, a very handsome little lady. In August, 1874, he hired to Landrum to team, and moved to Crainville. He has always been a drunkard, and is illiterate.

During all the trial and fatigue of the prosecutions, he stood up without murmur or complaint. His fortitude never failed under the most searching cross-examinations, but mild, firm and confiding, he told the same story over and over. If he had refused to testify, or had broken down, the blood of other men would have stained the soil of this county. He said he got into this thing when he was drunk, and had no idea of killing anybody, and now he had done more than justice, he had not been selfish from passion or principle; but had told the whole truth. His case went to trial April 17th, 1876, defended by myself alone, Allen and Duff for the People, who proved his confession, etc.

The defense was that the confession was made under the influence of hope, and not proper evidence. After the argument, the jury took the case, and was out twenty-one hours, and failed to agree; eleven being for acquitting, and one for conviction. And the case was set down for trial on the 21st. By that time I was afraid to try to clear him again, lest I failed, and it poisoned the public mind against him. Thus far it had been his faithful friend, and the prosecution now threatened to be severe. So, the danger of turning public sentiment against him, was greater than the hope of clearing him. And, if I had failed, and the people turned against him, there would have been no hope of pardon. So, I was forced to agree to a verdict of guilty, and 'a term of fourteen years. Beveridge told B. F. Lowe and J. W. Landrum that what ever they wanted done with Musick he would do. He, also, wrote to Duff and Allen, when he employed them, that they might say to Musick, if they thought best, that if he stood firmly by the truth throughout all the trials, he would be the subject of executive clemency. And the people supposed that he would make it a point of honor to keep this promise. A petition was sent him, signed by the parties designated, asking Musick's pardon; but he refused to interfere in the case.

At the April Term, Samuel R. Crain was indicted as accessory to the murder of Spence. He was arrested, but being in the last stages of a pulmonary disease, was bailed in the sum of $5,000.

Milton Baxter had been indicted for the murder of Hinchcliff, and he had been arrested and confined in jail a while. At this Term the People *nolled*. He, nor his brother, were connected with the Vendetta, no further than being strong friends to Russell and "Texas Jack."

With this, I seal the volume, and turn my eyes away from the bloody acts of depraved men, hoping with all the fervor of which my soul is capable, that God will add no other plague to our county. Enough has been done, to teach the world that sorrow is the first result of ambition, malice or revenge. The first gun of the Vendetta that rang out in the air, betokened a coming storm, and since then crime's destiny and miseries' tale has been unfolded with the stencil plates of blood on the souls of men. Many have become bankrupt on the pathway to shame. The different phases of human life display with unmatched and unequaled clearness to our senses the great wrongs and sins of mankind, and when we, in the course of our lives and professions meet them, we are startled from our unusual composure, and always do take them for warning in the future. I wish they would not occur to attract our notice. I wish we could be spared the recital of such crimes, revealing, as they do, one after another the sins and depravity of society. But justice demands that the guilty should bear the reproach, and that the stain should be washed away from the innocent. And while a man has a right before God to protect his own life, he cannot become the aggressor without blame. It was not that spirit of barbarism which kills men in Kansas, that governed the Vendetta, but that spirit which fights duels in Louisiana. It was the knock-down style of the West, coming in contact with the code of the South. The men who killed Bulliner would have fought him a fist fight, but they would not fight a duel; and they knew that it was death to insult a Bulliner and then face him. So, they laid down all rules, and that is why the shooting commenced on the other side. It never would have commenced on the Bulliner side; and it is not to be wondered at if they accommodated themselves to this mode of fighting in the bushes.

The age of chivalry is gone, but it has left its traces on their hearts, and it may be that they chose to exercise it in a more murderous, but less public way. The chastenings of honor inspired both parties with courage, and mitigated their ferocity; for they did not rob or steal, but simply killed. Their common cause gave them unbridled and unfettered alliance, each acting in subordination to the other. They held secret meetings, where powder and lead was the toast, and where they rejoiced over the death of an enemy like a conquering gladiator in the Roman Coliseum, with the fire of revenge roasting in their eyes. And so deep-laid were their plans, that treachery alone succeeded where stratagem and ingenuity had failed. The judgments against these parties stand out resplendent with the light of noonday as a beacon of warning that they will be duplicated whenever occasion requires it. At this time, but one side of the Vendetta has been punished. All on the other side have escaped.

Joseph W. Hartwell, the State's Attorney, served the people well in these prosecutions, and they have rewarded him by re-electing him. He was born in this county, and raised a poor boy. When the war came up, he joined the Thirty-First Regiment Illinois Volunteers, and was at the battles of Raymond, Champion Hill , Vicksburg, Kennesaw and Atlanta. July 21st, 1864, at Atlanta, his left arm was taken off by a twelve-pound howitzer ball. He came home March, 1865, and that fall was elected County Treasurer. He lived very hard, having a large family, and studied law under many disadvantages, but was admitted to the bar in December, 1866. It 1868 he was elected Circuit Clerk, and again ran in 1872, but was defeated. In 1874, he was elected Mayor of Marion, and May 15th, 1875, elected State's Attorney.

The people owe a debt of gratitude to Benjamin F. Lowe, for his bravery, skill and firmness. He was born in Effingham county, in 1838, moved to Marion in 1850. He was raised a poor boy, and worked around promiscuously. During the war he went South to see the boys from this county there, and on returning was arrested as a spy, but after a month's confinement, escaped his guards, and went to Canada. But he was not a spy, only having brought some money and letters through the line for the friends of the boys. Since the war he has lived at Marion and Murphysboro, serving as City Marshal at both places. In 1866, he married Miss Letha McCowan, and is a fine looking man, tall, slim, black hair, whiskers, and dark complexion. He is very pleasant, witty and an agreeable, reliable man. He is a professional gambler, and makes most of his money in that way; but he is a peaceable, sober, quiet man, and a man whom the people have great confidence in, in emergencies. He took hold of our troubles when it seemed like death to do so; but the people rallied in solid phalanx to his assistance.[113]

All men agree that the man who coolly and deliberately takes the life of his fellow-man is not fit to live, and the Judge or jury who lets such a man go unpunished richly deserves the wrathful condemnation of mankind. Yet, Judge Crawford assumed a responsibility that no Judge in our country ever

---

[113] For his efforts Lowe received $7,100, but claimed only $1,500 was over and above expenses. *Source*: Lind 1:87; quoting the April 19, 1877, edition of the *Marion Monitor*.

before took, that of hanging a man who plead guilty. And when Judges and juries take the responsibility of trying and punishing criminals like this, the law will become a terror to evil-doers.

The practice of carrying concealed weapons, which grew out of the war, and which led to so much bloodshed, will soon be ended if juries will convict the guilty parties. At the April Term, 1876, twenty-two indictments for this offense were found.

Williamson county has vindicated herself. She not only furnished the men to suppress crime, but she spent $13,032.79, besides jail fees. We are now beginning to have bright hopes of the future. Men of property would not come among us as long as the pistol and gun were used to redress wrongs, and men were allowed to go a "gunning" for human scalps. This has ceased in this county, and now if those editors who labored so hard to traduce our characters and disgrace our county, will do as much to restore it, soon peace and prosperity will be printed on the mangled tape of our county, and soon that odium that hangs around our name, like clouds around a mountain, will disappear, and Williamson county will stand forth resplendent in the light of a new civilization, conspicuous and honorable, and take the rank her sons and resources entitle her to.

EXPENSES OF THE VENDETTA.

Expenses exclusive of Bailiffs and dieting Prisoners	$ 670.24
Witnesses to foreign counties	1,523.55
Guarding jail	2,991.00
Rewards	4,000.00
Attorney's fees	3,650.00
Hanging Crain	100.00
Coffin and shrouding	38.00
Scaffold	10.00
Clothing for "Big Jep" and "Black Bill"	50.00
	13,032.79

Illustrated Historical Atlas of the State of Illinois

CARTERVILLE LANDMARK — James W. Landrum's mills served as a landmark in the western portion of Williamson County. Samuel Musick worked for Landrum as a teamster and Erwin later wrote that Musick and the Crains met near the mill to discuss items taken during the shooting of William Spence. The sketch above was first published in 1876 suggesting it was drawn a bit earlier, possibly during the time Musick worked for Landrum.

Chapter 16. **Ku-Kluckle Chuckle**

IN JANUARY WHILE MARSHALL CRAIN WAITED TO SWING the Ku Klux Klan made another appearance in Williamson County – or did they? The incident took place near Crab Orchard east of Marion. Residents had seen the Klan ride one night, though no one knew for certain whom all they were targeting. The local justice of the peace, John W. Peebels, investigated the various accounts and reported to the governor on February 11, 1876.

> There was something like unto the nature of "Ku-Kluxing" transpired about the Middle of last month near our little village and I think it is probably that the Klan can be raised if there is any reward for the arrest and conviction of Parties Known to be in disguises going around looking for men stating that they want to settle with them.
>
> I will stall the case. There was fourteen men dressed in White Robes, long caps, went to the residence of a Farmer inquiring for a certain young man all armed with Double Barrel guns.
>
> I want to hear from you on the matter as I think the Klan can be raised. I hope you will keep this matter secret as I am aware of the parties know that I know anything about it they would go for me. Hoping to hear from you. [114]

The good J.P. wasn't the only one corresponding to the governor. W. F. Spain sent two letters, the first of which came 15 days after Peebels' on February 28. Spain didn't have to investigate. He knew the parties involved and more importantly, he knew the motive and intent.

> Sir, I address you for information concerning a little trouble in this neighborhood. The trouble is this: The report is in circulation that one James Miles or Frank Miles, or both had went before one John W. Peebels that there is a band of Ku Kluckles in this

---

[114] John W. Peebels. Feb. 11, 1896. Letter to Gov. John L. Beveridge. Governor's Correspondence Files. February 1876. Illinois State Archives.

neighborhood committing various depredations, and that the same has been forwarded to you & upon this report there is a great excitement among the boys in this neighborhood for fear of being arrested and taken to Springfield.

Now upon the honor of a man I tell you there is not, nor never has, been a Ku Kluck in this neighborhood.

What this grew out of is simply this. The said Frank Miles was courting a girl in the neighborhood and because he went so often the boys in the neighborhood thought they would have a little fun out of him. So accordingly one light night in January – I do not remember the exact date – they made them some paper hats and taking some 2 or 3 sheets they went to the girl's house but the said Frank Miles was not there that night so there wasn't any one frightened or hurt, the family knowing all about it with the exception of the girl.

Now this is all the Ku Klucking that has ere been done in this neighborhood. These facts can be proved by B. F. Ensminger, James Miles, W. F. Scoby, F. M. Spain & judge of the Court R. W. Parks and all other good citizens of the neighborhood.

I want a copy of all that has been sent to you concerning this matter so that it can be thoroughly sifted before the grand jury. Write soon and give me satisfaction.

Spain actually sent the governor two letters apparently back to back though the surviving second one is missing pages. What's left explains Spain's need for Peebel's correspondence as it appears that the victim had decided to seize the opportunity presented to him by his "friends."

> … the reason I make this request of you is this. There are parties here at work at this thing that want to make money out of it. James Miles has told some of the boys, so I am informed, that if they would make him up $2,000 that he would drop it.[115]

The governor took no action and the matter was apparently dropped.

---

[115] W. F. Spain. Feb. 28, 1876 and c. Feb. 1876. Letters to Gov. John L. Beveridge. Governor's Correspondence Files. February 1876. Illinois State Archives.

Chapter 17. **Cleaning Up**

THUS WITH THE TOTALING OF EXPENSES incurred by Williamson County in fighting and prosecuting the Bloody Vendetta, Milo Erwin ended his account. But the trials weren't completely over. The confessions of Crain and Musick as well as the testimony presented at the various trials in Jackson and Williamson counties had shed light on a number of unsolved mysteries, especially the 1862 murder of John Burbridge by Terry Crain

That year Crain had enlisted with the ill-famed "Whang-Doodle" 128th Illinois Regiment that had been organized by initially pro-Southern, and some formerly vocal pro-secession Democrats, in order to prove their loyalty. As the regiment marched from Marion to Carbondale where they would catch the train, Crain met Burbridge in the road at the bridge and ended an apparent long-standing dispute between the two of them. He attacked and killed him. As a newspaper noted, "the case passed without an arrest until the exposure of the vendetta in this county by Sam Musick, and the apprehension of the parties concerned, which led to the exposure of Terry Crain's murder."

During the summer of 1875, the Jackson County grand jury indicted Crain for the murder. Following his arrest the court set bail at $15,000. As the Vendetta murder trials took precedence and most of the court's time, Crain found his trial pushed back to August 1876. There in Murphysboro, a jury sentenced him to 15 years in the penitentiary. Three jurors wanted a life sentence, but considering his age of 42, they agreed that 15 years would be enough.

The newspaper noted that "Let no guilty man escape," seemed to be the watchword of the day and that, "'the way of the transgressor is hard,' is clearly demonstrated."[116]

Although the paper identified Crain as an uncle to Marshall Crain, census records indicate otherwise. He appears to have been a first cousin, though one 15 years older than Marshall.[117]

------

[116] August 17, 1876. *Marion* [Ill.] *Monitor.*

He didn't stay in prison too long though as the governor pardoned him the following April. A newspaper article at the time identified the murder weapon used as a stone thrown by Crain at Burbridge.[118]

Four years later in 1880, while Thomas Russell was still hiding in exile, his brother John shot another man near Carterville in what was described both as a "trifling matter" and an "outgrowth of an old family feud."

> On the 11th of May, 1880, John Russell, brother of Thomas, of Vendetta fame, and Henry Stocks, who were close neighbors, had a difficulty over a trifling matter, and met one day on the road about a mile and a half from Carterville, when Russell shot and killed Stocks.[119]

Newspaper accounts immediately following the shooting provided additional details.

> Russell returned from Carterville and met Stocks near the Russell grave yard, two miles from Carterville. Stocks called out, "Get down off your horse and we will settle this matter right here." Both dismounted and Russell pulled a gun and said, "Defend yourself," and fired twice. The first ball entered on the left side, near the heart, killing him almost instantly. He was dead before Dr. Ferrell, 50 yards away, could get to him. Russell fled and has not been found. Stocks was about 50 years old and leaves a family, four grown sons among the number. Russell is about 28. Russell was justified as Stocks had threatened to kill him on sight.

The following week the newspaper corrected itself about describing the shooting as justified.

---

[117] 1850 Census of Williamson Co., Illinois; and the 1860 Census of Williamson Co., Illinois. Terry was the son of Jasper U. Crain and Marshall was the son of William B. Crain.

[118] Lind 1:88; quoting the April 26, 1877, edition of the *Marion Monitor*

[119] 1887. *History of Gallatin, Saline, Hamilton, Franklin and Williamson Counties, Illinois.* Chicago: Goodspeed Publishing Company. 486.

... justified is an error as Russell did the shooting while Stocks was begging for mercy and unarmed.[120]

Stocks' widow was the former Sophonia E. Russell, the daughter of James Stewart Russell, the uncle to the shooter John Russell.[121] Thus Stocks was the husband of Russell's first cousin. Besides the family relationship they apparently were neighbors as Stocks' household and Russell's mother's household appeared one after another in the 1870 census.

The horrors of the Vendetta seemed to be hovering over the county as the authorities swept into action, still remembering the painful lessons of the past. Immediately Sheriff Duncan brought together a posse of 14 men from Marion and added to it as he passed through Crainville and Carterville to search for Russell. In a matter of days rewards had been posted totaling $1,000 for his arrest; $200 by the governor, $400 by the county board and $400 by Stocks' family.

Meanwhile residents called for calm and support for the criminal justice system. Even Stocks' lodge took the step of going public with a plea against any vigilantism.

We will never under any circumstance express an opinion of a crime, yet will at all times assist the law in its course and condemn any unlawful action.[122]

By June though with Russell still at large, the remaining members of Stocks' family went into hiding apparently as the census enumerator didn't list them on June 9, 1880, when he counted heads in the area west of Carterville where they should have been found. The other Stocks family, however, were found.[123]

---

[120] Lind. 2:73; quoting the May 13, 1880, issues of the *Egyptian Press* and the *Marion Monitor*, both of Marion, Illinois, as well as the May 20 issue of the *Egyptian Press*.

[121] The Illinois Statewide Marriage Index, 1673 – 1900, shows Henry and Sophonia marrying in Williamson County on Feb. 1, 1851. She appears in James S. Russell's household in the 1850 census.

[122] Lind. 2:73; quoting the May 20, 1880, issues of the *Marion Monitor*.

[123] 1880 Census of Williamson Co., Illinois.

As the summer progressed without any success at bringing Russell to justice the fears of a Vendetta-like reprise began to find evidence in a series of attacks. In late July, the victim's son attacked the home of Russell's brother-in-law Madison Bolin.

> On Thursday, July 22, Wes Stocks, son of Henry Stocks, who was killed by John Russell, went to the home of Mat Bolin, one mile west of Carterville and shot at him and his house…

Stocks missed hitting his target, but his last shot grazed his cousin Harriet (Russell) Bolin's "head and took away some of her hair." Following the incident Wes went into hiding.[124] Nine days later his brothers Albert and John Stocks took off on their own offensive in order to either garner information on Russell's whereabouts or to try to flush him out with attacks on others.

> In another incident on the 31st, Albert and John Stocks, brothers, met Webb Lewis and threatened his life near the scene of the other affair. The Stocks boys are in a desperate state of mind since their father's death.[125]

The census that summer showed Webb Lewis living in the household of the widow Rebecca Russell, the mother of Harriet, Thomas and John. He was working on Rebecca's farm. Their household was just three away from Bolin's. He was 26 that year.

Finally in September authorities arrested Russell 15 miles northeast of Waterloo, Illinois. A. J. Miller captured him while he was working with a threshing machine.[126] Brought back to Marion, he faced trial, but won an acquittal from the jury and freed.[127]

---

[124] Wes is a nickname rather than a given name if he's Henry's son. He's either Walter or Marion Stocks.

[125] Lind 2: 85; quoting the Aug. 5, 1880, issues of the *Egyptian Press.*

[126] Lind 2: 90; quoting the Sept. 16, 1880, issue of the *Marion Monitor.*

[127] *History of Gallatin, Saline, Hamilton, Franklin and Williamson Counties, Illinois* 486.

Three years after John Russell faced down the prosecutor in court, his brother's partner and co-defendant in the David Bulliner murder case reappeared on the scene in January 1883.

> Sam Pleasant, connected with the vendetta, who fled the county with Tom Russell six or seven years ago, surrendered to authorities in Murphysboro. We believe he stands indicted for complicity in the murder of Dave Bulliner[128]

Three months later Pleasant walked out of the Jackson County Jail on a $1,000 bond.[129] The following January 17, 1884, Thomas Russell returned to Southern Illinois.

> Tom Russell who killed George Bulliner on the Marion Road near Carbondale on the night of December 12, 1873, and has been a fugitive since then, gave himself up last week to Jackson County authorities.[130]

In April a Jackson County jury found him guilty and sentenced him to 50 years in the state penitentiary. A newspaper at the time headlined the story appropriately as "The Williamson County Vendetta — Closing Scene in the Bloody Drama." Though Russell had been indicted for George Bulliner's murder in March 1878, the state couldn't prove it. However, the jury did believe enough proof existed to find him guilty for the murders of David Bulliner and Vincent Hinchcliff.[131]

With his conviction Russell became the last major defendant to be tried. The area newspapers reported the conviction scorecard.

---

[128] Lind 3:34; quoting the Jan. 11, 1883 issue of the *Egyptian Press*.

[129] Lind 3:44; quoting the Aug. 19, 1880, issue of the *Marion Monitor*.

[130] Lind 3:53; quoting the Jan. 24, 1884 issue of the *Marion Monitor*.

[131] Lind 3:58; quoting the April 10 and April 17, 1884, issues of the *Marion Monitor*.

John Bulliner and Allen Baker for the murder of George Sisney. Both received 25 years, John was pardoned July 4, 1882. Allen remained in Joliet Prison.[132]

Marshall T. Crain for the murder of William Spence, he also confessed to the murder of George Sisney. He was hanged January 21, 1876.

Big Jep and Black Bill Crain, both sentenced in February 1876 to 25 years in Joliet Prison for the murder of William Spence.

Samuel Musick confessed to his part in the murder of William Spence and in April 1876 he was sentenced to 14 years at Joliet Prison.

James Norris was convicted of the murder of James Henderson in April 1876. He was sentenced to 17 years at Joliet Prison. It was after found he was probably not guilty and he was pardoned on July 4, 1882.

Other than Russell's murder of Stocks, only two other killings occurred in Williamson County between the end of the Vendetta in 1876 and 11 years later in 1887 when a new multi-county history was published. The lack of widespread deadly violence noted a commentary by the editor of that volume.

Williamson County has a long record of crimes committed therein, but since the days of the "Vendetta," a general peace has been resorted, and at present writing the surviving members of the families connected with that affair are all on friendly terms. The spirit of revenge has been subdued, and past offenses forgiven. The people have suffered much on account of the bad men who happened to be among them. Without doubt there was a time when justice was not fairly administered. The pleas of alibi, and self-defense, have no doubt cleared criminals who ought to have been severely punished. This seems evident from the fact that when the State began to

---

[132] During July 1877, Joliet authorities discovered a plot by inmates to escape out of the penitentiary. Baker and William Davis of Jackson County were among the ringleaders. *Source*: Lind 1:97; quoting the July 19, 1877, edition of the *Marion Monitor*. This is probably why the governor didn't pardon him.

prosecute with vigor, through the instrumentality of such attorneys as Hartwell, Allen and Duff, and the people determined to bring criminals to justice, the commission of crime suddenly ceased in a very great measure.

It is true three homicides have taken place since that time, but with a few exceptions Williamson County has always been a safe place for those who were not disposed to be quarrelsome. The good people of the county have been slandered and vilified by the papers far and near, on account of their misfortunes. But the dark cloud has passed away, and the light of a brighter day is shining, and a good feeling among the people everywhere prevails. Williamson is as safe a county in which to live as any other county in the United States.[133]

A year after the publication of the new county history, Russell petitioned the governor for a pardon. Despite widespread support Gov. Richard J. Oglesby refused.

I partially examined this case when it was first filed in September 1888; a more careful re-examination of the case to-day [Nov. 26, 1888] satisfies me that it would not be proper, certainly at this time, to pardon or commute the sentence of the said Russell. The evidence, a synopsis of which is before me, together with a statement of the facts by the State's Attorney who prosecuted the case; a careful examination of the evidence, as shown from these two sources, I feel would not justify me in coming to the conclusion that said Russell was innocent of the crime charged in the indictment. There certainly is evidence enough to justify the finding of the jury in the case; although it is what is termed circumstantial evidence, the jury were perhaps justified in the verdict they rendered. Nine of the jurymen join in the petition for pardon, six of that number, however, subsequently join in a protest against executive clemency and that they are satisfied that Russell was guilty of the crime as found in the verdict of the jury, and that they signed said petition under a misapprehension or misstatement. The Judge who tried the case

[133] 1887. *History of Gallatin, Saline, Hamilton, Franklin and Williamson Counties, Illinois.* Chicago: Goodspeed Publishing Company. 486-487.

recommends that the sentence be commuted. He states, however, that he does not remember the testimony, and regards it in the light of an offense or crime committed as the result, not so much of personal malice as of a feud or vendetta.

It is true the petition is very largely signed by responsible persons and prominent citizens have written letters urging pardon in the case. The man, Thomas J. Russell, asks in his petition for pardon and promises to live an exemplary life hereafter. His reputation seems to have been good prior to the commission of the crime; his conduct as a prisoner in the penitentiary has in all respects been exemplary; still Russell in his petition does not frankly deny his guilt. He states; "He is not guilty of the crime charged." The tone of his petition and specifications do not leave the impression on my mind that he is free from guilt of the crime for which he was sentenced to the penitentiary. It may be he did not fire the fatal shot; it may be he was not present at the time. The jury, however, believed that he did fire the shot and was present at the time with another person who committed the crime, and as I have before stated, and again repeat, there appears to be evidence enough to sustain the finding of the jury. If said Russell was entirely free from connection with said crime he ought to state so frankly; if not entirely free connection with said crime, I think he ought also to state the fact as frankly, and then ask for clemency on the ground and argument he and others, even the Judge uses, that it was the result of a feud or vendetta, and not an ordinary case of murder.

Without going into the case at any great length, for I have not time to do so, I feel that I would not be justified in exercising the pardoning power in his behalf. It seems to me it would be premature to consider the question of commutation at this time. He was sentenced for 50 years; he has not yet been in prison five. In declining to commute the sentence in his case I do not wish my act to be considered as obliging any one to take the same view of the subject I do, nor to cause embarrassment to the petitioner on account of the exercise of the executive power. I simply feel obliged to pass upon the case, and for that reason have expressed the views above. Pardon and commutation are, therefore, refused.[134]

Three years later Russell tried again, this time with a new governor, Joseph W. Fifer.

> ...I have examined with great care the most important part of the evidence on which Russell was convicted. I have also carefully and patiently examined all the other papers filed in the case. The impression made upon my mind is that there is doubt as to the guilt of Russell. His previous reputation had been good and his conduct since his confinement in the penitentiary has been exemplary. The pardon is asked for the by the judge who presided at the trial, by the Hon. George Smith, member of Congress from that district, who prosecuted the case, by a majority of the jurymen who convicted the defendant, by all, or nearly all, of the county officers and by hundreds of the very best citizens of the community where the crime was committed.
>
> In view of the foregoing facts I shall not grant a pardon as asked for but will commute the sentence of the petitioner to a term of 12 years, the Secretary of State will make out the papers accordingly.

It's not clear what happened next. Even with the commutation Russell would have still faced five more years on his shortened term, yet possibly for time served with good behavior, he returned to his family three months later during the first week of July 1891. His visit to Marion the following Monday allowed the local newspaper to once again look back at the Vendetta that had ended 15 years earlier.

> Thos. Russell, one of the first arrested under a complaint as being connected with the unfortunate troubles originating in this county in 1873 between the Sisney, Bulliner and Russell families, returned home last week and was here Monday last. He was sentenced from Jackson County to 50 years, but has been reprieved.

---

[134] R. J. Oglesby. Nov. 26, 1888. "In the case of Thomas J. Russell." Thomas J. Russell File. Executive Clemency Files, 1874-1911. Illinois State Archives.

Somewhat surprisingly the newspaper provided another postscript to the Vendetta as to what had happened to those who had been imprisoned for their part in the killings.

> Not one of those on either side of the affair is now in prison and be it said to their credit, those who have returned are good citizens.
> The curtain has long since been rung down on the last sad act of the scene since which another generation has almost come upon the stage.[135]

---

[135] Lind 4:68; quoting July 16, 1891. (Marion, Ill.) *The Leader.*

Chapter 18. **Aiken Gang's Last Ride**

IN BOTH ERWIN'S ACCOUNTS of the Vendetta and his county's criminal history as well as contemporary newspapers in their stories concerning the Klan, writers frequently referenced the Aiken Gang of outlaws. Led by George Aiken who lived in the northwestern corner of Williamson County, they often based their operations at the edge of the various counties and away from the seats of power. Thus relatively few details have emerged even though Erwin blamed them for dozens of attacks.

George Aiken served as the postmaster of Blairsville, the town often mentioned as the site of various murders in the 1860s and 70s. His first entry into history came in 1862 following the formation of the 128th Illinois Infantry regiment, a unit comprised mostly of Democrats, seeking to prove their loyalty to the rest of the state. Of the officers involved it might have helped their cause if they hadn't included Aiken in the bunch. Later he tried to turn over the keys to the city of Cairo to the Confederate army.

> While at Cairo, George Aikin, the Quartermaster of this regiment, went over to Jeff. Thompson's army, and proposed to assist them in capturing Cairo. He agreed that this regiment should all understand it, and not fire on them. He made two trips for this purpose, and had a gentleman with him one time. The last trip, a lieutenant from Thompson's army came with him to view the situation. The intention was for Aikin and his confederate to post all the soldiers, and for Thompson to send soldiers over and capture the city.
>
> Aiken commenced his insidious work of informing the boys of his plot. About the first man he told it to was Dr. J. Clemison. Clemison went immediately and told Colonel Hundley all about the infamous plot, and Hundley indignantly vetoed the whole thing. This regiment was composed of as good material as any in the service, but they were badly treated. The Chaplain said:
>
> "That there were men in this regiment that would have turned their guns against the Government I have no doubt, but the majority

of them would have made as good soldiers as lived, under favorable circumstances."[136]

The 128th mustered into federal service on November 4, 1862, with 860 men. In five months the regiment lost nearly 700 men almost entirely to desertion. Almost five months later by order of the Secretary of War, the Army disbanded the regiment discharging on April 4, the officers, including Aiken, not for his treason, but for their "utter want of discipline" in allowing the regiment to drop to just 161 men. The few remaining men, including two lieutenants and an assistant surgeon were transferred to another Illinois regiment.

Aiken and the disgraced officers returned home that spring where they found a company of the 35th Iowa Infantry stationed in the county. "They were paroled prisoners off military duty, said to be, and were sent here to assist the enrolling officer," Erwin recalled, "but the county was not enrolled."

In July federal troops again occupied the county as the Third Battalion of the 16th Illinois Cavalry under the command of newly minted Maj. Charles H. Biers encamped at the old fairgrounds at Marion, which were then included the ground now bounded by West Main Street on the north, South Russell Street on the west, Cherry Street on the south and Bentley Street on the east.

> He was sent here to arrest deserters, suppress sedition, and enroll the county. He put the town under martial law, with Capt. Wilcot as Provost-Marshal, who stationed guards on all the principal streets.

The occupation dragged into August until the county commissioners either in an act of spite, stupidity, or evidence of their corruption, named George Aiken to the grand jury.

> At the August Term, 1863, of the Circuit Court, George Aikin, then foreman of the Grand jury, swore before that body that Biers and some of his men came to his house in the day-time, took him out

---

[136] Erwin 278-279. The chaplain quoted was Archibald T. Benson.

and whipped him, and then tied his hands behind him to a long pole, and then left him in a grove of thick saplings. Upon this evidence Biers was indicted, and a bench warrant issued for his arrest, and placed in the hands of Sheriff Spencer, who executed it by his deputy, Alex. Manier, without any resistance.

But Biers' men soon heard of his arrest, and they formed on the Square, and told the Sheriff that he must release Biers. Spencer said he could not do that, as he had a warrant, but that he could not fight a regiment. Biers then walked out. The soldiers had just started to leave the county, when the Grand jury adjourned. Biers arrested Aikin, who, when he started off, halloed out to the people, "Now you see where your liberty has gone to."

They took him to Springfield, where he remained about a month, then came home and got a good start, and ran away.

Erwin obviously didn't like Aiken and certainly didn't believe his story.

He was a very mean man. I have elsewhere spoken of the "Aikin gang," of which he was the leader. Aikin might have got whipped, but that United States soldiers did it is preposterous. [137]

It's during this time that the murdering and horse-thieving by the gang got out of hand, especially after Aiken's return sometime within the following year. Erwin didn't provide any details to this criminal activity, but James Goddard's obituary in 1878 recalled his robbery of $800, most of it in gold, by Aiken's son John and two other accomplices 15 years earlier.[138]

Still, the best account of the gang dealt with a murder not in Williamson County, but in White County, two counties to the east during the last week of winter in 1864. It didn't involve the senior Aiken, but one of his sons and other members of the gang.

---

[137] Erwin 281-282.

[138] Lind 1:118; quoting the Jan. 17, 1878, edition of the *Marion Monitor*. Goddard was born on Nov. 12, 1789, in Henry Co., Virginia, and would have been around 74 or 75 years of age during the robbery.

March 19, 1864, Augustus Stewart was a farmer in easy circumstances, living near the southern line of White County, about three miles west of the town of New Haven, in Gallatin County. His family consisted of himself and wife, his daughters Barbary, aged seventeen; Louisa, aged fifteen; Sarah, aged thirteen, and Phoebe, aged eleven; a boy named Edward Pratt, aged about sixteen years, who was working for him at the time, and a boy named Albert Raglin, about eight years of age, who was sick.

About an hour before sundown, on the day above mentioned (it was Saturday), a man riding a small black pony came to the house of Stewart, pretended to be a traveler, and desired to stay all night. Mr. Stewart, with his accustomed hospitality, put up the stranger's horse, and welcomed him to his house. The family ate supper about seven o'clock, after which they gathered around the fire in the sitting room, which was the south room of the house. While thus sitting, a little before eight o'clock, the stranger went out of the house, was absent ten or fifteen minutes, returned, and taking a book, sat down and appeared to be engaged in reading. In a few moments the family heard the sound of persons running from the front gate into the porch, and instantly the door of the room was thrown open, and two men (one larger than the other), with faces blackened, coats turned wrong side out, each presenting a revolver, rushed in, shouting in a loud voice, "Surrender!" Stewart, who was sitting in front of the room, was startled at the strange appearance. He turned his face toward the intruders, raised himself to his feet, and stood facing the assassins. The two disguised men rushed toward him, and the larger man, who was a little in advance of the other, placing his pistol against the breast of Stewart, fired. His clothes took fire, and the murdered man fell, with his feet toward the fire place, and his head in the door leading from the south room into the hall, from which point, amid the agonizing screams of his wife and children, he crawled through the hall out to the back porch, where he lay until carried in by the family after the murderers left. At this instant the smaller assassin turned upon the screaming family and the traveler who came to stay all night and who pretended to be greatly frightened, and with his pistol presented, huddled them in one corner of the room, threatening to kill any of them who should make any outcry, or interfere with the robbery they came to accomplish.

The large man then demanded of Mrs. Stewart the money that was in the house, saying he knew there was money, and for that they had come, and if she did not at once give up the last cent there was in the house he would serve all the family as he had served him (pointing to Stewart), at the same time taking some fire from the fire-place, he attempted to throw it on the body, but was prevent by one of the daughters. Mrs. Stewart replied that they had no money. One of the daughters told their mother there was some money in the house; the mother said she would speak to her husband about it, which she did, going out to the porch guarded by the larger man. Her husband was dying from the effects of the wound, and also suffering from his burning clothes. He told her to give up the money. She returned, and with the large man, whose pistol was constantly presented at her head, went into the north room and got the money, some $430, and gave it up.

Mrs. Stewart said to the robbers, "You are not Negroes, but white men blackened." The large man replied, "We know that, and I know you, too, d--n you." The large man then took a black coat of Stewart's, three or four pairs of socks and a bed-blanket. The traveler went into a small room in the porch and got Stewart's double-barreled shotgun, when they all three left the house. A few moments afterward the traveler came back to the door, and apparently in great alarm exclaimed: "Are they gone? My God, we'll all be murdered before morning!" and then disappeared. In a moment or two the family heard a great commotion at the barn; their horses and mules were running around the barnyard as though greatly frightened. All of the stock had been put up in the stable before dark.

While the men were in the house Stewart called to his family to come and put out the fire in his clothing, which was burning his flesh. Some of the children pleaded for permission to go to their dying father, but the blackened demons sternly refused, threatening to shoot the first one who should attempt to leave the room. At length the children asked if the traveler (whom at this time did not suspect) might not go to their father. Consent being obtained, he went out and extinguished the burning clothes of Stewart.

Edward Pratt immediately ran to the neighbors and gave the alarm. In a few moments Viol Saulsberry and Jonathan B. Dagley came to the house, and Stewart, who had been brought by his family into the south room and laid upon the floor where he was shot, died in about five minutes after they came. As Saulsberry was approaching the house he heard the noise of horses rapidly running about one-half mile to the west of the county road, and also found Stewart's horses and mules loose in the barn-yard in great commotion.

The next morning (Sunday, March 20), as soon as it was light, the neighbors, who had gathered at Stewart's during the night, began to examine the premises to see what traces of the ruffians could be found. They found where the lock on the barn door had been broken, and a saddle of Stewart's of a peculiar make had been taken out of the barn and carried away, while the one that had been brought to Stewart's house the night before on the black pony remained. This pony had been led out of the stable, across the barn-yard, and out of the gate, making distinct tracks which, from his size and appearance, were plainly distinguishable from any of Stewart's animals. These were carefully measured by Saulsberry and Dagley. The pony was traced across the road into a piece of open wood lying west of Stewarts house. Some sixty yards west of the gate they found signs of the two others horses having been hitched, one to an old wagon and the other to a sapling; these three tracks then left off together in a southwesterly direction through the wood about a fourth of a mile, when they entered the county road and turned eastward they were easily tracked to Eldorado in Saline County, some 25 miles west of Stewart's, when those in pursuit lost all trace of them at the time.

On the afternoon of the murder, about an hour before sundown, Viol Spaulding met these men on the county road, about one and a half miles west of Stewart's. There were one large man and two small men walking eastward and leading their horses. One of them had on a soldier's blue overcoat; one of the horses was a small black pony; the other two were sorrel or bay mares. Just as he passed them he heard one of the men say, "I know that man." A little farther west and few moments before Eldorado, Elbert M. Smith met three men and horses answering the description given by Saulsberry.

With this clue, those in pursuit of the murderers followed westward, and found that the three men had taken dinner and fed their horses at the house of Mrs. Minerva Randolph, who lived six miles west of Stewart's, about 1 o'clock on Saturday; that the same party had called for dinner about noon of the same day at Moses Kinsall's, who lived about a mile south of Mrs. Randolph's, and been refused.

The pursing party then went to the house of Burrell Bramlett, who lived southwest of Eldorado in Saline County, and learned that this same party had stayed there on Friday night, March 18, and obtained a better and fuller description of the men and horses. Shortly after this they proceeded to Blairsville, Williamson County, the home at that time of the defendant and the two Glides (suspicion had fallen upon these three). At Blairsville they found in the lot of George W. Aiken, father of the defendant, a small black pony, whose feet were measured and found to correspond exactly with the tracks found at Stewart's. The pony was also positively identified by Bramlett as the one which had been at his house on the night preceding the murder. Bramlett also found in the stable of Mr. Aiken the sorrel mare with the peculiar white feet, and identified her as being the one at his house on Friday night. The two Glides were tracked to their father's house in Blairsville; but while the pursuers were gone to a magistrate for a writ, they escaped and were never heard of afterward.

A week or two after this, George W. Aiken and the father and mother of the Glides were arrested for assisting in the escape of the murderers, and brought to White county; the black pony was also brought along by its owner, Willis Mulkey, a young man who was at that time living with Mr. Aiken. The pony's feet were again measured by those who had measured the tracks, and positively identified by those that had seen it at Stewart's; and young Mulkey at this time picked out of some forty or fifty others the saddle that was upon his pony when it left Blairsville the Thursday before the murder.

A reward having been offered for the murderer of Stewart, the prisoner, John Aiken, after remaining concealed a week or two near this home in Blairsville, was arrested near DeSoto, and persons from White County went there and received him. They arrived at the house of the Stewarts on Wednesday evening, April 13, 1864, nearly a month after the crime was perpetrated. At this time the prisoner was seen by Mr. Bramlett, Moses Kinsall, Mrs. Randolph, Saulsbury and Smith, and recognized as one of the men that stayed all night on Friday at Bramlett's; that called for dinner at Moses Kinsall's, six miles west of Stewart's, on the day of the murder; that took dinner at Mrs. Randolph's; that was general appearance, size and build, corresponded with the large man of the three, in the opinion of the persons in the house when the murder was committed.

Aiken, in conversation with various parties while at Stewart's, detailed with great particularity the events that happened in the house the night of the murder, giving the conversation of Mrs. Stewart and himself about looking for the money, and other things, all of which was known to those present on the night in question to be true, even to minute circumstances and incidental remarks.

On Friday, after Aiken was brought back on Wednesday, while standing out in the road with his guards, he was asked by one of the by-standers, "You were blacked when here before, were you not?" Aiken replied, "Yes," and said he could show them the place, and pointing down into the woods said, "It was right down there by that big log." One of the men who heard him went to the place indicated, and just beyond the log, in the edge of a paw-paw thicket, found the remains of a fire, of which no one had heard up to this point.

Willis Mulkey, the owner of the black pony, was at this time boarding at the house of George W. Aiken, attending school. On Wednesday, March 16, the latter told Mulkey that the boys were going to Franklin County to buy cattle, and asked if they could have his pony to ride. Mulkey replied that if Hal Glide (the smaller of the three) would ride it, they could. The next morning Mulkey saw the horses saddled, and the three men around the premises of Mr. Aiken preparing to leave, and went himself and examined the saddle upon his pony to see if it would hurt him; then left for school. On Sunday evening, March 20, about an hour before sundown, Mulkey, who was out in the barnyard, saw Charlie Glide come riding around through the field to the barn lot, making his horse jump the bars into the lot. He had a double-barreled shotgun in his hands, and his horse seemed nearly exhausted with hard riding. Mulkey asked where the other boys were, and Glide replied that he pony had given out; they were back some distance, but would be in shortly. Between sundown and dark Mulkey saw the prisoner and Hal glide coming into town from the east. The horses seemed fagged out, and Mulkey went to his own pony, took off the saddle and threw it over into the yard of George W. Aiken, after which he never saw it again.

Timothy Clark, aged about sixteen, was living with George W. Aiken, taking care of his stock. His story in regard to the two Glides and John Aiken going away with the horses, ostensibly to buy cattle, corroborated the statement of Mulkey. On the Monday following Clark saw John Aiken with a roll of money in his hand, and said to him, "John, how is it that you always have money and work so little? There must have been a fire somewhere." John laughed and said he had been to a fire. Some others in Blairsville saw the same men during their expedition.

The next day after John Aiken was brought to the house of the Stewarts, he held a conversation with Viol Spaulding, in which he confessed to being a participant in the deadly affray, but stoutly denied being the one that fired the shot at Stewart; told Spaulding about meeting him the night of the murder, and admitted that he was the man that remarked to his companion, "I know that man."

The witnesses having arrived about noon, the prisoner was taken to the barn before two magistrats for trial. The charge was stated to him, and he was asked by the justice if he was ready for trial. He answered that he was, but he would like to talk some if he could have the privilege. The court granted his request, and he made a public confession of the whole matter, but did not admit that he did the shooting; after which, that same evening, he was taken to New Haven, where Thomas S. Hick took down his confession at length, including not only the murder of Stewart, but many other robberies and crimes that no one in that vicinity had ever heard of.

At the August term, 1864, of the White county Circuit Court, the prisoner, together with the two Glides, was indicted but the same fall [of 1864] the prisoner [John Aiken] broke out of jail and made his escape… [and] could not be found.

It wasn't until after the Vendetta had ended and Sheriff Mason broke the back of the Klan in Franklin County did justice return for the friends of Stewart in the summer of 1877.

Thirteen long years had passed away, the wife of the murdered man had gone to her grave, the children scattered, and the awful crime had almost faded from the memory of the public mind amid the ever-changing scenes and busy strife of the world. There were those, however, among the neighbors and friends of Augustus Stewart, who saw this weltering corpse as it lay upon his own hearthstone, who could neither forget nor forgive the murder of their friend, but believed that in God's own good time justice would be done. It is due to the exertions of these men, and the vigilance and courage of Thomas I. Porter, Sheriff of this county, that John Aiken was recaptured.

In June 1877, Sheriff Porter, having satisfied himself that the defendant was in the southern part of Colorado, procured a requisition upon the Governor of that State, and, entirely alone, started upon his desperate mission of meeting and bringing out of the wilds of the Rocky Mountains a man known to be a desperado, and supposed to be surrounded by men of the same character.

He reached Denver June 28, and procuring the necessary papers from the authorities of Colorado, started for Cannon City, the county seat of Fremont County, where he arrived the next day. At this place he learned from the sheriff of the county that Aiken lived about 25 miles southeast, in a place called Babcock's Hole, up among the Rocky Mountains; and to effect his capture the greatest caution and vigilance would be required, as he was considered a dangerous man, and should he have warning of his attempted captured he could not be taken without a desperate struggle. Porter thought it better, therefore, to make the attempt at night. Taking with him two men furnished by the sheriff, he left Cannon City about three o'clock in the afternoon in a spring wagon, and reached Greenwood (a country store and post office three miles from Aiken's residence) about dark, when they put up their team and ate supper. Here they learned that Aiken was at home, but that it would be exceedingly difficult for persons unacquainted with the trail up the mountains to reach his ranch. Taking Morgan, the keeper of the store, as a guide, they started on foot up the Cannon about ten o'clock at night. When within a mile of Aiken's house, the guide refused to go farther, and the party were compelled to rely upon themselves. Learning that Aiken had a large family, Porter decided that it would be better, if possible, to get him away from his house before making the arrest, thereby avoiding the risk of hurting other members of the family.[139]

It was therefore agreed that they should represent themselves as a party from Chicago who, in looking around the country, had become lost, and desired to be piloted out of Greenwood. Going up close to the house, which was a low double-log cabin. Porter called until Aiken came to the door and inquired what he was wanting. Porter told the story that had been agreed upon, and proposed paying him $5 if he would go with them to Greenwood. To this he agreed. He dressed himself, came to the door, and looking at the men outside for a moment, went back into the house (to arm himself the party supposed), came out, and walking beside Porter with the two men in the rear, started down the mountain path, guided by the uncertain light of the moon, which was just breaking over the huge mountains and down into the dark valley. The defendant strode bravely on, little thinking that the iron grasp of the law was quietly but surely closing around him from which he should never more escape. Long had he evaded the punishment due to his crime. Many times since his escape from prison had he doubled on his track, until that amid the solitudes of these great mountains he undoubtedly felt secure. But a moment more and the delusion of safety which he had so long hugged to his bosom would vanish.

When the party had gone about a mile from the house and reached an open glade where the moonlight shone full upon them, according to prearranged program, one of the assistants walking

---

[139] A *Denver News* report reprinted in the *Marion Monitor* of July 19, 1877, noted that Aiken had been living in Custer County for some years where he had "75 to 100 head of cattle and a family of nine children." *Source:* Lind 1:96.

behind suddenly, in a deep, stern voice, cried "Halt!" The prisoner turned to see what it meant, and at the same instant Porter, presenting his gun to his head, ordered him to throw up his hands, which he did, and the shackles were put upon him and he was informed that he was arrested for murder. As he stood there so near his mountain home, yet so powerless, chained, and guarded by a power irresistible, with the sudden announcement that his crime had at least overtaken him, no wonder that he trembled. As his troubled conscience brought before his eyes the form of his murdered victim, and from whose accusing spirit he had been fleeing so many years, he could exclaim with Eliphaz the Temanite:

> "Fear came upon me, and trembling, which
>   made all my bones to shake.
> "Then a spirit passed before my face; the hair
>   of my head stood up:
> "It stood still, but I could not discern the form
>   thereof; an image was before mine eyes;
>   there was silence."[140]

After sending one of the men back to inform Aiken's family of his arrest and procure a change of clothing for him, the party proceeded to Greenwood, and leaving there the same night arrived at Cannon City about six o'clock Sunday morning, July 1, where Aiken was put in jail until Monday morning, when Sheriff Porter started with him for Illinois.

Without any assistance, chained to his prisoner, sitting by his side during the day, and sleeping at night with the same shackles around his own arm that fastened the defendant to him, this brave officer safely brought his prisoner a distance of 1,500 miles and placed him in the Carmi jail, from which he had escaped so many years before. The prisoner at all times denied his identity, refusing to recognize men with whom he had been acquainted for years, and while admitting that his name was John Aiken, denied that he was the man that had formerly been arrested for the murder of Stewart,

---

[140] The verses are from the Bible, specifically Job 4:14-16 (King James Version).

until several weeks after he had been placed in jail his sister-in-law visited him, and seeing that it was impossible longer to deny it, admitted his identity.

At the November term, 1877, of the White County Circuit Court, the prisoner [John Aiken] obtained a change of venue to Gallatin County, was tried in the court of that county the December following, found guilty and adjudged to suffer the penalty of death. The court, learning that the jury decided the case by lot, set aside their verdict and ordered a new trial. The case was accordingly thoroughly investigated at the next term of court, and the accused was sentenced to imprisonment for life, and he is now at Joliet, Ill., toiling his weary hours away.[141]

When the county history of Gallatin County was being written in 1887, the Aiken murder trial remained a hot topic as it recalled the scandal of the verdicts and described Sheriff Porter as "one of the quietest and most courageous of men." Here's what it recalled of the verdicts:

A change of venue was taken to Gallatin County, where the trial took place before the following jury: John B. Walters, John H. Crow, William Willis, Jasper Bowling, Thomas Frohock, Albert Hill, A. M. Hannah, James J. Williams, John M. Thomas, John Fitzgibbon, William R. Tate and John Wilde.

The verdict of the jury was as follows: "We, the jury, find the defendant guilty of murder and fix the punishment at death." A motion was made for a new trial, and on hearing of that motion it was developed that the jurors, before arriving at their verdict as recorded above, had all been in favor of finding him guilty of murder, but one of them was opposed to the infliction of the death

---

[141] 1883. *History of White County, Illinois.* Chicago: Inter-State Publishing Company 366-375. As Aiken had confessed to the crime a decade earlier before escaping to Colorado, there was little question to his guilt, especially since two of Stewart's children and a hired hand who witnessed the shooting still lived in the area to testify. *Source:* Lind 1:96; quoting the July 19, 1877, edition of the *Marion Monitor,* which in turn had reprinted a story from the *Denver News.*

penalty.[142] As this one would not yield his opposition to this penalty, it was arranged that two members of the jury, the one opposed to hanging and another, unwilling to agree to anything else, should draw straws for the verdict, the long straw to win. The result of the drawing was that the juror unalterably in favor of hanging drew the long straw, and hence the fixing by the jury of the death penalty. Upon the development of this fact, a new trial was granted, and the jury which had adopted the novel methods recounted above of arriving at a verdict were punished as follows: the four engaged in the drawing of the straws, the one who procured them, the one who held them and the two who drew them were fined, three of them being fined $100 each, one of them $50 and the remainder of the jury were acquitted.

Upon the second trial the following were the jury: John Eskew, Samuel Simpkins, Thomas Martin, Richard Sweeney, Edward Young, Moses McDonald, James A. Jones, William Clayton, George B. Stilly, Price Williams, Charles Mock and Thomas McKee. They brought in a verdict of guilty of murder and fixed the punishment at imprisonment in the penitentiary at hard labor for life.

As of 1887, Aiken's accomplices of Henry and Charles Glide still had not been apprehended.[143] Overall, the trial cost White County between $2,500 and $5,000, according to the newspaper estimates. Fourteen years after the murder John Aiken left Carmi for the last time on his trip from the county jail to the state penitentiary.[144]

---

[142] Lind 1:136; quoting the March 28, 1878, edition of the *Marion Monitor* which reported the first jury's first ballot was one for hanging, 10 for life and one for clearing him.

[143] Jon Musgrave. 2003. *Handbook of Old Gallatin County and Southeastern Illinois.* Marion, Ill.: IllinoisHistory.com. 42-43; quoting 1887. *History of Gallatin, Saline, Hamilton, Franklin and Williamson Counties, Illinois.* Chicago: Goodspeed Publishing Co.

[144] Lind 1:136; quoting the March 28, 1878, edition of the *Marion Monitor.*

Chapter 19. **Jennings Gang**

OF ALL THE TWISTS AND TURNS of those involved in the Vendetta, the character and family of State's Attorney Jennings certainly stands out. Erwin made it clear what he thought of the man who absconded with public funds.

> He was very popular, and the secret of it was his manners, saying and opinions. He was a professional doctor, lawyer, preacher, fiddler, horn blower and a libertine. When he made music on the square, a crowd would swell around him. When he preached, they all went to hear him, from the talented aristocracy down to the boot-black. He was a rowdy among the rowdies, pious among the pious, Godless among the Godless, and a spooney among the women.
>
> He would get up in a sermon and rattle away until the shrouds and lanyards of conscience must have fairly quacked under the strain, and then go, get on a drunk. He was a clerical blackguard, whose groveling passions assumed full sway at all times. Lost to every Christian restraint, degraded in his tastes, villainous in his nature, corrupt in his principles, how wretched was such an apology for a State's Attorney!

In later years both Jennings and his sons remained familiar with the ins and outs of the criminal justice system while active practitioners of the law as attorneys and judges, but also as frequent breakers of the law. Topping it all off, one of Jennings' outlaw sons eventually ended up in Hollywood acting and consulting for the film industry's early westerns.

John D. F. Jennings, Sr., the man who served as the people's prosecutor during the Vendetta claimed Virginia as his state of nativity, Tazewell County to be exact according to one sketch with known inaccuracies.[145] Census records do back up that sketch's statement of April 23, 1830 as his

---

[145] 1901. *Portrait and Biographical Record of Oklahoma.* Chicago: Chapman Publishing Co. 1059. According to one of his descendents, Lorena Curtis, his full name was John De La Forrest Jennings. *Source:* E-mail to the author July 13, 2006.

birth date. That 1901 account provides his parents' names as William R. and Mary (Chapin) Jennings.[146]

In 1853 he married Mary Scates, a woman whose middle name is sometimes given as R. and sometimes as Elizabeth. By the mid 1850s after they had two children, one who died as an infant followed by a boy named William Zebulon, Jennings moved his young family to Greene County, Tennessee, on the western side of the Appalachian Mountains. John Jr. was born in Tennessee around 1856 and his brother Edgar, or Edward E., as it appeared in later years, came three years later. It was there in the area served by the Caney Branch post office that the enumerator found Jennings in 1860. At the time he worked as a physician and owned $500 worth of real estate and $100 in personal property.[147]

Jennings' youngest son, Alphonso, later claimed his father served as a Confederate officer under Robert E. Lee during the Civil War.[148] One sketch published during Jennings' lifetime claimed he had served in the 61st Tennessee Infantry and was captured at Vicksburg.[149] Another source claimed him a surgeon with the 41st Virginia Infantry.[150] Like many points of Jennings' history, none of the claims can be confirmed though there are a number of John Jennings who did served in Confederate units in Tennessee and Virginia. Still, census records do indicate that the family moved back to Virginia after the war began as another son Francis was born in Tennessee around 1861, and Al was born in Virginia in 1863.[151]

Although the census records suggest a move without drama, Al Jennings' semi-fictional autobiography provides a far more harrowing, if certainly less believable account.

---

146 *Portrait and Biographical Record of Oklahoma* 1059.

147 1860 Census of Greene Co., Tennessee.

148 Harry Sinclair Drago. 1998. *Outlaws on Horseback*. U. of Nebraska Press. 279.

149 *Portrait and Biographical Record of Oklahoma* 1059.

150 Beatrice M. Doughtie. 1961, reprinted 2001. *Documented Notes on Jennings and Allied Families*. Reprint privately published by Ann Blomquist of Orlando, Fla. 660. Doughtie's information on Jennings came from a biographical sketch of his son Al in the following book: Joseph B. Thoburn. 1916. *Standard History of Oklahoma*. Chicago and New York: The American Historical Society. 1682.

151 1870 Census of Williamson Co., Illinois.

A wilderness of snow — wind tearing like a ruffian through the white silence — the bleak pines setting up a sudden roar — a woman and four children hurrying through the waste.

And abruptly the woman stumbling exhausted against a little fence corner, and the four children screaming in terror at the strange new calamity that had overtaken them.

The woman was my mother — the four children, the oldest eight, the youngest two, were my brothers. I was born in that fence corner in the snow in Tazewell County, Virginia, November 25, 1863. My brothers ran wildly through the Big Basin of Burke's Gardens, crying for help. My mother lay there in a fainting collapse from her five days' flight from the Tennessee plantation.

The Union soldiers were swooping down on our plantation. My father, John Jennings, was a colonel in the Confederate army. He sent a courier warning my mother to leave everything, to take the children and to cross the border into Virginia. The old home would be fired by the rebel soldiers to prevent occupation by Union troops.

A few of the old negroes left with her. They were but an hour on the road. They looked back. The plantation was in flames. At the sight the frightened darkies fled. My mother and the four youngsters went on. Sixty miles they tramped, half running, half walking, and always beset with alarms. Frank was so little he had to be carried. Sometimes they were knee deep in slush, sometimes they were slipping in the mud. The raw wind cut to the bone. It was perhaps as terrible and as bitter a journey as a woman ever took.

I was born in a snow heap and reared in a barn. They picked my mother up and carried her in a rickety old cart to the mountains. Jack and Zeb, the two oldest, had sent their panicky clamor through the waste. A woodsman answered.

The loft of an old log cabin in the Blue Ridge Mountains was our home in those hungry years of the Civil War. We had nothing but poverty. There was never enough to eat. We heard no word from my father. Suddenly in 1865 he returned and we moved to Mariontown, Illinois.[152]

In another version Jennings claimed he was born in an abandoned schoolhouse as a battle raged outside. Nonetheless, Al's reference to Tazewell Co., Virginia, is backed up from county marriage records showing his father as performing the ceremony, a task he still performed at least as late as September 30, 1865.[153]

Although Al referenced the family home as a plantation, the census record showing a value of just $500 for the real estate argues against Jennings' account. Likewise, the reference to the family slaves abandoning the family is difficult to believe when the enumerator failed to count any slaves in the family that year.

It's not known exactly when Jennings made his way to Southern Illinois as he's still in Tazewell County at the end of September 1865, even though two of his biographical sketches claimed he moved to Marion "at the cessation of hostilities" or sometime in 1865.[154] At any event he's found in the newspaper advertising sermons in Marion by the summer of 1867 when his son Al was four.

> There will be preaching at the courthouse on the next Sabbath at 11 o'clock A.M., by Dr. J. D. F. Jennings.[155]

Like the story of his birth, Al Jennings couldn't help but dwell on the poverty of the family once they arrived in Marion.

> I remember our home there. I remember our habitual starvation. We lived in an empty tobacco barn. There was hardly a stick of furniture in the place. Frank and I used to run wild about the bare

---

[152] August/October 2004. "More About J. D. F. Jennings and Hs Son Al." *Springhouse.* 21:4/5. 70; quoting from Al Jennings. 1921. *Through the Shadows With O. Henry.*

[153] Aug. 22, 1917. "Once in the Limelight." Lincoln Daily Star (Lincoln, Nebraska). 5.

[154] *Portrait and Biographical Record of Oklahoma* 1059; and Doughtie 660.

[155] Lind 1:5; quoting the June 13, 1867 edition of *Our Flag* (Marion, Ill.)

rooms. I know that I was always longing for, and dreaming of, good things to eat.[156]

By the 1870 census, Jennings' oldest son had either died or left the household. The enumerator counted Jennings' family living in what's now East Marion Township. He was listed as 40, a physician with $800 in real estate and $150 in personal property and a native of Virginia. His wife Mary was 36, keeping house and also a Virginia native. Children included four boys, John, 13; Edward, 11; Francis, 9; and Alphonso, 7.[157] A daughter Mary Dell would come later that year.[158]

> Before the war my father was a physician. A little sign on our barn tempted a few patients to try his skill and gradually he built up a meager practice. All at once, it seemed, his reputation grew and he became quite a figure in the town. He had never studied law, but he was elected state's attorney.[159]

Jennings' change of station in life can likely be attributed to a new state constitution adopted in 1870 that changed the method of selecting state's attorneys. Prior to the 1872 election each state's attorney served an entire judicial circuit. The new constitution recognized the population growth of the state and created a state's attorney position for each county. Also, unlike in earlier years when the position was appointed, 1872 saw the first county wide election for the spot. Jennings ability as a slick talker proved enough to win the race in a then small county with few practicing attorneys.

Sometime in the early 1870s Jennings' wife died, probably after the election.

> It was as though a fairy charm had been cast over us. And then my mother died. It broke the spell.
> There was something grim and fighting and stubborn about her. In the misery of our pinched days I never heard her complain. She

---

[156] "More About J. D. F. Jennings and Hs Son Al." *Springhouse.* 21:4/5. 70.

[157] 1870 Census of Williamson Co., Illinois.

[158] Doughtie 661.

[159] "More About J. D. F. Jennings and Hs Son Al" 70.

was perhaps too strong. When she died it was like the tearing up of a prop. The home went to pieces [160]

Al's autobiography suggests that his mother died at Marion. Other sketches of his father written by him or members of his family note the mother's death in Ohio in 1874. Erwin didn't tell exactly when Jennings left Williamson County other than to describe it as after Vincent Hinchcliff's assassination on October 4, 1874. The office itself wasn't declared vacated until the following April which might represent a legal necessity of a six-month waiting period. A biographical sketch of his son Al published in 1916, claimed that the father left Williamson County on "account of ill health" and had intended to relocate to Virginia. However, "his wife died in Adams Co., Ohio, and he abandoned the journey."[161]

Although Al never mentioned his father's scams and attempts to extort money, it's likely that his mother's death played a role in the senior Jennings' unraveling. He left abruptly at the end of winter in 1875. By April the county declared his office vacant. In August rumors circulated that Jennings had resigned rather than simply abandoned his post, a contention the newspaper quickly countered.

> Who ever heard of J. D. F. Jennings resigning? He never did resign, but left here because he did not do his duty.[162]

By October 1877, the *Marion Monitor* had reported a sighting of the "defaulting" Jennings as living in Rome, Ohio.[163] After the sighting in Ohio, Jennings may have next moved to Appleton City, Missouri, in the Ozarks, but he's not found anywhere in the 1880 census. According to accounts published decades later in 1939, Jennings and his boys had moved back east to Ripley, West Virginia, by late 1880 or 1881, where they once again ran into trouble with the law.

---

[160] "More About J. D. F. Jennings and Hs Son Al" 70.

[161] Doughtie 660.

[162] Aug. 26, 1875. *Marion* [Ill.] *Monitor*.

[163] Lind 1: 105; quoting the Oct. 25, 1877 issue.

It was about 1881 that the Jennings family located at Ripley and the Jennings drug store was established there. The family was understood at the time to have come from Missouri. They stayed in Ripley some four years before moving to Charleston, They found so many drug stores here that "Doctor" Jennings did not undertake to open one. With his usual occupation gone, they did not remain here long.

Before leaving Ripley nearly all the men and boys in the family had been arrested.[164]

While living in West Virginia, Al Jennings did accomplish one thing. He attended law school, and even graduated if his accounts can be believed. Jennings and his boys didn't stay long in Charleston for by the spring of 1885, they had traveled west again to the frontier in Comanche County, Kansas, and the new town of Coldwater.

Cash Cade was a cattleman and an organizer of Coldwater who found his plans for the town upset by Jennings.

We left all the land around Coldwater for the settlers. We took a section for the town site… We started to make Comanche co. a cattle county like Barber, but J. D. F. Jennings and others arrived near Coldwater about this time and the first election we had was a herd law and anti-herd law ticket. Jennings won, of course — he was the farmer, the downtrodden farmer. He was in favor of letting the people rule and putting the plutocrats out of business.[165]

At another time Cade provided a few more details about that April 2, 1885 election.[166]

[164] George W. Summers. June 11, 1939. "Al Jennings, Ex-Charlestonian, Famed for Banditry." (Charleston, WV) Charleston Daily Mail. 4

[165] Cash M. Cade. Feb. 25, 1921. "The Early Days of Coldwater." *Western Star.* http://www.rootsweb.com/~kscomanc/cade_cm.html.

[166] Coldwater Diamond Jubilee Committee. 1959. *Diamond Jubilee Coldwater, Kansas, Aug. 30-31 Sept. 1-2.* Coldwater, KS: Western Star.
Online at http://www.rootsweb.com/~kscomanc/diamond_jubilee.html..

In the early days of Coldwater, politics cut no "ice." The Coldwater Town Company was for a cattle country, like Barber.

J. D. F. Jennings appeared upon the scene and located at Reeder north of Coldwater, and after he looked the situation over, figuring on getting an office, he at once took up the fight of two room house "Peepul" and organized a herd law ticket and was nominated and elected Probate Judge.

Thus the man who abandoned his post as state's attorney during the Vendetta could now be called "judge." Cade also recalled another story involving Jennings that showed off his rusty lawyering skills.

We had lots of fun in the early days...

We had mock trials. When a "dude" struck town, he was arrested for some offense. J. D. F. Jennings and A. K. Cook would defend and Geo. W. Vickers and Bob Palmer prosecute. A trial was in progress in Justice of Peace court trying a stranger for horse stealing, as he had just arrived in town. He was found guilty and J. P. was about to pass sentence fixing the date when he should be hung when a young lawyer looking for a location entered and stated to the Squire that it was not an offense for which the penalty of death could be attached, when some one in the audience hollowed, "Hang him, Hang him." Some cowpuncher threw a lariat rope and in place of catching the prisoner caught the young lawyer. While they we were going downstairs, the lawyer kept protesting that they had the wrong man. He got the rope loose and walked or ran to Kinsley, Kansas.[167]

By February 1886, the Jennings boys (father and sons) had yet to be run out of town and were performing several acts in the "Coldwater Mokes" the community's first minstrel show.[168] Though the show received good reviews, the Jennings found that it was soon time to move on as Al later recalled.

Cash M. Cade. March 17, 1922. "Memories of Early Days." *Western Star.* Online at http://www.rootsweb.com/~kscomanc/cade_cm.html.
[168] Evelyn Reed. 1984. Coldwater Centennial Notebook.
Online at http://www.rootsweb.com/~kscomanc/centennial.html.

The Middle West was wild, new country then. We moved from Kansas, took up land in Colorado, built the town of Boston, sold town lots, cleared $75,000 and lost every cent of it in the county-seat fight.

Crumb-clean we went into Oklahoma in 1889. The settlers were all bankrupt. The government even issued food to them. Frank and I were both athletes. We supported the family with the money we earned at foot racing.

Just about this time one of the periodic swells in our fortune swept my father into Woodward County, where he was appointed judge by Governor Renfro, John and Ed opened law offices in the same town. I was elected county attorney of El Reno. Frank was deputy clerk in Denver.[169]

The Jennings boys managed to stay relatively clean until 1896 when a tavern shoot-out following a legal dispute in Oklahoma Territory left one brother dead and another wounded.

Deadly Affray

Woodward, O.T., Oct. 10. — Yesterday Lawyer Ed Jennings of Woodward was shot dead, and his brother John Jennings, was mortally wounded. The men who did the shooting were ex-State Senator Temple Houston of Texas, the eldest son of General Houston, and ex-Sheriff Jack Love of Woodward.[170]

John and Ed had served as defense attorneys for some cowboys arrested for stealing barrels of beer. Houston worked for the prosecution. During the trial the brothers became so emotional they began yelling at Houston who accused them of being "grossly ignorant of the law." Ed responded slamming his hand down on the table and calling him "a damned liar." The three of them nearly had a shoot-out in the courtroom had they not been restrained.

---

[169] August/October 2004. "More About J. D. F. Jennings and Hs Son Al." *Springhouse.* 21:4/5. 72; quoting from Al Jennings. 1921. *Through the Shadows With O. Henry.*

[170] Oct. 10, 1896. "Deadly Affray." *The Marion Daily Star* [Marion, Ohio]. 1.

Later that night Ed and John entered the Cabinet Saloon in Woodward and found Temple and Love playing cards in a side room. They drew their weapons and entered the room. Temple stood and motioned for Ed to follow him outside where they could settle everything peacefully.

> Jennings was apparently drunk. He shouted at Houston: "See me here and now, you s.o.b.!" Both men pointed their guns, as did John Jennings. Houston fired six shots at both Jennings brothers. John was hit in the arm. Ed was struck in the head by a stray bullet from his brother's gun. When two more of Houston's bullets struck Ed Jennings he fell dead onto the barroom floor. John Jennings staggered out of the bar with half his arm in shreds. Though John Jennings had accidentally fired the shot that killed his brother, Houston was charged with murder.[171]

Depending on which version he told Al managed to get himself involved in the middle of this story. At the least he may have been in town visiting his father and assisting his brothers in the trial. Unable to stop his sons' inability to control their tempers earlier that night, Judge Jennings at least talked Al out of going after Houston out of revenge. There was still a chance the courts would convict, just not a very good one.

> Ex-Senator Houston Acquitted.
> Wichita, Kan., May 18. Ex-Senator Temple Houston, son of the first president of the Texas republic, was acquitted of the murder of John Jennings, in a terrible duel in a saloon at Woodward, O.T., last fall, and the wounding of Ed Jennings, John's brother. Mr. Houston is the best revolver shot in the West. He is a brilliant orator and a literary man, and public sentiment was with him.[172]

Thus when the jury acquitted Temple on grounds of obvious self-defense in May 1897, Al stopped listening to his father and became an outlaw, despite

---

[171] Jay Robert Nash. 1994. *Encyclopedia of Western Lawmen & Outlaws*. De Capo Press. 189-191.

[172] May 18, 1896. "Ex-Senator Houston Acquitted." *Bismarck Daily Tribune*, [Bismarck, N.D.]. 1.

his utter incompetence as one. Al rode off joined by his brother Frank. Riding into southern Oklahoma they met up with several members of the Doolin Gang – Richard "Little Dick" West, and possibly Richard "Dynamite Dick" Clifton – as well as the brothers Sam and Morris O'Malley who were cowboys and possibly even ex-Deputy U.S. Marshals according to one source.[173]

Nearly three months after Houston's acquittal Al, Frank, Little Dick and the O'Malleys stopped a southbound Santa Fe train at Edmond, but failed to get the safe open.[174]

The Jennings Gang made its second attempt at a train robbery a few nights later when Al stood in the center of the tracks holding a lantern and frantically waved a red flag trying to get the engineer to stop. He didn't, but Al at least leaped out of the way in time. On their third attempt Frank and Al tried to race the train on horseback "firing their six-guns in the air" but also to no avail. The engineer simply waved hello as the Jennings' horses gave out.

For their fourth attempt, they made an important change in their plans. Since they didn't have much luck in stopping trains, they decided to rob one already stopped. Their luck turned when they found a southbound Rock Island passenger train stopped at a water station eight miles south of Minco at 11 a.m. October 1. They boarded the baggage car and quickly found the safe, which they could not open. Unlike their first attempt they came prepared this time with dynamite.

> "I've been waiting for that," Al Jennings said and he produced several sticks of dynamite. He tied these together, struck a long fuse into one stick, lit it, and placed it alongside the safe. The baggage car clerk and the outlaws leaped from the train car and ran some distance from it, waiting.
>
> "How much dynamite did you use, Al? Frank Jennings asked his brother.

---

[173] The Sept. 13, 1894, edition of the *Guthrie State Capitol* noted that Deputy Marshals Sam and Morris O'Malley and Rufus Cannon came in with a batch of prisoners from the Creek country. Online at http://www.coax.net/people/lwf/DOOLIN.HTM.

[174] Nash 189-191.

"You got to use a lot of dynamite to dent a big safe like that, "Al Jennings answered knowingly.[175]

A few seconds later, the entire car blew up, sending a shower of wooden and iron splinters in all directions. There was no safe, let alone money, to be found. The frustrated gang members then went through the passenger coaches and robbed everyone down to their last dollar. They also took diamond stickpins, women's jewelry, even a new pair of boots from a traveling salesman.

Fleeing into Indian Territory the gang laid low until they robbed the till of the Crozier and Nutter Store in Cushing netting just $15, or a piddly $3 per outlaw. At some point in October or November they also robbed a small post office at Foyil, I.T., which brought federal authorities on their tail. On either November 30, or December 1, 1897, deputy U.S. marshals caught up with the gang at the Spike S Ranch on the Duck River. According to Al's later accounts they "engaged in battle" and made "a miraculous escape in the face of a withering rifle fire from *hundreds* of deputies."[176] Jennings was known to exaggerate. When he said "hundreds" he must have really meant "two."

It was [Paden] Tolbert and [Bud] Ledbetter that surrounded the Jennings gang at the "Spike S" ranch and after shooting a house all to pieces drove the bandits out and captured them after a chase of sixty miles, arresting Al and Frank Jennings and Pat and Morris O'Malley.[177]

Ledbetter captured the Jennings brothers on Carr Creek near Onapa in present-day McIntosh County after receiving a tip that the brothers were hiding in a covered wagon moving through the Indian Nation.

---

[175] Other accounts suggest Little Dick handled the dynamite instead since he theoretically would have had the most experience since he'd been a member of an outlaw gang for three-and-a-half years already joining the Doolin-Dalton "Wild Bunch" gang at least by April 1894.

[176] Aug. 22, 1917. "Once in the Limelight."

[177] Emily Jordan. trans. March 29, 2006. "1904 Deaths Pt 2 - Oklahoma County, Oklahoma." Oklahoma County Archives. USGenWeb Project; quoting Tolbert's obituary.   Online   at http://www.rootsweb.com/~usgenweb/ok/oklahoma/oklahoma.html.

The boys meekly surrendered and Ledbetter captured them without firing a shot. He threw them a rope and ordered them to tie each other up. Thus hog-tied, Ledbetter threw them over the backs of horses and led them ignominiously to town. This was the end of the Al Jennings gang, an outlaw band that never really got started and one that earned its members less than $200 each.[178]

The irony didn't end there. Once back at Guthrie the Jennings hired the best attorney they knew to represent them in court. They retained Temple Houston for the position.[179] Newspapers far and wide reprinted the articles on the trial, especially the newspaper back in their old home of Williamson County.

These boys will be remembered by our older people as once being citizens of Marion. Their father, Dr. Jennings, was elected states attorney in this county, and without any notice, left the country before the expiration of his term of office. By their dislike to law and order the boys have been known from youth up. [180]

Even the judge knew about their past in the Prairie State.

Judge Thomas reminded the prisoners he knew a number of their people in Illinois, all of whom are highly respected and told them they ought to know better than to disgrace the family by being outlaws. He set their bonds at $5000 each.[181]

Although they were not financially successful in their law-breaking itself they did break enough laws to secure five-year sentences for the O'Malleys and Frank Jennings, and a life sentence for Al. Sent to the federal penitentiary at Columbus, Ohio, Jennings had the good fortune of sharing a cell with

---

[178] Nash 189-191.

[179] Dec. 10, 1897. "Houston to Defend Jennings." *Atlanta Constitution*. 1.

[180] Lind 6:108; quoting the Dec. 16, 1897, edition of *The Leader* of Marion, Illinois.

[181] Lind 6:110; quoting the Jan. 6, 1898, edition of *The Leader* of Marion, Illinois.

William Sydney Porter, whom the world would later best remember as the author O. Henry. Legal appeals shortened his sentence and finally President Theodore Roosevelt pardoned him, but his story didn't end there. Once out of prison his natural showmanship combined with Porter's literary encouragements made him quite a character when he hooked up with the nascent motion picture industry and its thirst for westerns. Al also published two books about his legendary exploits, one of which served as the basis for the early 1914 Western, "Beating Back."

In 1908, he played himself in the 19-minute feature, "A Bank Robbery", a short movie where for once the actors playing the lawmen and outlaws were actually lawmen and outlaws. Other stars included famed U.S. Marshal William Tilghman and Sheriff Heck Thomas, gunfighter Frank Canton, and Indian leader Quanah Parker. The first movie adaptation of his life came about six years later in 1914 in the film "Beating Back" that featured both him portraying himself and his brother Frank acting as another character. Both brothers also played themselves in the 1918 film, "The Lady of the Dugout" and the 1925 film, "The Tryout." The last two Al also produced. Frank also played the sheriff in the 1929 film, "The Three Outcasts." Al also wrote the story for the 1917 film, "Hands Up!" as well as the screenplay for the 1936 film, "Song of the Gringo."

Between 1917 and 1939, Al acted in 13 Westerns, sometimes as minor characters, other times uncredited. The biggest film of this period was the 1939 Western, "The Oklahoma Kid", which in a strange casting move starred James Cagney in the title role and Humphrey Bogart as the outlaw leader. He also served as a consultant and technical adviser on many other projects. He never gave up his self-promotion. In his 88th year he saw his book remade into a second biographical Western, "Al Jennings of Oklahoma" that came out in 1951.

Al Jennings died on December 26, 1961, at the age of 98, not bad for a real-life gunslinger.[182]

---

[182] "Al J. Jennings" and "Frank Jennings." IMDb.com (Internet Movie Database).

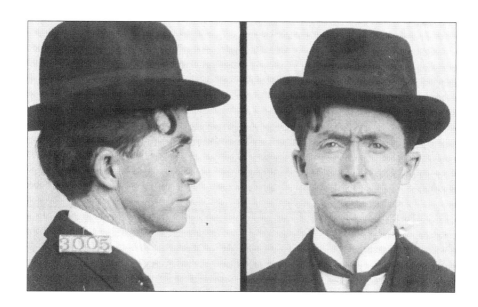

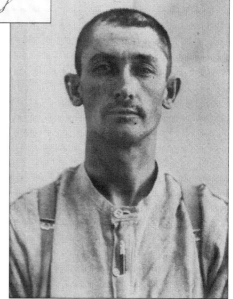

National Archives, Kansas City

JENNINGS GANG MUGS —
Al Jennings poses for his official mug shot from Leavenworth Penitentiary above. His brother Frank's is to the right. In between is their father and former Williamson County State's Attorney J. D. F. Jennings' signature from a letter he wrote to the warden on Frank's behalf.

Chapter 20. **One More Killing**

WHICH CENTURY MATTERS NOT. Young male criminals often come from broken families with histories of violence. On May 31, 1895, Jackson County authorities hung two such Carterville men.

They were Frank Jeffries and Arley Douglas "Doug" Henderson -- foster cousins each with a connection to the assassinated James Henderson. Jeffries had been the dead man's 7-year-old foster son who stood guard the day of the murder. Doug was James' nephew, the son of divorced parents who had remarried. His father was Patrick "Pad" Henderson, an ex-con and the one son of William Henderson Milo Erwin had not considered either honest or fair in his dealings. His mother, the former Arminda R. Sanders, daughter of Isaac and Martha Patsy (Gower) Sanders, had divorced the father then later remarried and divorced him again.

Pad served time at least twice. In October 1875, during the time of Marshall T. Crain's trial, he was arrested one week and sentenced the next to one year at the Joliet penitentiary for malicious mischief. "His time in jail was short, and he was soon informed what it costs in this county to ax a cow." He returned to Marion the following September.[183] In 1883 he faced another year in the pen at Chester.[184] Doug was 23 when he died. At the age of 10 he had moved in with his grandfather. After his grandfather died about 10 years later he married Nora Greathouse in 1893.

Jeffries was about five years older than Doug. Born May 20, 1867, he lost his father James while a baby. Not found in the 1870 Census, Erwin described him as Henderson's "foster son" in 1874. Though his mother remarried twice; to Matthew R. Tippy in 1876 and James Dobson in 1881, Jeffries fell through the cracks of the county's limited relief efforts. By the age of 12 he worked in a coal mine and must have been out on his own because he didn't live with his

---

[183] Lind 1:38, 63; quoting the Oct. 21, 1875, issue of the *Marion Monitor*, and the Sept. 28, 1876, issue of the *Egyptian Press*.

[184] Lind 3:48; quoting the May 31, 1883, issue of the *Marion Monitor*. "Elvira Wilburn and Pad Henderson were taken to Chester Penitentiary Monday, she for 14 years and he for one year."

mother the following year during the 1880 census. By 1894 the two were laborers by day and robbers by night.

> [The two] also admitted that they were the parties who held up and robbed Richard Swain near Big Muddy; Wm. Nichols west of town and they had their plans to "do up" A. K. Ellis the night they were arrested. They further claim that there is a third party interested in the crimes, but refuse to divulge his name.

On the morning of Thursday, December 20, 1894, the pair met James Towle, 46, a widower and resident of Ledford in Saline County, who had been working the past week or so at a farm near Carterville. Towle was on his way to Makanda to visit his sister Jane Land. The two watched him go into a store in Carterville where he made some purchases. When he left and started walking down the railroad track toward Carbondale, they followed. At one point Henderson outlined a plan to Jeffries.

> "That fellow has stuff and it would pay to get it from him."
> Jeffries objected and thought the matter had been dropped.

They soon caught up to Towle and eventually the three men walked single file down the tracks with Towle in between.

> A short time later [Jeffries] was in front, Henderson behind and Towle walking second, when he heard a pistol shot, and turning saw Towle turn around and say to Henderson, "what do you want?" when the last named fired a second shot striking Towle in the forehead and killing him instantly. Henderson then turned the pistol on him and commanded him to search the dead body, after which he compelled him to help drag the body away and secrete it.

Another newspaper printed a similar version.

> [Jeffries] says he heard a pistol shot and turned around, Towle being shot in the back of the head also turned and was again shot in the forehead by Henderson; that he and Henderson then dragged the body off and threw it into the field where it was found. Henderson's

tale was about the same except that he claimed he was in the lead when Jeffrey fired the shot, that Towle fell against him and he said to Towle, "Partner, he has done you up, hasn't he?" Jeffrey then run around in front and again shot Towle.

Before hiding the body, the duo emptied Towle's pockets looking for loot. Instead they found 20 cents in silver coins and three small apples.

The body was in a thicket about fifty yards from the railroad track. On the ties east of the track blood and brains were found, and there was a distinct trail from the spot across the track and into a ravine and to the clump of bushes which concealed the body. Two wounds, one in the back of the neck, the other in the forehead, gave evidence that the man had been murdered in cold blood.

A boy, Marion Claunch, saw the body that afternoon but thought it a tramp sleeping. The next day his brother came across the body while hunting and "gave the alarm" as a messenger hurried to find the coroner.

While the coroner was investigating Officers Ryder and Robertson were seeking a clue to the murderers. It was observed that two men had participated in the crime, as the tracks were plainly visible along the trail made by dragging the body through the soft earth at the side of the railroad and along the ground. These tracks continued from the thicket through a field to a strip of woods, and from the length of the strides, the men ran away from the scene of their bloody work.

On Saturday, Lee Brandon of Carterville traveled to Carbondale and identified the body as that of his uncle James Towle who had been working on his farm the previous week. Later that day his father, Lewis Brandon, provided a second confirmation, as law enforcement authorities in both Jackson and Williamson counties closed in on the killers.

It was to be seen by the movements of Sheriff Wells, of Murphysboro, and Marshal Walker of Carterville, last Saturday evening, that something important was in the wind.

By the end of the day the authorities had interviewed enough witnesses, including Nichols who had been robbed a few days earlier, and found that all the descriptions pointed to Jeffries and Henderson.

Saturday morning Sheriff Wells and Marshal Ryder repaired to the place where the Carbondale officers had left the trail of the two men the evening previous. They followed the trail to the Carterville road. While on route the sheriff was informed that two men had been seen the day before going across the field toward the road. A description of the men was secured. Further on several parties were found who had seen the men.

About one mile west of Carterville Mr. William Nicholls resides. This gentleman while returning home Monday night of last week had been held up by two men, but no money was found on his person. Sheriff Wells now visited Mr. Nicholls and obtained from him a description of the robbers who had waylaid him. The two descriptions allied exactly. The sheriff also obtained a glove that had been dropped at the scene of the robbery.

Meanwhile Walker arrested the suspects at his end in Carterville.

In the meantime the officers and people at Carterville had been active. Jeffries and Henderson had been suspicioned as the murderers and were arrested separately and prevented from having any conversation with each other. Then parties who had seen the three men together the previous day identified Jeffries and Henderson as two of them. The sheriff brought the glove mentioned to Carterville, and one of the merchants identified it as one of a pair he had sold to Jeffries a short time before.

At this juncture Mr. James H. Conner gave valuable assistance to Sheriff Wells. Mr. Conner had Jeffries brought to his store, where he began a most rigid "seating" process. Conner cross-questioned the man most unrelentingly, and got him very badly mixed up. He then presented the glove and boldly charged him with being one of the robbers of Nicholls as well as one of the murderers of Towle.

"What's the use of lying!" asked Mr. Conner.

"We have arrested Doug Henderson and he has given the whole thing away. Henderson says that you helped to rob Nicholls and that you shot Towle. You might as well own up, for we've got all the evidence we want."

Upon this Jeffries wilted, and told the story of the robbery and murder, implicating Henderson as the principal in both cases. Then Mr. Conner put Henderson through a similar process and succeeded in getting from him exactly the same story as told by Jeffries, except that Henderson claimed that Jeffries had done the shooting.

With the confessions in hand Sheriff Wells transported the two to the Jackson County Jail in Murphysboro where they were arraigned the following Monday and a trial was set for later in the winter.

Sheriff Wells did not trust to memory for anything, but has a record of everything connected with the affair down to the smallest detail, and had there been no confession he had succeeded in securing a chain of circumstantial evidence that would have a great deal of weight. Too much credit cannot be given the sheriff for the promptness and clever manner in which he handled the case.

Before the trial could commence though, Jeffries escaped the county jail in February but was soon recaptured near the Mississippi River.

In March, a special term of the Jackson County Circuit Court convened to try the pair. Between their confessions and the eye-witness accounts to their presence in the area with Towle, the jury didn't take long to convict, sentencing both to hang. At first the impact of the sentence didn't faze the two. After the jury handed down the verdict Jeffries turned to Henderson.

"What do you think of that, buddy?"

Later on the way to the jail, Jeffries talked with sheriff, as he began to realize what the sentence meant.

"That is the first time I was ever sentenced to be hung."

The sheriff, probably with at least a hidden grin, quickly retorted.

"And in all probability it is the last."

Though newspapers after the trial reported that "little concern is shown by either party" they like Marshall Crain before them realized that in facing death they still had one more decision to make. Early in May, Henderson's mother came to town from St. Louis, the first time she had seen him in eight years. Together with her son and Jeffries, they repented of their sins and asked Jesus Christ to be their personal Lord and Savior.

> Arly Douglas Henderson and Frank Jeffrey, the convicted murderers, who are to hang on May 31, have professed religion, have been received into the membership of the Free Will Baptist church, and on Friday afternoon at 4 o'clock they will be baptized by the Rev. J. F. McBride in the shallow waters of the Big Muddy river under the shadow of the Chicago & Texas railroad in the southern portion of the city. It was at first intended to have the ceremony occur in the jail, but the men desired that it occur in public and wanted it to be witnessed by all. Sheriff Wells consented to this arrangement and barring accidents it will occur as above stated.

On May 17, McBride baptized the two men and Henderson's mother. She first, then Henderson and Jeffries waded in, chained at the ankles.

> Without doubt the largest crowd that ever witnessed a baptizing in Jackson county, was the one which assembled on the banks of the Big Muddy river Friday afternoon to see Arley Douglas Henderson and Frank Jeffrey, the convicted murderers of James Towle, immersed by the evangelists who claimed these men have repented their grievous sins and have been converted. No doubt the fact that the converts were in just two weeks to expiate their terrible crime upon the scaffold had the effect of attracting the throngs to the river, and when Sheriff Wells' party in closed carriages and on horseback, reached the scene of the ceremony, the crowd of curious and eager humanity which lined either bank would easily number 4,000.
>
> It was just ten minutes past four when Henderson and Jeffrey manacled together, hand and foot stepped from the closed carriage into the water. Jeffrey had been quite observant all the time and shook hands and smiled pleasantly to several acquaintances. Henderson on the other hand was sad and silent. He apparently took no interest in the proceedings and recognized no one. The ceremony was quite brief, and the men quietly entered the carriage and were hurriedly driven back to the jail from whose dark portals they will

never again emerge until on Friday, May 31, when they will be led to the gallows.

Meanwhile the sheriff readied for the event. He secured the same scaffolding used successfully a few months earlier at the Cantrill hanging in Belleville, and two years earlier at a double hanging in Nashville, Illinois, of two African-American men convicted of murder.[185] He also had to build a stockade around the gallows and print tickets for the honored and chosen few who would have the opportunity to view the execution.

On Friday, May 31, 1895, a week after their baptism, the two hung by the necks until dead. Their families buried Jeffries at a cemetery near Carterville and Henderson in the new cemetery at Marion. Both men left widows. Henderson left a baby girl who had been born in between the trial and the execution. His widow married his uncle Felix Henderson the following year at the courthouse in Marion, "and the happy pair repaired to their cozy home in Johnston City." The newlyweds' bliss didn't last. They divorced two years later. She later married four more times.

Nurtured in the violence of the Vendetta, neither Jeffries nor Henderson respected the law or valued human life. In the end they hung for the sum of a dime a piece and a few bites of apple.[186]

---

[185] George Cantrill had pled guilty to the murder of Fred Kahn of East Carondalet, Illinois, which he and Kahn's wife had done the previous spring. The hanging was Nov. 30.

[186] Darrel Dexter, trans. "Index to Obituaries and Death Notices in the Jonesboro Gazette, 1893-1896." GSSI. http://www.rootsweb.com/~ilgssi/obit_1893-1896.htm; Lind. 5:37-38-40-58-59-71; May 21 and 28, 1895. "Facts and Fancies, Chronicled by Sprightly Exchanges of Other Counties." *Edwardsville Intelligencer* [Ill.]. 2; Illinois Statewide Marriage Index; 1870 and 1880 Censuses of Williamson Co., Illinois; LeeAnn R. Henderson. Oct. 4, 2003. Letter to Jim Redden. James E. Redden Collection; and Susan Cook, trans. "The Hanging of Henderson and Jeffries for the murder of James Towle, Murphysboro, Ill., 1895." Jackson Co. Illinois Trails. www.iltrails.org/jackson/henderson_jeffries_hanging.htm.

Chapter 21. **The Final Mystery**

THE LAST MYSTERY OF THE BLOODY VENDETTA has never been solved, that being what ever happened to Milo Erwin. By the 20th Century it had become accepted as truth that he had been run out of town and chose to go into hiding.

> It was a foolish thing to write this history so soon after, as he later found out. The people involved and then living were still filled with hatred and bitterness toward one another. They had not forgotten nor forgiven their enemies [even] in 1904. Many were living who vividly recalled those dark and bloody times. And this book was just new fuel for the smoldering fires. As soon as the book came off the press, both sides were on the verge of going gunning for Erwin. He had set down the real names of his characters, shielding no one. He had been warned of the dangerous consequences of writing the story and he soon envisioned what would happened to him, so the story goes, that he departed shortly, suddenly and unannounced, for parts unknown to anyone. He never showed his face again in Southern Illinois. [187]

The only problems with this story are the facts. While it's assuredly true that some in the Vendetta would rather the book not come out, it's doubtful he named any names that hadn't come out in trial and been splashed across the newspapers of the Midwest. Marion was a two-newspaper town and both covered the minute details of the violence.

Only one detailed threat against Erwin still circulated a half century after the book publication. James Hartwell Duncan threatened to kill Erwin if he published anything about him "killing old man Kennedy."[188] Erwin didn't, though the incident may have taken place, or was at least tried, in Franklin County, placing it outside the scope of Erwin's book.

---

[187] Trovillion 1943.

[188] Nannie Gray Parks. [n.d.] MS notes. Erwin Family File. Nannie Gray Parks Collection. Williamson County Historical Society.

Instead of running off to the wilds in hiding after publication, the only trip historians have confirmed is a week-long visit to his brother-in-law in March 1877.

> Milo Erwin has been spending the week at his brother-in-law's, John H. Rummage in Crab Orchard.[189]

It likely wasn't a pleasant visit as three of his nieces and nephews all had scarlet fever. At least three, and possibly four other children in Crab Orchard had died already from the disease during this particular outbreak. Though he told the *Egyptian Press* he thought his relatives would recover his five-year-old nephew Charley Rummage succumbed to the disease three weeks later.[190]

Even while compiling information for his county history, he ran for the state legislature in 1876. He lost, but he kept at it running again in 1878, and finally, with the Klan having stopped assassinating Republicans Erwin found himself sent to Springfield following the 1880 election. Two years later voters re-elected him again, thus making him an incumbent politician just 10 years after he graduated law school at the University of Michigan and eight years after running the first time for the legislature.

By 1877, he was single, 30 years old, five years out of law school, had served as defense attorney in major murder trials, served a term as Marion's city clerk, ran twice unsuccessfully for the legislature, and had published a book, which went up in flames mostly. It was time for something new.

His March visit to Crab Orchard must have laid the groundwork for his next move. He entered into partnership with his brother-in-law in a mill and helped him operate a 200-acre farm and as one historian also noted, "was the speaker at a Fourth of July celebration at Crab Orchard, was superintendent of the art exhibit at the county fair and served his part as congressional district committeeman."[191]

His election in 1880 set the stage for the next chapter in his life. As a lawmaker in Springfield he was able to see greater opportunities elsewhere in

---

[189] Lind 1:79; quoting the Mar. 15, 1877, issue of the *Marion Monitor*.

[190] Lind 1:79, 83 and 86; quoting the March 15, 1877 issues of both the *Marion Monitor* and the *Egyptian Press*, as well as the April 12, 1877, issue of the *Marion Monitor*.

[191] Helen Sutt Lind. December 2003. "A Man and his Book" *Springhouse*. 35.

the state. Also, the call of the law once again appealed to him as a February 1888 articled noted.

Milo Erwin has gone to Peoria to practice law.[192]

His stint in Peoria isn't believed to have lasted long as he turned his back on the law and returned to his love of writing taking a job with the St. Louis *Globe-Democrat*. It's at this point the mystery begins.

After a few years on the paper's staff, more than a decade after he published what was remembered as his controversial history, he disappeared, dropping completely off of Williamson County's radar until his death in December 1894.

One family story recalled he had returned just once to Williamson County after leaving the newspaper. One 20th Century informant told a historian he had been "living with the Indians." In the end, he ended up in Forrest City, Arkansas, a community roughly halfway between Little Rock and Memphis.

In all actuality, his disappearance wasn't that unusual. People moved all the time, almost as much as they do now. For Milo, the mystery came in his re-appearance, not under his own name, but that of "Mark Stanley," an elected official in Arkansas.

Here's what the Marion paper clipped from the *Forrest City Times*.

> All that remain mortal of Mark M. Stanley, county surveyor, was consigned to mother earth Monday afternoon. Mr. Stanley died quite suddenly and unexpected last Thursday. He was taken with a chill which seemed to yield to remedies and on Saturday morning he went into Henton's restaurant for his meal, when he was taken ill and retired to a bedroom in the rear. Nobody seemed to realize how ill he was until Sunday morning when he was found in an unconscious condition. A physician was called, but too late to do any good, as he was in a congested state. He was removed to the residence of G. B. Mosley where all attention was paid him, but all in vain and his spirit returned to its maker at 9 o'clock Sunday eve. Mark M. Stanley was a man of considerable ability and the high

---

[192] Lind 3:84; quoting the Feb. 18, 1884, issue of the *Marion Monitor*.

compliment has been paid him that he was perfect in his work. He has relatives living in Illinois who have been notified of his demise.

That was the first article the Arkansas paper published. The following week they revealed the mystery.

Last week's issue of the *Times* contained an account of the death of Mark M. Stanley, who in life was county surveyor of this county. His friends and acquaintances knew little of his past history and little dreamed of the developments printed below:

The Thursday night train from the east brought to this city, R. P. Erwin and G. H. Romage,[193] who introduced themselves as father and brother-in-law of him we knew as Stanley. The gentlemen are from Marion, Ills. The father, though bending under the years of more than man's allotted time, came with a heart full of affection and tender devotion, eager to learn "where is my wandering boy tonight." A *Times* representative met the gentlemen and from them learned the true name and a bit of interesting history of the prodigal son.

Some twenty years ago, Milo Erwin (Mark Stanley) was enjoying a happy home with his parents in Illinois. He had been a close student and had graduated in an eastern university. Returning home from school he took up the practice of law in which he made headway and soon found his lot to be that of a representative to the Illinois Legislature, in which capacity he served two terms. He then accepted a position on the staff of the *Globe-Democrat*, in which position he was distinguished for several years.

As the mileposts of time were passed, financial distresses visited his home and a relief from the scenes of crumbling fortune, he sought refuge from the sorrowing cup. Prompted by his high sense of pride and honor, he resolved to bid adieu to home and friends and seek his fortune in different lands and eventually drifted into this community under the name Stanley. He had made this county his home for several years and has earned honors as a most efficient civil

---

[193] Should be John H. Rumage or Rummage, different sources provide different spellings.

engineer, having been elected to the office of county surveyor twice in succession. He was a Royal Arch Mason and was well up in the Blue Lodge.

Fortunately, after death a letter was found on his person disclosing the name of his parents and residence and a letter notifying them of his death resulted in their visit and the disclosures of the past history of the once Mark Stanley.

The Marion paper continued with their own eulogy of the long-missing county historian.

> The name of Milo Erwin is well known in and around Crab Orchard. He was well liked and highly esteemed for the many kind deeds done through life. He commenced his education here at this place and finished it in the east, climbing three university ladders to the top round. He was an apt scholar and could talk several languages fluently. He was a brilliant writer, being the author of the "History of Williamson County."
>
> While in the legislature he made many telling speeches and was chairman of several important committees, among them the committee on education.
>
> He leaves a very aged father, R. P. Erwin, one sister, Mrs. Mary Rumage, wife of John H. Rumage and one younger brother, W. F. Erwin who now resides at DuQuoin, Ills., his mother having died several years ago. Milo Erwin's demise will end a long wished for return by his many friends. J. S. N.[194]

Erwin had already been buried by the time the family arrived. Because of that, and possibly due to the season, Erwin's father made no decision to remove his son's body back to Illinois. However by the spring his decision changed as the *Forrest City Times* reported.

> The remains of Milo Erwin who died of congestion some four months ago was disinterred Tuesday for shipment to his old home, Crab Orchard, Ills. Jno. H. Rumage, a brother-in-law of the deceased,

---

[194] Lind 5:42-43; quoting the Jan. 17, 1895, issue of The *Leader* (Marion, Ill.).

was here and attended to the arrangements. Mr. Rumage is a pleasant gentleman and was pleased to hear nothing but good words for the surveyor while he lived in this community, notwithstanding his eccentricities.[195]

The disinterment would have taken place on April 23, 1895. Rumage arrived back home with his brother-in-law's remains three days later, in time for a large funeral planned for the following Sunday, April 28. At first, local residents didn't want to believe it was him. Years later Erwin's cousin Sarah McDonald recalled the scene.

> His body was brought to the home of his sister Mary Rumage near Crab Orchard. The casket was not opened. Many of the country people were in doubt that it was the body of Milo Erwin. Well Rummage said the body of Milo Erwin was sealed in a metallic casket & brought to Marion. His father saw the body in Ark. & was sure it was M. Erwin.[196]

Both local newspapers covered the event.

> The readers of the *Leader* know of the death of Hon. Milo Erwin which occurred last December. The father of the deceased, being unwilling for the remains of his dear son to remain in the west, sent Mr. John H. Rumage to bring the corpse here for reburial. On last Friday, Mr. Rumage returned, bringing the lifeless form. Friends were notified and the preparations made for funeral on Sunday at 2 o'clock P.M. When the hour came, one of the largest congregations of people that was ever seen at Mt. Pleasant had gathered from various parts of this and other counties to unite in paying the last tribune of respect to Mr. Erwin.
>
> After the singing of an appropriate hymn, Rev. Z. T. Walker offered a very earnest and touching prayer. The Marion bar showed its respect for one of its ablest ex-members by an address delivered

---

[195] Lind 5:66; quoting the May 9, 1895, issue of *The Egyptian Press* (Marion, Ill.).

[196] Parks MS notes. McDonald was a cousin of Erwin's mother who was living in the mother's household during the 1870 Census of Williamson Co., Illinois.

by Judge Young. The eulogy of the Judge, though largely extemporaneous, was both interesting and instructive. The casket was placed beneath the sod and the concourse of people dispersed.

We are no longer permitted to know the Hon. Milo Erwin as a citizen of our county. We can only remember him as one who has written his history and gone to the long home which awaits us all. The memory of the deceased will long be cherished. In bold type did he write his name on the pages of history. His name stands forth as that of one who well served his people in the Legislative branch of our state government; as that of one who was a successful lawyer, a noted orator and a brilliant writer.

We dare not say that our subject was without fault. Look not among men for perfection. "To err is human." By the Creator, Saviour and preserver of mankind, we are gloriously freed from judging of man's destiny. Let us forever bury his frailty and make his virtues our own. J. M. S.[197]

Dr. G. R. Brewer also attended the funeral that day as a young man.

The climatic event at the funeral and burial of this young man, to me as a young man, was a final song that was sung as the old friends and acquaintances were gathered about the grave, entitled, "Oh Wait, Meekly Wait and Murmur Not." The deep voice of a Mr. Askew of Marion so thrilled me that an impression of the song, the singer and the surroundings was imbedded in my mind where it lingers yet.[198]

---

[197] Lind 5:64; quoting the May 2, 1895, issue of The *Leader* (Marion, Ill.). The *Egyptian Press* also reported the funeral, though only in a short brief.

[198] Lind "A Man and his Book." 36.

Williamson County Historical Society photo

VENDETTA HISTORIAN — Milo Erwin did more than just account for Williamson County's early history, his witness to the events of the Vendetta made sure it would be preserved for posterity.

Vendetta Timeline

July 4, 1868	Hendersons and Bulliners fight over card game.
April 26, 1870	Sisneys and Bulliners hold shoot out over oats crop.
1872	T. J. Russell and J. Bulliner both court Sarah Stocks.
Dec. 12, 1873	George Bulliner assassinated.
March 27, 1874	David Bulliner ambushed and shot, dies next day.
May 15, 1874	James Henderson assassinated.
August 9, 1874	George W. Sisney ambushed, but survives.
October 4, 1874	Vincent Hinchcliff assassinated.
December 1874	George W. Sisney shot again, but survives.
July 28, 1875	Third time's a charm, Sisney finally assassinated.
July 31, 1875	William Spence assassinated.
August 1, 1875	Allen Baker fired upon, survives.
July 21, 1876	Marshall T. Crain hangs for murder in Marion.

Parties to the Vendetta

Democratic	Republican
Bulliner Family	Henderson Family
Crain Family	Russell Family
Vincent Hinchcliff	Capt. George W. Sisney
— — — —	— — — —
Allen Baker	Gordon "Texas Jack" Clifford
Timothy Edward Cagle	David Pleasant
Wesley Council	William Spence
Samuel Musick	
James Norris	

Jon Musgrave photo

MURDER WEAPON? — Manufactured in 1862 for the Civil War, this .32 caliber Smith & Wesson Model 2 Army revolver later belonged to Felix G. "Field" Henderson and still remains in his family. The late Henderson descendent Jim Redden wrote his father, "seemed to think that Felix probably shot a couple of guys with this revolver" during the Vendetta.

Postscript

Now that *The Bloody Vendetta of Southern Illinois* has reached its second printing there's one more story to add. In the decades following the Vendetta the story often would bubble to the surface. In 1922 following the Herrin Massacre, it managed to break into the papers once more. That summer Tom Russell, now an old man, served on the jury that brought the indictments against the rioters.

Then, one day, his former nemesis John Bulliner, his opponent for Sarah Stocks' affections, "walked into the grand jury room as a witness and there came face to face with his enemy of feudal days."

Bulliner had a story to tell, not about the massacre outside Herrin, but the ambush and attempted massacre the day before on the Marion-Carbondale highway that ran by his farm south of Carterville..

Asked to tell what he knew, "I will tell you all I know," he responded.

On the morning of the 21st a group of men called on him.

"John, we are going to kill some of those scabs and want you to get your gun and come along."

Bulliner told them to wait as he went back into his house to get "something to back up my argument," he explained to the jury.

Back outside on the porch presumably he gave the mob his answer: "Now, you fellows get out of here a good deal faster than you came. You say you are going to kill somebody. Well I will have nothing to do with it. I don't want to get into any more trouble. Now go."

And they did, ambushing a truck carrying guards and replacement workers who had just arrived at the Illinois Central railroad station in Carbondale and were on their way to the infamous strip mine.

As the newspaper reported, "Russell, the juror, leaned forward to hear the story, nodding at times. He knows and everyone knew that when John Bulliner told a story it was true."[199]

---

[199] Oldham Paisley, comp. 2006. *Newspaper Articles from Oldham Paisley's Scrapbooks. Volume 1-A & 1-B Riot.* Marion, Ill.: Williamson County Historical Society. 59-60; quoting Philip Kinsley. Sept. 9, 1922. "Soil at Herrin Dedicated Long Ago to Crime." undated and unidentified newspaper clipping.

Bibliography

1883. *History of White County, Illinois*. Chicago: Inter-State Publishing Co.

1887. *History of Gallatin, Saline, Hamilton, Franklin and Williamson Counties, Illinois*. Chicago: Goodspeed Publishing Co.

1901. *Portrait and Biographical Record of Oklahoma: Commemorating The Achievements Of Citizens Who Have Contributed To The Progress Of Oklahoma And The Development Of Its Resources*. Chicago: Chapman Publishing Co.

Beatrice M. Doughtie. 1961, reprinted 2001. *Documented Notes on Jennings and Allied Families*. Reprint privately published by Ann Blomquist of Orlando, Fla.

Coldwater Diamond Jubilee Committee. 1959. *Diamond Jubilee Coldwater, Kansas, Aug. 30-31 Sept. 1-2*. Online at http://www.rootsweb.com/~kscomanc/diamond_jubilee.html. Coldwater, Kan.: Western Star.

Harry Sinclair Drago. 1998. *Outlaws on Horseback*. U of Nebraska Press.

Milo Erwin. 1876, Reprint 1976. *History of Williamson County*. Marion, Ill.: Williamson County Historical Society.

Barbara Burr Hubbs. 1939, reprint 1979. *Pioneer Folks and Places of Williamson County, Illinois*. Marion, Ill.: Williamson Co. Historical Society.

Helen Sutt Lind. 1994 – 2005. *Events in Egypt: Newspaper Excerpts, Williamson County, Illinois*. Private published and available at the Williamson County Historical Society in Marion. Helen has published 10 volumes so far covering the years of 1856 to 1912.

Jon Musgrave. 2002. *Handbook of Old Gallatin County and Southeastern Illinois*. Marion, Ill.: IllinoisHistory.com.

Jon Musgrave. 2005, Rev. Ed. *Slaves, Salt, Sex & Mr. Crenshaw: The Real Story of the Old Slave House and America's Reverse Underground R.R.* Marion, Ill.: IllinoisHistory.com.

Jay Robert Nash. 1994. *Encyclopedia of Western Lawmen & Outlaws*. De Capo Press.

William Henry Perrin. 1883. *History of Alexander, Union and Pulaski Counties, Illinois*. Chicago: O. L. Baskin & Co., Historical Publishers.

Joseph B. Thoburn. 1916. *Standard History of Oklahoma*. Chicago and New York: The American Historical Society.

Warner & Beers. 1876. *Illustrated Historical Atlas of the State of Illinois*. Union Atlas Co.

Articles

Feb. 7, 1946. "Manuscript of History Owned Here." *Marion Daily Republican*.

Cash M. Cade. Feb. 25, 1921. "The Early Days of Coldwater." and March 17, 1922. "Memories of Early Days." *Western Star*. Online at http://www.rootsweb.com/~kscomanc/cade_cm.html.

Andy Hall. July 1923, reprinted April 2002. "Ku Klux Klan in Southern Illinois." *Springhouse*. 19:2. 13-15. In this article publisher Gary DeNeal introduces the topic for six long paragraphs before reprinting Hall's original 1923 article on the Klan that had been copied in the July 19, 1923, edition of the *Daily Independent* of Murphysboro, Illinois.

Andy Hall. 1953. "The Ku Klux Klan in Southern Illinois in 1875." *Journal of the Illinois State Historical Society*. 363-372. More details than the 1923 story the editors still left out material.

Andy Hall. February 1970. "Ku Klux Klan and the battle at John B. (Jack) Maddox Farm." *Outdoor Illinois*. 8-15, 38. This is the most comprehensive version by Hall as it appears to be the unabridged version of what he submitted to the Illinois State Historical Society.

Helen Sutt Lind. Summer 2002. "Milo Erwin alias Mark M. Stanley." *Footprints in Williamson County, Illinois*. Quarterly of the Williamson County Historical Society. 5:3. 21-25.

Helen Sutt Lind. December 2003. "Milo Erwin: A Man and his Book." *Springhouse*. 20:6. 35-36.

[Helen Sutt Lind]. Summer 2004. "The Murder of Isaac Vancil." *Footprints in Williamson County, Illinois*. Quarterly of the Williamson County Historical Society.7:2. 12-14.

Charla Schroeder Murphy. Spring 2002. "The Cash and Stanley Family Feud." *Footprints in Williamson County, Illinois*. Quarterly of the Williamson County Historical Society.5:2. 14-18.

Hal Trovillion. March 19, 1943. "At the Sign of the Silver Horse." *The Egyptian Republican*. (Herrin, Illinois). 8.

Newspapers

Alton Daily Telegraph. [Alton, Ill.] Accessed via the Newspaper Collection at Ancestry.com.

Atlanta Constitution. Accessed via the Newspaper Collection at Ancestry.com.

Bismarck Daily Tribune [Bismarck, N.D.]. Accessed via the Newspaper Collection at Ancestry.com.

Burlington Hawk Eye. [Burlington, Iowa]. The Hawk-Eye ran numerous accounts of the Vendetta and the Ku Klux Klan activities that originally ran in the St. Louis *Globe-Democrat*. Accessed via the Newspaper Collection at Ancestry.com.

Decatur Daily Republican [Decatur, Ill.]. Accessed via the Newspaper Collection at Ancestry.com.

Decatur Republican [Decatur, Ill.]. Accessed via the Newspaper Collection at Ancestry.com.

Edwardsville Intelligencer [Edwardsville, Ill.] Accessed via the Newspaper Collection at Ancestry.com.

Egyptian Press. [Marion, Ill.] Available on microfilm.

Leader, The. [Marion, Ill.] Available on microfilm.

The Marion Daily Star [Marion, Ohio]. Accessed via the Newspaper Collection at Ancestry.com.

Marion Monitor. [Marion, Ill.] Available on microfilm. Generally contained the most news coverage of the Vendetta and the Klan compared to its competition, the *Egyptian Press*.

Correspondence / Miscellaneous

Masatomo Ayabe. 2005. "The Ku Klux Klan Movement in Williamson County, Illinois, 1923-1926." Dissertation. Champaign-Urbana, Ill.: University of Illinois. Excellent research into the 1920s-era Klan and local politics, including editor Hal Trovillion's role.

Lorena Curtis. July 10, 13, 25, 26, 2006. "Re: Al Jennings." E-mails to Jon Musgrave. Curtis is a descendent of J. D. F. Jennings.

Jeana Gallagher. Oct. 19 and Oct. 23, 2005. "Re: Isaac Vancil." E-mails to Jon Musgrave. Besides the latest e-mails Gallagher's correspondence concerning Isaac Vancil and his stepson and her great-great-grandfather Pleasant M. Finney, have been incorporated into at least two different genealogy sites online dealing with the Vancil family, including a page on the Vancil section of the Ikard Family genealogy site at www.ikardfamily.com/vancil_fam/index.htm.

Internet Movie Database. "Edward Jennings." IMDB.com.

Nannie Gray Parks Collection. "Erwin File." Williamson County Historical Society.

Jim Redden Papers. A descendent of "Field" Henderson, Redden had long been interested in the Vendetta and family history. His papers include letters both as well as information on Field's revolver. The papers are in the possession of his son in Marion.

Hal Trovillion. Dec. 1, 1914. "By Way of Explanation." Introduction included at the beginning of his reprints of *The Bloody Vendetta: Embracing the Early History of Williamson County, Illinois*. ix.

Herb Weiner. March 29, 1996. "Perpetual Calendar." Online at http://www.wiskit.com/calendar.html. This is an excellent simple site used often in the preparation of this book to determine the dates of actual events only referenced as "last Thursday" or such. Users simply enter the month and year and the calendar appears.

Index